MUSICAL
GROWTH
IN THE ELEMENTARY
SCHOOL

MUSICAL GROWTH IN THE ELEMENTARY SCHOOL
Second Edition

BJORNAR BERGETHON
University of Illinois

EUNICE BOARDMAN
Wichita State University

HOLT, RINEHART AND WINSTON, INC.
New York Chicago San Francisco Atlanta
Dallas Montreal Toronto London Sydney

ACKNOWLEDGMENTS

Holt, Rinehart and Winston *Exploring Music* series for piano accompaniments to the following songs: "See Saw, Margery Daw," "Who Will Come with Me?" "Dance in the Circle," "Ha Ha Thisaway," "Shoheen Sho," "Twilight," "Poor Bird," "Three Pirates," "Haul Away, Joe," "Chebogah," "Come Tend the Geese," "Clouds," "Tinga Layo," "Donkey Riding."

Holt, Rinehart and Winston, Inc., and for "Twilight" from *Exploring Music,* Book 1, by Eunice Boardman and Beth Landis, copyright © 1966 by Holt, Rinehart and Winston, Inc.; for the words to "Dappled Pony" from *Exploring Music,* Kindergarten, by Eunice Boardman and Beth Landis, copyright © 1969 by Holt, Rinehart and Winston, Inc.; for

the words to "Chebogah" and the music to "Clouds" from *Exploring Music,* Book 3, by Eunice Boardman and Beth Landis, copyright © by Holt, Rinehart and Winston, Inc.; for the words to "Pretty Pena" from *Exploring Music,* Book 5, by Eunice Boardman and Beth Landis, copyright © 1966 by Holt, Rinehart and Winston, Inc.; for the arrangement to "Ghost of Tom" and the music to "The Night Piece" from *Exploring Music,* Book 6, by Eunice Boardman and Beth Landis, copyright © 1966 by Holt, Rinehart and Winston, Inc.; Gulf Music Company for "Farewell, My Own True Love," for the music to "The Sun" and "Windy Night," by William S. Haynie. Used by permission.

ISBN: 0-03-083577-1
Printed in the United States of America
3456789 005 98765

Preface

The enthusiastic reception accorded the first edition of *Musical Growth in the Elementary School* by college teachers and students of music education, as well as teachers and administrators of music in the elementary schools, have encouraged us and our publisher to present this new edition. We hope it may serve as a blueprint for continued nourishing of the kind of musical growth which every child deserves.

The original purpose and plan of the first edition has been retained in the second edition. Each step in the growth of musical awareness and understanding is carefully set forth in the development of the book; the prospective user may study this method of presentation in the section *How to Use This Book* that follows. However, many changes and additions have been made in the content and scope of the book. A section devoted to musical growth in the kindergarten has been added. A variety of new songs have been selected for the other grades. Added emphasis has been placed on the se-quential presentation of musical concepts, moving from aural awareness to an understanding of musical notation as the symbolic representation of these concepts. The listening program has been expanded with additional lessons included in each grade; representative examples of music from the baroque to the twentieth century are included. Some of these compositions that are not easily available, as well as a number of songs, are included in a supplementary recording that is available from the publisher.

Before we undertook revision of the first edition, a number of college teachers from various sections of the country were consulted. Their comments on their use of the book and suggestions for improvement of the new edition were exceedingly helpful. We hope that many of these music educators will find their ideas incorporated in this second edition. We would like them to know our deep appreciation of their assistance.

The Authors

How to Use This Book

An effective music program in the elementary school should be based on a cumulative sequence of musical experiences that will nourish the continuous growth of children in musical understanding, skills, and knowledge. The purpose in writing this book has been to show how such a music program can be organized and to suggest teaching procedures that may be utilized for promoting specific musical learnings.

The book is designed to be used as a text for music methods classes made up of future music specialists, future classroom teachers who have a background in music fundamentals, or members of in-service classes in music methods for the elementary schools. Present and future classroom teachers who have had little previous musical experience can gain the necessary musical skills and understanding needed for teaching music as they utilize the materials and techniques included in this text. School administrators, curriculum directors, and parents may also use this book to help them evaluate ongoing programs of music education in the elementary schools.

In this book we have sought to provide the teacher with a guide for translating music education objectives into day-to-day learning experiences and for fashioning year-by-year goals of musical attainment on the part of children. The latter are presented graphically in six Musical Growth Charts at the end of Part I, *Planning for Teaching Music,* which gives a philosophical orientation to the teaching of music. These charts show the sequential development of musical skills and concepts that children should exhibit from grade to grade. They are organized so that the teacher can evaluate the children's musical attainments in six areas of musical activities: listening, singing, playing, moving, creating, and reading. *In studying these charts it is important that the attainments outlined for each grade be seen as year-end accomplishments; skills and concepts may, in some instances, be introduced prior to the grade level at which they are first mentioned.*

Individual classes will vary greatly in musical attainment; the instruction must always be adjusted to the children's present stage of musical development. Careful scrutiny of the Musical Growth Charts will enable the teacher to determine the particular stage of development his class has reached and to plan future musical experiences accordingly. Subsequently, the charts may be used to indicate the direction in which future musical growth should proceed.

Part II, *Guiding Classroom Musical Experiences,* presents materials and teaching suggestions for a sequential program of music instruction in the elementary school. For each grade, a chart of teaching directions that parallels the Musical Growth Charts of Part I has been prepared. The teaching directions are in the form of "lesson plans," which the teacher might follow in presenting the material to the class.

These lesson plans should be considered as guides rather than dictums. They should be studied carefully and adapted to the particular group for which they are used. The individual plans have not been outlined in the sequence in which they must necessarily be followed. For example, when teaching a new song the teacher might have the children participate in all the *listening* activities suggested under the various *concept* categories (melody, rhythm, harmony, and so on). Later, the children may be engaged in all the *reading* activites, and so forth. It is not assumed that the teacher will use all of the teaching suggestions for any particular song or recording, nor should he attempt to incorporate too many of the suggestions in any one lesson. The music at hand should be reintroduced periodically, each time discovering some new aspect of it or exploring previously presented ideas in greater depth.

To make the plans in Part II as clear and usable as possible, the authors' comments directed to the teacher have been printed in text type, while the teacher's comments directed to the children have been set in **bold.** Possible answers to the teacher's questions, supplied by the children, have been placed in parentheses following the questions. The musical concept or the new term or symbol that is to be stressed in a particular lesson has been set in SMALL CAPITAL letters. The comments are not intended to be used as written, but should only be considered as models that the teacher can adapt to his own situation. It should also be pointed out that the lesson plans for Grades 2-6 are based on the assumption that the children are using a typical music book from one of the elementary series and that they therefore would see only the voice part, or parts, and not the full score as printed in this book.

We should like to stress that the ultimate value of these lesson plans will not be realized until the teacher, whether "in training" or "in service," adapts the procedures suggested to new materials of his own choice. Teachers of methods classes should encourage their students to make many such applications to materials selected for use at the particular level that interests them the most.

Part III, *Planning for Musical Learning,* deals with ways and means of teaching music in the elementary school. Procedures, materials, and equipment for the teaching of listening, singing, playing, moving, creating, and reading that have been found useful and effective are discussed more specifically. It is intended that the teacher should use this part as a reference for any teaching problems that may arise in presenting the materials contained in Part II. For this reason it is suggested that Part III be perused before proceeding with Part II, in order to facilitate the integration of these two sections of the book in making class assignments.

Finally, we should like to emphasize the theme of this book, *Musical growth comes from musically oriented teaching.* Only out of classroom experiences that are musically meaningful can the aims of those concerned with the musical education of children be attained: to help children discover, understand, and enjoy music as an art and as a means of self-expression.

B. B.
E. B.

Contents

PART I
PLANNING FOR TEACHING MUSIC

Preparation of the Teacher

You have chosen to embark upon one of the most exciting of all careers: helping children to learn—helping to evoke in them the desire to know, the need to discover, and the ability to explore. Yours will be the privilege of seeing the fruits of your labors, not in wood or stone, but in changed human beings. On some days it will seem that the fruits are sparse and stunted, or unbelievably long in maturing. But there will also be the days when the wonders and joy on a child's face as he realizes his increasing capacity to *do*, to control and change his world, will remind you once more that yours is at once the most challenging and the most rewarding of all professions.

The teacher's task is indeed an awe-inspiring one, for dealing in human lives cannot be taken lightly. Whether or not each individual attains his own potential and realizes the possibilities of himself and his world, depends in great measure on you, his teacher. For this reason, you will need to consider carefully and plan thoughtfully, not only for the day-to-day contacts between you and your children, but for the "long view" as well. What are your ultimate goals? What kind of changed human being do you hope to see as the child becomes an adult? *Why* do you teach children? *What* is most essential for them to know of their world? *How* can you be sure that they learn these essential concepts? *When* is the appropriate time for specific learnings to take place?

You, as a classroom teacher, will have to answer these questions in relation to every classroom experience: mathematics, social studies, or language arts. This book has been planned to help you as you seek answers to these questions in relation to musical learning: "Why teach music? What should you teach? How should you teach? When should you teach?"

WHY TEACH MUSIC?

The charting of a course of study, whether in music, mathematics, or nuclear science, must be soundly based on a knowledge of, and a commitment to, the reasons for teaching that subject. A teacher who is not sure *why* he is teaching is likely to be equally unsure of how, when, or what he should be teaching. The first question facing the potential teacher of music therefore must be, "Why teach music?"

Any answer to this question will depend at least partially on what is conceived as the purpose of all education. Views as to the purpose are as varied as they are numerous. Essentially, however, the role of education seems to be to equip the individual with the knowledge, skill, and insight that will help him control and adapt to his environment most adequately and that will prepare him for acceptable membership in his society.

As the history of man lengthens and the knowledge considered necessary for environmental control broadens, the problem of the educator becomes increasingly complex. He is faced with the necessity of sifting and sorting the mass of knowledge man has acquired and of selecting from it that which is essential and which will enable the individual to grow and adapt with a changing environment. The teacher must take care to ensure that each selection has been included only if it possesses the potential for generative rather than terminal learning, and that it offers unique alternatives to action. Ever-multiplying demands on the contemporary educational system make it imperative that such criteria be established. Crowded curriculums can no longer provide a place for the teaching of content that does not generate further learning or help provide the insights for continued growth. Neither is there a place for content that does not contribute uniquely to environmental control. Any subject, or segment of a subject, should retain a place in the curriculum only if it provides the individual with alternatives to action that no other subject might offer.

Recognizing the necessity of making selective choices, the teacher's first task must be to satisfy himself that music *does* provide something unique to man's well-being. He cannot hope, he should not try, to develop a music program until he has determined the contribution of music to the total human experience. Through the years a variety of views have been proposed as to the nature of this contribution. The following views are three that endeavor to show ways in which music does contribute uniquely to man's ability to control and adapt to his environment, thus satisfying our previously established criteria. Three possible answers to our first question, "Why teach music?" are: because it is part of the world about us, because it is part of our heritage, and because it is a means of personal expression.

Music—part of the world about us

Music's first claim to a place in the curriculum lies in the simple fact of its existence. If one function of education is to acquaint the individual with his environment, then surely music must be included, for it is an integral part of that environment. There is no phase of man's struggle for existence that has not been accompanied, communicated, and extended by music. From the most primitive to the most sophisticated of cultures, music has been central to every ritual. It has been the voice by which man gave praise and supplication to his God or gods, sang thanksgiving for the bountiful harvest, and voiced his pride in the traditions of his society. From dawn to dusk, from birth to death, in work or at play, musical sound surrounds him. Every significant event in man's personal life has had its accompanying musical expression.

In primitive cultures this musical expression was most often a personal involvement. The individual actively participated in the creation of the musical expression; he danced around the campfire, beat the drums, and chanted his praises and entreaties. The Indian boy created his own personal tune and played it on his flute to woo the maiden of his choice. The slave poured out his weariness and loneliness in song as he labored in the cotton fields; the mother rocked the cradle and sang of her love for her child as she rocked. Today one does not dance about the campfire or chant incantations to the gods; one is more likely to respond to the expression of others. Yet, music still surrounds

man. Baby is lulled to sleep by a mechanical music box. Music is piped throughout the factory for all to hear, whether or not it fits one's "expressive need" at the moment. Individuals have become, except for the professional, primarily "reactors" rather than "actors" in our society.

Still, music—for recreation, for communication, or for emotional expression—is as important in the life of modern man as it was in the life of the savage. Even the economic system bends to its force—listen to the daily assault of the advertising jingle. Music is used to sell products, to increase efficiency in factories and offices, to provide therapy for the ill, to commemorate every important occasion from the Homecoming parade to the Centennial pageant. Music is a part of the world about us, a part of our lives.

Music—part of our heritage

The history of music is the history of mankind. Woven into the musical fabric of the centuries is a tale of man's striving toward a better and richer life. In many subtle ways music provides a record of how man has reacted in his struggle with his environment, of what he had held dear, and of what he has seen as important to his well-being. Music reflecting national pride did not arise in the nineteenth century by happenstance; it was a direct reflection of a period in which national states were becoming solidified and in which patriotism was an emotion held dear by the man in the street as well as by the composer.

Similarly, the fact that Mexican music is often confused with the music of Spain is not a coincidence. Here is an example of events far removed from the concert hall or theater influencing dramatic expression. Mexico was a country with a long, proud history, including a rich musical culture; a country whose own civilization was almost completely obliterated by its foreign conqueror. So in Mexico City today one hears, not the drums of the Incas, but the castanets of the Spaniards—a living memorial to a conquering people.

In the culture of America the history of the westward movement comes alive in song. "Meltingpot" becomes more than a catchword, as one listens to the English folk songs of the Appalachian mountains, the plaintive tunes of the cowboy and the Sooner, and the provocative melodies of the Negro, the Latin, and the Oriental. One becomes truly alive to the priceless and varied musical heritage that belongs to him.

This musical heritage is composed not only of the music of the folk, however. Musicians keep searching for better ways to organize and control the elements of sound, just as others have searched for ways to control different elements within their environment, each trying to satisfy a particular human need for food, for shelter, or for beauty. As the search continues, specialists develop: scientists, architects, and musicians. The modes of control become more sophisticated. Out of the primitive musical expression, and side by side with it, grows a more subtle musical utterance. Where there once occurred a simple, spontaneous outpouring of the daily fears and desires of the individual, the expression that now appears is less immediate and personal. As in a more primitive culture each man spoke of "my loneliness" or "my fear," the musician now speaks of "loneliness" and "fear." Thus his music, by speaking for all, takes its place beside the music of the folk as part of the cultural heritage.

Music—a means of personal expression

There is no desire or emotion felt by man that is not reflected in his art. Regardless of the simplicity or complexity of the culture, the emotions common to all men find expression through artistic form. The love of parent for child, man for woman, or patriot for homeland is revealed through the lullaby, the serenade, the patriotic song. The sorrow from loss of home, departure of loved ones, or tragedy of war finds release through the medium of music. Humor, weariness, awe—all are portrayed through musical sound. If there is a universality of music it lies in the unanimity with which men through time have responded musically to the same human expressions and experiences.

This ability of man to express his emotions through some kind of symbolism (words, musical sounds, color, and line) might well be considered his highest attainment. Music contributes to the life of feeling in a way that language cannot. It is not bound, as are words, by specific meanings. In music each can find his own expression and create his own interpretation. The composer of "Three New England Sketches," Walter Piston, tells of a man who asked him if he minded that he "smelled clams" during the first sketch. Mr. Piston replied, "I don't mind at all, they're your clams!"[1] And so it is with music—what one takes from it will depend on what he brings to it. The response may occur on different levels; one may "smell clams" while another responds purely to the organization of the musical elements. Each response is legitimate, though one might remain more satisfying than the other. Everyone will respond at different levels at different times, depending on the type of music and on his mood at the moment. The level of response will also depend on his acquaintance with the elements of musical organization, just as his ability to grasp a foreign language depends on his familiarity with its idioms.

Implications for teaching music

Three answers have been given to the question, "Why teach music?" Music is a force within our daily lives; it is a part of our heritage; it provides us with a means of personal expression. The acceptance of these answers as the reasons for music's place in the curriculum will provide shape and direction to the musical experiences the teacher plans for his children.

The teacher will know that it is his responsibilitiy to help pupils discover ways to participate more fully in their musical environment. He will help them learn how to listen to music with understanding and discrimination. He will strive to assist them in acquiring the necessary musical skills and in finding the joy that comes from adequate musical performance. He will aid them in their exploration of the realm of creative music as an expressive medium. He will show them ways to continue their musical growth after they are away from the classroom by encouraging them to use their increased knowledge and insight in selecting records, attending concerts, or choosing television programs. Furthermore, as children are introduced to various types of music, the teacher will help them to grasp the relation of music to people, to see music as a record of man's most personal impressions and expressions.

The teacher will also remember that each

[1] Walter Piston, "Can Music be Nationalistic?," *Music Journal,* October 1961.

musical selection used in the classroom must be chosen with care. Man's heritage is so rich and so vast that no one can possibly learn it all. Criteria of representativeness, authenticity, and musical value must be applied in the selection, for time cannot be wasted on music of little consequence.

Finally, the teacher will be mindful of music's potential as a personal mode of response and expression. Musical expression and responsiveness occur on various levels from the simple to the highly complex. A lack of understanding of how music is organized commits the individual to the lowest levels of musical response indefinitely. Also, the teacher will remember that children discover the value of music as an expressive vehicle by exploring music that is of expressive value.

It is the teacher's responsibility to introduce his pupils to the possibilities of musical performance and response, the literature of their heritage, and the elements of musical organization so that they may use them to satisfy their own needs for personal expression and increase and deepen their capacity for discriminating musical response. Only to the degree that teachers make children alive to these possibilities, and help them gain the needed skill, knowledge, and insight can a music program be considered successful.

WHAT SHALL WE TEACH?

The acceptance of the conclusions offered as answers to *why* teach music immediately gives a particular focus to one's decision regarding *what* to teach. An individual can become sensitive to music in his life, but it will remain a potent force for him only if he has acquired an understanding of the concepts involved in musical organization, some functional skills of musical performance, and a wide knowledge of musical literature. Thus, there are three clear answers to the question, "What shall we teach?"

Basic concepts of musical organization

The philosophy of this book is based upon the belief that musical maturity and independence are dependent upon the possession of those concepts that give an insight into expressive musical organization. These concepts must form the central core of the elementary music curriculum.

The conceptual structure of music is concerned with the elements of music—melody, rhythm, and harmony and their formal, expressive, and stylistic organization. Specific concepts relating to the organization of each of these elements are essential to musical understanding, whether the music to be comprehended is a simple folk tune or an intricate fugue.

It is possible to introduce basic musical concepts in a meaningful manner in the early grades. When presented to the young child in a vocabulary and in a context suited to his maturity, they become clear and comprehensible to him, and remain valid and useful as he continues his education in music. Such an approach to musical learning is truly developmental for it is based, not on the introduction of new and different knowledge at each stage of learning, but on a sequence of experiences involving the same concepts investigated in ever-increasing depth and breadth.

As the individual grows in his understanding of the complexities of musical organization, he also needs more precise terminology to help him identify and define these elements. So with increased comprehension of musical structure must go an increasingly sophisticated vocabulary and an understanding of notation as symbolizing the musical concepts he already grasps. The ability to use these symbols with an understanding of their meaning is essential if he is to perceive the musical ideas of others or to communicate his own.

The following listing of musical concepts is not intended to be absolute or all-inclusive, nor are the concepts arranged in the order of increasing difficulty. The child will be growing in awareness of many concepts simultaneously, moving gradually from an awareness of the obvious to a comprehension of the hidden.

CONCEPTS OF RHYTHMIC ORGANIZATION

Rhythm is a sequence of sounds and/or silences of varying duration creating a pattern controlled by an underlying pulsation. The concepts necessary to an understanding of rhythmic organization include:

BEAT. Rhythm is usually governed by a pulse (beat) which is steady, continuous, and "ongoing" even throughout silences in the music.

ACCENT GROUPINGS. Beats may vary in that some are heavy and some are light. The sequential order of heavy–light beats determine the "accent groupings" (meter). Music may move in accent groups of twos (heavy–light), or threes (heavy–light–light), or a combination of these groups: fours, fives, and so forth.

PATTERN. Rhythmic patterns are groupings of sounds and/or silences of related durations.
1. The relationship of sounds and/or silences within rhythmic patterns are perceived as longer, shorter, or the same. These relationships are always 2-1 (♩ ♩ = 𝅗𝅥 , ♫ = ♩ , ♫ = ♪) or 3-1 (♩ ♩ ♩ = 𝅗𝅥. , ♫♩ = 𝅗𝅥. , ♫♫ = ♪).

2. Rhythmic patterns may be even (♩ ♩ , ♩ ♫ , 𝅗𝅥. ♫♫) or uneven (𝅗𝅥. ♪ , ♩ ♪♪ ♪ , ♩. ♫♩. ♫).

RHYTHM OF THE MELODY. Melodic movement is rhythmically controlled. A melody may move with tones that sound with the beat, are shorter than the beat, or longer than the beat. Rhythmic patterns within the rhythm of the melody may be primarily even or uneven.

CONCEPTS OF MELODIC ORGANIZATION

Melody is a succession of tones (pitches), the movement of which is rhythmically controlled. An understanding of melodic organization involves an awareness of the entity, "This progression of sounds that I hear is a melody." Concepts involved in melodic organization are:

UP-DOWN-SAME. Melody is tonal movement. Tones may move upward, downward, or stay on the same level (melodic direction), creating an over-all "shape" or melodic contour.

STEP-SKIP-SAME. Tonal movement may progress by steps (whole, half), by skips (thirds, fourths, and so on), or by repetition of the same tone.

RANGE. The melodic entity may include tones that are near together or far apart. The over-all extent of pitches included in a melody determines its range, which may be narrow or wide.

HIGH-LOW. There are actually two concepts involved here. We speak of a violin as being a "high" instrument and of a cello as being a "low" instrument; or of a soprano voice as "high" and a bass voice as "low." Each of these instruments or voices, however, may execute a melody in which tones are higher or lower in terms of pitch progressions. In the first case, "high" and "low" are absolute; in the second case, they are relative.

TONAL ORGANIZATION. All melodic movement is governed by some kind of tonal organization: scales (major, minor, pentatonic, whole tone), modes, tone row, and so on. Melodies based on major and minor scales are related to a tonal center or key tone (tonality).

CONCEPTS OF HARMONIC ORGANIZATION

Harmony is used here in its broadest sense to describe music in which there is a melody with chordal accompaniment (homophonic), as well as music having, simultaneously, two or more independent melodic lines (polyphonic), as in a round or a fugue. An understanding of harmonic organization is dependent on the realization of the existence and possibilities of these combinations. The following concepts are basic to this understanding:

MULTIPLE SOUNDS. Multiple sounds are created by sounding two or more tones simultaneously. They may be perceived as intervals or chords related to the tonality that governs the composition.

REST-UNREST. Multiple sounds produce feelings of rest and unrest. Some sounds are tension-producing and require resolution, whereas other sounds are restful because they do not demand immediate movement. These qualities of rest and unrest depend on the intervallic relationships used and on the context in which they are placed.

TEXTURE. Musical texture is the relationship of vertical (harmonic) and horizontal (melodic) elements of music. When a single melody is accompanied by chords, the texture is described as homophonic; when two or more prominent melodies are sounded simultaneously, the texture is said to be polyphonic. The texture may be "thin" or "thick," depending on how many tones are sounded at the same time and how they are spaced vertically.

CONCEPTS OF FORMAL ORGANIZATION

Form is the organization of musical ideas into meaningful designs of "tone in time." Form gives continuity to a "musical whole" by the successive ordering of recognizable musical segments. Concepts essential to understanding formal organization include:

MOTIVE. A motive is the smallest musical segment. It is brief and fragmentary, and may be either a rhythmic or melodic pattern.

PHRASE. A phrase is a musical thought or idea, the end of which is marked by a point of rest (cadence). A phrase may be composed of a combination of motives, or it may be a single continuous pattern. Phrases may vary in length (two, three, four, or more measures) and may be combined in various ways to form larger musical segments or a musical whole.

REPETITION–CONTRAST. Musical form is based on the principle of repetition and non-repetition (contrast). A musical pattern may be repeated or it may be followed by a new contrasting pattern. Variations of the first pattern may function either as contrast or as repetition. Repetition provides unity within a musical design; contrast offers variety.

CONCEPTS OF EXPRESSIVE ORGANIZATION

Expressiveness is that quality of music which conveys a "way of feeling." This is communicated through the organization of melody, rhythm, harmony, tempo, dynamics, and tone color within the musical totality. An awareness of music's expressiveness depends on the realization that all of these elements contribute to the expressive purpose of the music.

MELODY. The choice of tonal organization, the number and sizes of intervals within the melody and its over-all range contribute to the expressive character of the music.

RHYTHM. The choice of accent groupings, the relation of the rhythm of the melody to the underlying beat, the regular or irregular movement of the rhythmic pattern help to determine the nature of the musical expression.

HARMONY. The type of texture, the frequency and placement of harmonic changes contribute to impressions of stability or instability, thus reinforcing the expressive qualities of rhythmic and melodic organization.

TEMPO. The speed at which the beat recurs may be described as the tempo. Music may move at varying rates of speed (fast-slow). Not only is there a basic tempo that contributes to expression, but this tempo may be altered within the musical whole. One section may be faster than or slower than another; also, within any section the tempo may be gradually speeded up (accelerando) or slowed down (ritardando).

DYNAMICS. The degree of loudness (loud-soft) of a musical performance helps to determine its expressiveness. This expression may be affected by contrasts between sections—louder than or softer than—and/or by the music becoming gradually louder (crescendo) or gradually softer (decrescendo) within sections.

TONE COLOR. The same pitch will give a different expressive impression when played by different instruments or sung by different voices. An individual instrument or voice may also alter the tone color by changes in tone production. The manner in which various tone colors (timbres) are combined also influences the expressive character of the music.

CONCEPTS OF STYLISTIC ORGANIZATION

Style in music has a variety of meanings; it may characterize music of different cultures, periods, or composers as well as types, methods, and mediums of compositions. It is the unique organization of elements that creates a particular musical style.

MELODY. Melody helps to determine style by its tonal organization (tonality), total range, number and sizes of skips, tonal movement, spacing of cadences, and placement and height of climax.

RHYTHM. Rhythm helps to determine style by the nature of its underlying organization (meter), its characteristic patterns, and the way in which rhythmic lines are combined.

HARMONY. Harmony helps to determine style by the kind of tonal organization upon which it is based, the type of progressions used (harmony, counterpoint), the intervallic relationships of chord structure, and the speed with which chords progress from one to another.

FORM. Form helps to determine style by the length of phrases, the type and extent of repetition and contrast used, and the manner in which melodic and rhythmic motives are varied.

EXPRESSION. Expressive characteristics that help to determine style are basic tempo, the use or absence of acceleration and retardation, dynamics, and tone color.

A foundation of musical skills

One's ability to use music as a medium by which he may express his feelings about, or reactions to, the world about him is dependent upon an understanding of certain basic musical concepts. It was noted that conceptual understanding is dependent upon learning in and through a musical context that is meaningful to the child. Part of one's answer to "What shall we teach?" must therefore include a consideration of the kinds of activities that will best contribute to this understanding and that will provide the individual with skills of performance and response enabling him to reveal, and to use, these musical insights.

Recognizing that individuals may develop essential musical concepts in varying ways and that different skills contribute differently to the total musical understanding of the child, the teacher should include in music time as wide a variety of skill activities as possible. Such variety also allows the child to experiment with each skill until he can determine which is most satisfying for him as a mode of musical expression.

Each child should be given the opportunity to discover that there are different ways of producing music: it can be sung, individually or in groups, and it can be played on a variety of instruments, by oneself or with others. He should also have the privilege of exploring the different ways that music can be used as an expressive medium: he can produce his own music, he can reproduce music created by others, and he can respond to the reproductions of other individuals.

The following skills are commonly included as part of the content of the elementary music curriculum. It is through the exploration of these skills that children grow in musical understanding. Only if all of them are presented can each child find the medium best suited to his own abilities and interests, thus equipping him to give voice to his own feelings or to ascertain the feelings of others.

LISTENING. Listening is the most essential of all musical skills. Music is "sound" and it communicates its message aurally. An individual will become a sensitive performer or responder only if he listens to himself and to others with discrimination. This ability is a learned skill, which must be taught as carefully as any other skill.

SINGING. Singing is a skill that one may take with him everywhere he goes, all through his life. For this reason it is especially important that it be taught as an integral part of the music curriculum. Emphasis should be placed on learning:

1. To sing a melody accurately with good tone quality
2. To maintain a harmonizing part independently

PLAYING. The experience of playing common classroom instruments is an activity in which many may participate on varying levels of competence, each individual contributing an important part to the whole and each receiving satisfaction from that whole. There should be opportunities for:

1. Playing simple percussion instruments, such as the drum, sticks, and triangle
2. Playing simple melodic instruments, such as the resonator bells, xylophone, and recorder
3. Using the autoharp for chordal accompaniments
4. Exploring at the piano keyboard, including how to chord

MOVING. For some individuals, moving to music—responding with body movements rather than playing or singing—may be the most satisfying skill. Young children often learn certain concepts better through this mode of expression than any other. There should be occasions to experiment with:

1. Free interpretation and characterization

2. Fundamental movements, such as walking, running, and skipping
3. Singing games and folk dances

CREATING.   To produce one's own compositions is perhaps the ultimate, and certainly the most personal, of all musical expressions. While few children may ever produce compositions of lasting value or pursue this activity in later years, all should have the opportunity to experiment with improvisation and composition. Creative music should include such activities as:

1. Developing a simple percussive or melodic accompaniment
2. Composing a melody to fit a poem
3. Improvising within an instrumental ensemble
4. Writing instrumental compositions
5. Planning a dance
6. Contributing to a class project, such as an operetta

READING.   One's ability to progress in the development of many of the above-mentioned skills will be closely related to his growing ability to associate sound with notational symbols. If children are to attain musical skills that they can use independently, they must be able to interpret notation vocally or instrumentally and to notate their own compositional efforts. Attention should be directed to:

1. Symbols of pitch and tonality
2. Symbols of duration and meter
3. Symbols used for harmonization
4. Symbols used for expression

A basic repertoire of music literature

The child grows in conceptual understanding and in musical skills through the learning of a repertoire of suitable music literature. As the child grows in his understanding of musical organization and in his ability to perform and respond to music, his repertoire of songs and instrumental compositions should expand correspondingly. A third aspect of our answer to "What shall we teach?" must be concerned with the selection of this repertoire.

The choice of repertoire must first and foremost reflect one's reasons for teaching music. If it is the purpose of music education to help children become aware of their heritage, then the choice of music must reflect this concern.

Every song and every composition must have value as part of a nation's past or its present culture. In a sense, any music created honestly and sincerely for a musical purpose might be included if we use such a criterion.

The music literature selected must also help children realize that music is a mode of personal communication. In the opening section it was asserted that there have been few human activities or emotions that have not been accompanied by, or reflected through, music. The total elementary repertoire should include music that expresses or describes feelings and experiences such as love, religious fervor, patriotism, work, play, and festival observances.

If the aims discussed are to be realized, then the scope of the repertoire must be broad enough to include examples of varied types of literature as well as various media of musical expression. Examples from each of the following categories should be added to the child's repertoire sometime during his elementary school music career.

TYPES OF MUSIC

FOLK MUSIC

1. *Composer unknown.* This category should introduce children to the musical lore of all the cultures of the world, past and present. These are the songs whose origin is lost and whose composers remain unknown.
2. *Composer known.* "Folk-type" songs, such as the Stephen Foster songs and patriotic songs, fall in this category. These songs, with which people have identified closely, are often considered as part of our folk heritage. They are generally as simple and naive in their musical message as the true folk song.

ART MUSIC

1. *Time-honored.* Historically, art music gradually reached a more important position in man's music-making. Similarly, this music should gradually form a greater part of the repertoire of children. Works of the master composer, recognized by their permanence in our musical heritage, should be included, but because of their complexity they will probably be taught best through listening experiences rather than through singing and playing at the elementary level.

2. *Contemporary.* Children should also have the privilege of exploring the newer serious expressions of present-day composers. Contemporary music is as much a part of their heritage as is the music of the past.

Teachers should also share the responsibility of helping children to become aware of such uniquely American forms of music as jazz and musical comedy.

MUSICAL MEDIA

VOCAL. The repertoire of vocal music should include not only those songs that the children may sing themselves, but selections beyond their present performing abilities.

1. *Solo literature.* This should include folk and art songs, and songs from operettas, operas, and oratorio for all types of voices: soprano, alto, tenor, and bass.
2. *Ensemble literature.* This should include music representing various styles and periods for different types of ensembles: madrigal, cantata, opera, and oratorio.

INSTRUMENTAL. The repertoire of instrumental music should include the whole range of old and new literature.

1. *Solo literature.* Examples of compositions for all common solo instruments should be presented.
2. *Small ensemble literature.* Children should be introduced to the standard literature for string quartet, brass, woodwind, and percussion ensembles.
3. *Large ensemble literature.* Music composed for band and orchestra (symphonies, concertos, suites, tone poems, and so on) will form an important part of the elementary school repertoire.

When selecting representative types of music in various media, careful attention must be given to choosing music of good quality and to avoiding the musically mediocre. The quality of music is difficult to measure, but there are some clues one may look for when selecting music for children:

1. Is the total musical expression arresting, drawing and impelling?
2. Does the melodic line evolve naturally and logically, making it relatively easy to learn and to recall?
3. Is there balance between repetition and contrast: melodically, rhythmically, and harmonically?
4. Is there balance between movement and rest: melodically, rhythmically, and harmonically?
5. Does the music create patterns of tension and release—moving toward points of climax that are subsequently resolved?

When selecting songs we may ask:

1. Does the music fit the expressive meaning of the text?
2. Does the rhythmic flow of the music match the natural rhythmic flow of the words?
3. Does the accompaniment reinforce the expressive qualities of the melodic line?

When selecting instrumental compositions we may ask:

1. Is the composition a worthy representative of the type or form of music under consideration?
2. Is the composition idiomatic of the particular style or of the composer it is intended to represent?
3. Is the medium (instrumentation) suitable to the expressive intent of the composer?

IMPLICATIONS FOR TEACHING MUSIC

The three answers given to the question, "What shall we teach?" suggests that the teacher must plan the teaching of music in the elementary school in terms of the concepts, skills, and music literature which the children should learn. Consequently, there are three well-defined steps that the teacher must follow in planning for teaching:

1. The first step must always be to determine the concepts that are to be emphasized: "At what stage of conceptual growth are my children? What musical concepts are they now prepared to explore?"
2. The second step calls for the choice of skill(s) to emphasize: "By what means will my children best learn this concept? Which skill or combination of skills will most readily further their understanding of the concept in question?" As he determines the answers

to these questions, the teacher will also assure himself that over a period of time he has provided for the inclusion of a variety of skills.

3. Finally, the teacher will select the literature to be used. The choice of composition will be based first on its musical value and on its worth as part of the cultural heritage, as well as on the extent to which the music characterizes the particular musical concepts that are to be learned at the time.

If the preceding steps are followed consistently and carefully, we shall be assured that the content of the elementary music program will provide for the accumulation of understanding, skill, and knowledge essential to musical growth.

HOW SHALL WE TEACH?

In the discussion of musical concepts expressiveness was described as the quality of music that communicates a "way of feeling." Ultimately, this is what the teacher will want to share with his children: to teach so that music becomes for children a source of beauty and joy, and so that the making of (or listening to) music becomes a satisfying experience because it provides a very special kind of immediate, personal communication. This, then, will be the guide as the question "How shall we teach?" is considered.

We should teach so that the focus is ever on the music, on its expressive purpose, and on the organization of the elements that contribute to its expressiveness. We should teach so that every music time ends with that excited feeling of having accomplished something. Then the learning of music becomes an end in itself. *Music time* is time to explore, time to discover, time to share the wonders of music; the wonder that it can say in a new, and perhaps better, way that which one feels most strongly, whether it be the mystery of love, the fear of the unknown, or just the simple joy of being alive.

If this is to happen, there are certain principles that the teacher must keep in mind, else music time becomes stagnant and repetitious—a time for drill rather than discovery, imitation rather than exploration. Young children respond naturally to the expressiveness of music. Even a tiny child quiets at the sound of a lullaby and laughs with the gay tunes of the circus clown. If this responsiveness is to be kept alive, then his musical experiences must grow with him. Young children are growing physically, emotionally, and intellectually. They will also grow musically if we do not stunt that growth by forgetting that musical learning must keep pace with other learnings. *How* one teaches, therefore, will be guided by what one knows about children's growth. This knowledge will be used in the selection of musical content at each grade level and in planning the situation in which that content is to be learned.

Using our knowledge of physical growth

Until a child is physically mature enough to perform a task with reasonable facility and without prolonged drill, teaching that task may be inefficient, if not harmful. Consistent failure is not conducive to building favorable attitudes toward the task involved. With this in mind, the choice of musical experiences, and the manner in which they are taught, will be based on one's knowledge of the physical growth patterns of children.

Children in the kindergarten and first grade are just beginning to develop some degree of muscular coordination. Instruments used in these classes will be those that do not demand a high degree of physical control: simple percussion instruments, including step and resonator bells. Similarly, the rhythmic and tonal patterns used with these instruments will be simple and repetitious, well within the physical powers of children to perform easily.

As children grow they acquire the physical control needed to play a variety of classroom instruments. With maturation and previous experience in handling instruments, second, third, and fourth graders are ready to experiment with continually more complex tonal and rhythmic patterns. The song bells, the xylophone, the piano, and the autoharp are some of the new instruments that are suitable to these stages in physical development. By the fourth grade children will probably be physically ready for recorder-type instruments as well as many of the traditional orchestral instruments. Fifth and sixth graders can usually handle all classroom instruments easily, including the more "exotic" ones used for playing complex calypso and syncopated rhythms, with expressive results.

Decisions regarding what instruments to introduce at any grade level must be based upon musical as well as physical considerations. Is the time and effort involved in overcoming physical problems worth the musical product that results? Young children may be able to memorize complicated patterns and, in time, learn to execute them in an acceptable manner. Such sustained effort, however, often results in a mechanistic, lifeless product. A simple performance, done with musical sensitivity, may come closer to fulfilling the educational purpose of the music class. If music time is to be a musical time, the situation must contain that potential.

Our awareness of children's physical growth patterns will also be reflected in the types of movement to music that are used in teaching. Young children learn with their whole bodies, and moving to music is important to their over-all musical development. In using various forms of movement it must be remembered that muscular coordination is being developed and that musical demands must match, while at the same time nurture, the physical development.

Early experiments in moving to music will emphasize movements that are most natural to young children: fundamental movements such as walking, running, skipping, and so on, combined in a free and undirected manner. As children explore these movements, their attention will be directed to the rhythmic, melodic, and expressive features of the music. The music teacher is not concerned primarily with teaching children how to walk or to skip; he is interested in helping them to use such movements expressively in response to the musical stimulus.

As children become increasingly adept in coordinated movement, they are able to respond to more subtle nuances in the music. Whereas kindergarteners and first graders will respond primarily to the over-all feeling of the music with large gross movements, the second, third, and fourth graders are able to reflect their growing awareness of musical concepts through increasingly differentiated movements. Consequently, they should be encouraged to use this improving physical control to respond to more and more specific variations in rhythmic patterns and to use their bodies to reflect the rise and fall of the melodic line with more exactness. Later, the fifth and sixth graders should be helped to search for, and to respond to, changes in harmonic progressions, to variations in form, and to differences in musical style. Intermediate children are also ready to learn specific dance steps such as the polka and the waltz. As children enter the sixth grade, however, the spurt in physical development that takes place prior to adolescence may cause some boys and girls to find moving experiences both difficult and embarrassing. The sensitive teacher will take such changes into consideration in deciding when to use such activities.

A knowledge of physical maturation will also affect the teaching of singing. There are studies which show that young children's vocal ranges are quite limited, about five tones from d' to a':

In time, this range gradually extends both upward and downward. For this reason, many of the songs selected for use in the kindergarten and the first grade should be songs that are limited in range to the octave c' to c". Songs encompassing wider ranges may be introduced gradually in the intermediate and upper grades. At the sixth grade level, however, some voices are beginning to change, and songs must be selected to accommodate these changes. Probably more important than total range is the range in which most of the pitches of a song lie (the tessitura). A song that lies chiefly in the range from a' to e":

is more difficult for young children than one that lies mostly in a lower range, e' to b':

moving to higher pitches only occasionally.

Not only must the range be considered in the selection of songs, but the complexity of the melodic line is also important. For young children, songs with extremely wide skips may be difficult. Songs that use numerous repeated tones or that move by many half steps may also be hard for the young child to reproduce accurately. Whether this is a problem of physical and sensory maturation or of experience has not been precisely determined. It is known, however, that young children have difficulty in discriminating and in reproducing fine variations of pitch and duration. This knowledge will affect the planning of listening lessons as well. Young children will not be expected to perceive small intervallic progressions in the melodic line or subtle changes in tempo, dynamics, or form, with any degree of exactitude. As they mature and improve in sensory discrimination, the teacher will want to center the children's attention on these subtleties, for they contribute much to musical expressiveness.

Using our knowledge of emotional growth

Just as a child grows physically, so he also shows increasing emotional maturity. Musical experiences must be planned with this in mind if music time is to continue to meet each child's changing emotional needs.

The emotional life of the kindergartener and first grader is narrow and self-centered. He is concerned with the outer world primarily as it affects him. Keeping this in mind, the teacher should select musical experiences for him that reflect those emotions with which he has had some experience: love for mother, affection for pets, wonder at a story, the exuberance of special days, or the mystery of the night.

Musical activities will often include those that can be done individually: songs that can be performed alone or that call for solos and creative movements that do not require conformity to the group. At the same time, the teacher will select many activities that require group participation such as singing games, dramatizations, and dances, which involve several children.

As the child matures, his emotional life widens. The second and third grader is becoming aware of others, not merely as they affect him, but as individuals with personalities and interests of their own. His broadening awareness is reflected in his enthusiastic participation in activities that require cooperative effort. Now, too, his imagination begins to soar. Fantasy and daydreams are important parts of the second and third grader's life as he uses these means of traveling beyond his own narrowly bounded physical environment. Music

that allows his imagination free reign—songs of adventure, nonsense songs, and so forth—are favorite choices. Now is the time to encourage the child to explore all the imaginative possibilities of music. Dramatizing songs and instrumental compositions, planning dance movements, drawing pictures to music he has heard, making up songs to sing and to play (and presenting them before friends and parents) will be important activities during music time at this age.

By the fourth grade, the typical child has adjusted himself to his immediate environment and is ready to push his frontiers outward in time and space. The world of long-ago and faraway calls to him and with it the deeper emotions and interests that are part of this bigger universe. Pride in his country is reflected in the fervor with which he sings (and ever resings) his favorite patriotic songs. A curiosity about people of other times and places leads to an interest in their music. Eager, intent, and with a longer attention span, the fourth and fifth grader is ready for, and desirous of, new challenges. The teacher must recognize this in his choice of material and in his planning of a wide variety of activities that will meet these expanding interests. Projects covering a long span of time, such as units covering the music of a country or of a period of history, can now be proposed.

By the sixth grade, new and strange things may be happening to some children's bodies. Emotional stability, recently secure, may totter and must be regained. A larger world has brought the sixth grader nearer to larger emotions which sometimes are more than he can absorb. Music can help him accept these emotions as he discovers that these feelings are shared by others, and that through music he can express doubts, fears, and longings that he did not feel free or able to verbalize. Too often it is at this age that school music experiences fail to meet the child's emotional needs and interests. If music is to remain meaningful to him, it must have grown with him. The sixth grader is ready at times to respond to music, to sing songs, which speak of more mature emotions. "Fun songs" and play-party tunes are not always enough. Sometimes he is ready for music that speaks of emotions of tenderness or of grief in more subtle ways. He is ready to discover new and more precise forms of musical expression.

Using our knowledge of intellectual growth

A knowledge of how children grow intellectually, of how they acquire concepts, has important and specific implications for decisions pertaining to teaching method. Understanding some of the principles involved in concept learning will help the teacher plan classroom experiences that allow for more efficient musical learning.

The process of conceptualization is the means by which an individual organizes his sensory experiences. Concepts allow him to generalize, to differentiate and to categorize classes of objects, qualities, or relationships. They provide the individual with tools for problem solving in new situations. The ability to conceptualize gives the individual the possibility for "progressive learning," that is, the building of new learnings on previously acquired conceptual organizations.

Although there is disagreement on exactly how concepts are acquired, there are certain principles that the teacher should take into consideration. Implied in each of the principles is the necessity for self-discovery. Teaching for concept development is more than providing for rote memorization. If conceptual knowledge is to be useful for the learner, it must be based on individual exploration and experimentation. Seven principles of conceptual learning may serve as guides when the teacher prepares daily lessons.

CONCEPT FORMATION IS DEPENDENT UPON THE ABILITY TO PERCEIVE

Certainly, the capacity of the individual to perceive, to register upon the defining characteristic of a concept, is basic. The relative ease with which a concept is attained is directly dependent upon the clarity with which the individual may perceive the features to be conceptualized. As a concept occurs at more and more perceptual levels (seeing, hearing, tasting, smelling, touching), conceptualization occurs more readily. Translated into music methodology this suggests the desirability of wide sensory experiences involving not only the ear, but the eye and the body as well. Active pupil exploration, where the child actually manipulates and experiments with stimuli, is superior to methods that provide only for verbal responses. Classroom activities should regularly include all kinds of musical participation: singing, playing, moving, listening, and seeing a variety of visual representations of music. Situations should be arranged in which individual children may have opportunities for exploration and experimentation with a minimum of teacher direction or control.

CONCEPT FORMATION PROCEEDS FROM THE CONCRETE TO THE ABSTRACT

Concepts involving concrete objects are most readily acquired by the young child. Many of the concepts of music are so abstract, so obtuse in that they borrow terminology and characteristics from other categories of concepts, that the importance of concrete experiences in music study cannot be overemphasized. The introduction of melodic concepts such as "up" and "down," "step" and "skip" must be planned around the use of materials and activities that make these concepts as concrete as possible. They can best be grasped if they are related to spacial concepts that can be concretely perceived: bodily movement, space instruments (such as step bells), and visual diagrams of all kinds. Concepts of "long" and "short," "fast" and "slow" can also be related to bodily movement (big and little steps, running and walking) and to spacial references that can be visually and kinesthetically experienced.

CONCEPTS ARE FORMED GRADUALLY

The formation of any particular concept is a long, slow process that moves from vague to clear, inexact to definite. Changes occur in the implications, relationships, and transfer possibilities that an individual sees within the concept as many sensory experiences gradually become synthesized or integrated into a single meaningful definition. Teachers should keep in mind that a single musical experience will not suffice for the development of musical understanding. Learning the concept of "accent groups" not only requires numerous concrete experiences, but experiences that are recurrent over a long period of time. Such repetition allows the child to test his vaguely formed definition in new situations. Each new experience should allow him to become more convinced of the validity of the principle he is evolving. Only by such recurrence will he develop a concept to the point that it becomes an independent tool useful in solving new musical problems.

CONCEPT FORMATION IS DEPENDENT UPON THE COMPLEXITY OF THE EXAMPLE

The amount of effort required to form a concept is directly related to the complexity of the examples from which the concept must be derived. Music, even in its simplest form, is still a highly complex art. The graspings of melodic, rhythmic, or harmonic concepts within the musical whole will be difficult at best. The selection of musical examples in which the concept to be studied is clearly evident is one of the most difficult, yet essential, tasks of the teacher. "Steps" and "skips" will be more easily grasped when the composition used for the introductory example illustrates both as clearly as possible. "My Pony" (p. 74) is a better choice for such study than "Hey, Betty Martin" (p. 62) because the two types of melodic movement (steps and skips) are clearly separated within the musical phrase.

CONCEPT LEARNING MOVES FROM THE SIMPLE TO THE COMPLEX

The thoughtful teacher will make sure that his children have first comprehended the simpler concepts before he attempts to introduce those that are more complex. For example, a young child may be ready to understand "high" and "low" where the differences are great, but far from ready to specify the differences between tones only a half step apart. The sixth grader may recognize the difference in quality between major and minor intervals, but not between minor and diminished. Concepts related to musical expressiveness or style are dependent upon the merging of simpler, less complex concepts, and will take on meaning for the student only as he grows in his comprehension of the more basic concepts of melody, rhythm, harmony, form, and so on.

CONCEPT LEARNING MOVES FROM GENERAL TO SPECIFIC AND FROM WHOLE TO PART

As a new idea is introduced, an individual first grasps the over-all configuration and only gradually becomes aware of specific details within the whole. Translated into a teaching principle, this suggests that in every new learning situation one must consider the problem in its entirety: the over-all contour of the melody, the generally even or uneven nature of the rhythm. Only after this has been experienced can one expect young children to begin to isolate individual patterns that combine to create the musical totality.

This principle also has meaning as children grow intellectually. The young child will grasp only the broad implications of a concept. He hears and responds at first only to the over-all "upness" and "downness" of melodic direction, or to obvious contrasts and repetitions of musical phrases. It is only as the child develops conceptually that he is ready to see more specific details. The kindergartener recognizes the unevenness of the rhythmic pattern, the first and second grader describes duration as longer and shorter, the fourth grader comprehends relationships of 2–1 and 3–1, the sixth grader applies this knowledge to the solution of more and more complex rhythmic problems.

CONCEPT FORMATION IS DEPENDENT UPON PAST EXPERIENCE

As children grow intellectually, concrete experiences are not as essential provided the concept to be learned builds on previous learnings. Situations introducing new ideas, however, or more complex aspects of familiar concepts, must be couched in as concrete and meaningful terms as possible, no matter what age the student. For example, the principle of scale organization that governs tonality is highly abstract, but it can be grasped by fourth and fifth graders readily if the introduction of the problem is presented in a concrete situation. Experimentation at the piano, or rearranging resonator bells, will help children form the concept of "scale" more quickly than any amount of drill in singing scales or in memorizing key signatures. Diagrams that help children visualize the consistent relationship of tones within the scale will provide another concrete dimension to the learning environment.

The learning of an appropriate vocabulary must accompany the development of a concept. Once concepts involved in concrete situations are attained, ease of conceptualization seems to depend upon the semantic efficiency of the verbal tools. Without the expansion of his musical vocabulary, the child is limited in his ability to expand and communicate his musical knowledge. However, the vocabulary learned will be useful only if it stands for concepts already possessed. Grasping the idea, the underlying principle, is the primary aim of learning. Once the idea is understood, the proper term can be added with ease.

The same sequence must also be followed in introducing musical symbolism: *notation.* To the child who has still not grasped the basic concepts of melodic and rhythmic movement —up-down-same, step, skip, beat, long-short— the symbols of musical notation can have no meaning. Just as the words in a child's first primer stand for ideas he already possesses, so must notation picture musical concepts he has already formed.

Using our knowledge of musical growth

At the beginning of this section it was stated that musical growth will result only if we teach for that growth. We must not teach only *for* musical growth, however; we must also recognize, and remember, that children *are* growing musically, just as they are growing physically, emotionally, and intellectually. The same content, the same kinds of activities, cannot be repeated year after year in music any more than one would consider repeating exactly the same arithmetic or reading assignments from one grade to another. The underlying concepts may remain the same, but the depth to which they are studied will increase.

In the discussion of intellectual growth it was noted that children's ability to learn moves from the simple to the complex, from the general to the specific, and from the concrete to the abstract. As they grow emotionally they move from the immediate to the remote and from the present to the possible. Their physical coordination moves from the general to the precise. Musical growth follows a similar path.

The child in the early primary grades responds to the simple, more obvious, musical expressions. His ability to perform is limited, but it is satisfying to him because his acquaintance with the possibilities of musical expression is equally narrow. The second or third grader is ready to expand his musical experiences. The use

of fundamental movements, repetitious instrumental accompaniments, and rote songs is not enough for him. He wants new ways to express himself if he is still to experience satisfaction in music time.

The teacher in the upper grades has special demands on him, because learning must move in a continuous upward spiral. Musical learning in the elementary grades too often moves in a circle instead, repeating the same experiences over and over, rather than moving always higher. Such experiences are stunting in their repetitiousness. The same problems may need to be returned to time and again, and the same skills must certainly continue to be practiced; however, like the spiral, the return must be to a position a little higher on the ladder toward musical understanding and achievement.

Children of elementary school age hear a great deal of music in the classroom and at home. They are developing standards of musical preference. The content of the music class must be geared to expand their knowledge of music as an art and to promote discriminating musical choices. This can be accomplished only if, each year, the children meet new musical challenges placed in new contexts and new music from which they can draw insights and through which they may improve existing musical skills.

To summarize, "How we teach" will be determined by what we know of children's physical, emotional, intellectual, and musical growth. The effective teacher will use this knowledge constantly in planning musical experiences for the children. Remembering that children mature at different rates, he will use his knowledge of individual children in planning: the immature will receive those tasks that are within their present abilities; the able will be presented with problems that are challenging; the contributions of each will be combined into an experience that is musically gratifying to all.

WHEN DO WE TEACH?

In the previous section it was suggested that musical growth follows a sequential pattern similar to the orderly development seen in other areas of child growth. Cognizance of this sequence is essential if the classroom teacher is to know when to introduce new material, when to emphasize previous learnings, and when to encourage deeper exploration of ideas already grasped. It is important that the teacher have in mind, first, the musical behavior that children should exhibit when they come to him and, second, the musical accomplishments they should gain under his tutelage so that they will be ready for subsequent musical experiences. He needs to know *when to teach what.*

The content of the music curriculum that has been proposed is both broad and deep, and includes the attainment of those concepts that are essential to musical understanding, a variety of musical skills, and a wide repertoire of vocal and instrumental compositions. Important parts of this content may be slighted, if not overlooked, unless the teacher is able to refer to some sort of sequential plan of presentation worked out in advance. For this reason, also, it is important that the question "When do we teach?" be answered.

Any program of instruction, in order to be successful, must be constantly evaluated in terms of its long-range objectives. Such an evaluation, whether of pupil accomplishments or of teaching procedures, must be based on criteria drawn from those objectives. The teacher of music possesses such criteria when he has in mind an ordered sequence of musical growth stated in terms of musical behavior.

The following "Musical Growth Charts" are designed to help the teacher determine the direction and the scope of his classroom music program and to provide criteria for evaluating that program in terms of the observable musical behavior of children. Of course, there can be no absolute time tables for the introduction of specific musical learnings. Individual differences and variations in previous experiences preclude that possibility, but we can call on our knowledge of children's physical, emotional, and intellectual development to outline a logical sequence of musical growth.

As the charts are studied, the teacher should bear in mind that they are to be interpreted in relation to the individual differences and previous experience of his own class. He should also keep in mind that *these are accomplishments to be attained during the year in which they are cited.* This does not mean that the concepts and skills mentioned may not be *introduced* in earlier experiences, but that their *acquisition* may not be completed until the grade level indicated. Finally, they are attainable only if the content of each semester, each month, each week, and each day is consciously and purposefully directed toward these ends.

Musical
Achievement
Charts

Musical Growth Through Listening

	Kindergarten–Grade I	Grade II	Grade III
SKILL	Is improving in ability to listen with discrimination.	⟶	⟶
LITERATURE	Is becoming familiar with diverse types of music: march, lullaby, brief descriptive selections.	⟶	Is expanding repertoire to include examples of small dance forms: waltz, minuet, and so forth. Is adding music based on stories, legends, and fairy tales to his repertoire of descriptive music.
CONCEPTS *Melody*	Identifies melodic movement in terms of up, down, same, high, low.	Identifies melodic movement in terms of step, skip, and scale-line pattern. Is aware of major and minor tonalities.	Reveals increasing recognition of scale-line and chord-line tonal patterns. ⟶
Rhythm	Distinguishes between beat and rhythmic pattern of melody. Identifies rhythmic patterns as "even" or "uneven" (made up of tones of the same length or longer and shorter tones).	⟶ ⟶ Is aware that music "swings" in twos or threes.	⟶ Recognizes simple 2-1 relationships within rhythmic patterns: $\quad\downarrow\ \downarrow = \downarrow,\ \sqcap = \downarrow,\ \sqcap = \downarrow$ Shows increasing awareness of accent groupings in relation to common meters.
Harmony	Is aware of the presence of multiple sounds (melodic, rhythmic, and harmonic).	⟶ Reveals awareness of need for chord changes in song accompaniments.	⟶ ⟶
Form	Identifies melodic and rhythmic phrases as same or different.	Recognizes repetition and contrast of phrases or sections in short compositions.	Recognizes structure of two- and three-part song forms.
Expression	Identifies obvious changes in dynamics and in tempo, and relates them to musical expressiveness. Identifies common orchestral instruments by tone color and as belonging to high-low categories.	⟶ ⟶ Associates instrumental tone color with musical expressiveness.	Is conscious of variation in tempo and dynamics as contributing to musical expressiveness. Identifies all common orchestral instruments by name. ⟶
Style			

Grade IV	Grade V	Grade VI
→	→	→
Is familiar with compositions exemplifying two- and three-part song forms, rondo, and variation forms.	→	Is familiar with examples of the larger instrumental forms (symphony, concerto, and so on) and of vocal forms (art song, madrigal, cantata, oratorio, opera).
Is adding examples of tone poems, suites, and incidental music to his repertoire.	→	→
Knows many compositions that he can identify by title, form, and composer.	Knows many compositions which he can identify by title, form, composer, and culture.	Knows many compositions that he can identify by title, form, composer, culture, and period.
→	→	→
Identifies tonality of melody as major, minor, or pentatonic.	→	Is aware of other tonal organizations, such as mode and tone row.
Recognizes tonal sequences in melodic line.	→	→
	Recognizes common melodic intervals.	→
→	→	→
Recognizes 3–1 relationships within rhythmic patterns: ♫♫ = ♩. , ♫♫♫ = ♪ ♫ , ♫♫♫♫ = ♩. ♪ and syncopated patterns: (♪♩).	Recognizes extended rhythmic patterns based on 2–1 and 3–1 relationships in various meters.	→
→	→	Is becoming aware of accent groupings in unusual meters (5, 7, 9, 12) as combinations of twos, threes, or fours.
→	→	→
→	→	→
Recognizes common harmonic intervals (thirds and sixths).	→	→
Recognizes I, IV, and V_7 chord qualities in major keys.	Recognizes I, IV, and V_7 chord qualities in minor as well as major keys.	Begins to be aware of secondary chord qualities (II, VI) and of chords built on intervals of seconds and fourths.
Recognizes structure of two- and three-part song forms, rondo, and variation forms.	→	Recognizes structure of sonata-allegro form and polyphonic music.
→	→	Identifies expressive qualities in melodic, rhythmic, and harmonic organization, and in changes of tempo and dynamics.
→	Recognizes common combinations of instruments: orchestra, band, ensembles.	→
→	→	→
Is aware of expressive qualities of tonality (major, minor).	→	→
Senses expressive purpose of musical climax.	→	Is aware of unity, variety, and climax as contributing to musical expressiveness.
Identifies obvious stylistic qualities of music in terms of cultural characteristics.	Bases recognition of individual styles (composer, cultural) on melodic, rhythmic, and harmonic organization.	Identifies style of music by historical periods, cultures, or composers.

Musical Growth Through Singing

	Kindergarten–Grade I	Grade II	Grade III
SKILL	Is improving in ability to sing on pitch within a limited range.	Is improving in ability to sing accurately within an expanding range.	————————————→
			Reveals improvement in tone production and in diction.
LITERATURE	Is building a repertoire of many types of songs.	————————————→	————————————→
CONCEPTS *Melody*	Reproduces simple melodic patterns accurately, revealing understanding of melodic movement.	Exhibits understanding of melodic movement in singing simple tonal patterns with numbers and/or syllables.	Sings scale- and chord-line tonal patterns with increasing comprehension, utilizing numbers and/or syllables.
Rhythm	Is improving in rhythmic accuracy when reproducing melodic fragments.	Reflects awareness of "ongoingness" of pulse and of rhythmic patterns.	Demonstrates understanding of accent groupings and of a variety of rhythmic patterns based on 2–1 relationships.
Harmony	Reflects awareness of multiple sounds in singing with accompaniment.	————————————→	————————————→
		Displays awareness of multiple sounds in singing chants and simple two-part rounds.	Exhibits increasing awareness of multiple sounds in singing chants, rounds, and easy two-part music.
Form	Reveals awareness of phrase as a melodic unit.	Demonstrates increasing awareness of phrase.	————————————→
Expression	Relates possibilities of altering tempo and dynamics to musical expressiveness.	Reveals sensitivity to expressive value of loud-soft singing.	Indicates awareness of expressive value of changes in dynamics and in tempo.
Style			

Grade IV	Grade V	Grade VI
Sings accurately and independently within range B flat to F':	⟶	Singing may reveal approaching voice change with consequent limitations in individual ranges.
⟶	Sings with increasingly expressive tone quality and with good diction.	⟶
⟶	⟶	Is building a repertoire of various types of songs, including art songs and songs from opera and oratorio.
⟶	Sings all common tonal patterns independently with numbers and/or syllables.	⟶
Exhibits understanding of accent groupings in common meters, of rhythmic patterns based on 3-1 relationships, and of syncopated patterns.	Reproduces increasingly complex rhythmic patterns in a variety of meters.	⟶
⟶	⟶	⟶
Demonstrates understanding of multiple sounds in singing rounds, descants, and two-part music.	⟶	Exhibits his understanding of harmonic relationships in singing two- and three-part music and polyphonic compositions.
Establishes feeling for tonality by singing tonic triad.	⟶	⟶
	Reflects sensitivity to chordal qualities through vocal chording (chord roots or triads).	⟶
Sings melodic phrase with adequate breath support.	⟶	Exhibits sensitivity to melodic line and balance of parts in singing polyphonic music.
⟶	Makes use of increasingly subtle variations of tone, tempo, and dynamics for expressive purposes.	⟶
		Reveals awareness of stylistic features by using appropriate tempo, dynamics, tone, and diction.

Musical Growth Through Playing

	Kindergarten–Grade I	Grade II	Grade III
SKILL	Is developing skill in playing simple rhythm and melody instruments.	⟶	Is improving in ability to play a variety of rhythm and melody instruments. Is developing skill in chording with the autoharp.
CONCEPTS *Melody*	Is revealing awareness of "up," "down," and "same" in reproducing melodic fragments on melody instruments. Associates "high-low" concept with "right-left" direction in playing keyboard instruments.	Plays melodic fragments on melody instruments by ear and by scale numbers.	Plays familiar tunes on bells and piano by ear and with the aid of scale numbers and letter names.
Rhythm	Reproduces short rhythmic patterns on percussion instruments by ear. Demonstrates awareness of basic beat and rhythmic pattern in playing percussion instruments.	Is developing ability to maintain simple rhythmic patterns as accompaniment. Demonstrates awareness of beat, meter, and even-uneven rhythmic patterns in playing.	Is increasing in ability to maintain rhythmic patterns independently. Demonstrates awareness of accent groupings and rhythmic patterns based on 3–1 and 2–1 relationships.
Harmony	Is developing awareness of multiple sounds through playing rhythmic and melodic accompaniments.	⟶	⟶ Demonstrates increasing awareness of chord qualities in playing autoharp accompaniments by ear.
Form	Indicates awareness of same-different melodic and rhythmic phrases by selecting same-different instruments for accompaniment.	⟶ Demonstrates developing concepts of introduction and coda through playing accompaniment.	Exhibits awareness of phrase structure in planning accompaniments. ⟶
Expression	Is developing sensitivity to the expressive possibilities of various instrumental combinations.	⟶	⟶ Uses awareness of tone color and variations in tempo and dynamics in playing melodies and accompaniments.
Style			

Grade IV	Grade V	Grade VI
————————————————→	Is developing ability to play diverse instruments, including Latin-American, Hawaiian, and so forth.	Plays all classroom instruments with facility.
Exhibits increased skill in chording with the autoharp and on the piano.	————————————————→	————————————————→
Is developing skill in playing the recorder or similar instrument (song flute, flutophone, tonette, and so forth).	————————————————→	————————————————→
Plays simple tunes on bells, piano, and recorder-type instruments by notation as well as by ear.	————————————————→	————————————————→
Reveals understanding of scale structure by playing major and pentatonic scales on piano and bells.	Reveals understanding of scale structure by playing major, minor, and pentatonic scales on piano and bells.	————————————————→
Uses autoharp, bells, and piano to establish tonality of songs.	————————————————→	————————————————→
————————————————→	Maintains complex rhythmic patterns independently on melody and percussion instruments.	————————————————→
Demonstrates awareness of rhythmic patterns based on 3-1 and 2-1 relationships, including syncopation.	————————————————→	————————————————→
Exhibits increased skill in playing ostinati and descants.	————————————————→	————————————————→
————————————————→	Uses knowledge of chords in major and minor keys in playing accompaniments on autoharp and piano.	————————————————→
Demonstrates recognition of repetition and contrast in planning melodic and rhythmic accompaniments.	Exhibits understanding of repetition, contrast, and variation in planning accompaniments.	————————————————→
————————————————→	————————————————→	Demonstrates understanding of polyphonic structure in planning accompaniments.
————————————————→	————————————————→	————————————————→
————————————————→	Reveals increasing sensitivity to melodic, rhythmic, and harmonic organization in playing expressively.	————————————————→
	Selects instruments and plans accompaniments showing consideration for cultural characteristics.	————————————————→

Musical Growth Through Moving

	Kindergarten–Grade I	Grade II	Grade III
SKILL	Is developing ability to interpret music through body movements, impersonations, and dramatizations.	⟶	⟶
	Is developing a vocabulary of fundamental movements: walking, running, skipping, and so on.	Possesses a vocabulary of fundamental movements.	⟶
LITERATURE	Is acquiring a repertoire of action songs and singing games.	⟶	⟶
	Is gaining a repertoire of suitable music for dramatizations and other expressive purposes.	⟶	⟶
CONCEPTS *Melody*	Uses hand levels and body movements to signify awareness of "up-down" and "high-low."	⟶	Adapts body movements to rise and fall of melodic contour.
Rhythm	Indicates awareness of beat by walking, clapping, and so forth.	Reveals recognition of beat, accent, and rhythmic pattern by clapping, tapping, stepping, and so on.	⟶
	Displays growing recognition of even-uneven rhythmic patterns in running, skipping, and so forth.	⟶	Demonstrates awareness of 2–1 rhythmic relationships through clapping, and so on.
	Reflects awareness of rhythmic elements through dramatizations and impersonations.	⟶	⟶
Harmony			
Form	Demonstrates recognition of phrase as an entity with appropriate movements.	Shows awareness of same-different phrases and sections in planning dance movements.	Reveals growing recognition of repetition and contrast (melody, rhythm, phrase) in planning dance movements.
Expression	Shows developing sensitivity to over-all mood through spontaneous movement.	⟶	Displays sensitivity to variations in tempo and dynamics in planning dance movements.
Style			

Grade IV	Grade V	Grade VI
Is developing a vocabulary of free dance movements to express variations in rhythmic nuance, tempo, and style.	⟶	⟶
Is developing a vocabulary of formalized dance steps for folk dances.	⟶	Is developing a vocabulary of formalized dance steps for period dances.
Is acquiring a repertoire of American folk dances and of folk dances from other countries.	⟶	Is acquiring a repertoire of period dances.
⟶	⟶	⟶
⟶	⟶	⟶
⟶	⟶	⟶
Demonstrates awareness of 3-1 rhythmic relationships and of syncopation in clapping, skipping, and so on.	⟶	⟶
Reveals sensitivity to rhythmic nuance through free dance movements.	⟶	⟶
Exhibits awareness of differences in rhythmic structure in executing folk dances.	⟶	Exhibits awareness of differences in rhythmic structure in executing period dances (minuet, gavotte, and so forth).
		Displays understanding of meter through use of basic conducting beats.
Exhibits awareness of cadences and countermelodies in planning dance movements.	⟶	⟶
Reveals awareness of two- and three-part form and simple rondo form in planning dance movements.	Reveals understanding of rondo and variation forms in planning dance movements.	Plans dance movements to reveal formal structure of polyphonic music.
Executes dance movements appropriate to formal structure of folk dances.	⟶	Executes dance movements appropriate to period dance forms.
	⟶	Reveals sensitivity to subtle variations in tempo and dynamics through increasingly precise physical responses.
Reflects awareness of cultural characteristics in executing folk dances.	⟶	Reflects awareness of period characteristics in executing dances such as minuet, gavotte, and waltz.

Musical Growth Through Creating

	Kindergarten–Grade I	Grade II	Grade III
SKILL	Uses voice and simple instruments to improvise own music.	———————————————→	Uses voice and simple melody instruments to create own melodies.
	Creates expressive movements in response to music.	———————————————→	———————————————→
		Creates simple accompaniments for class songs, using common percussion instruments.	———————————————→
CONCEPTS *Melody*	Reveals awareness of melodic contour in improvising melodic patterns.	Shows awareness of step and skip movements in creating melodies.	Demonstrates increasing awareness of scale- and chord-line tonal movement in creating own melodies.
Rhythm	Reveals awareness of contrasting rhythmic patterns when improvising own music.	———————————————→	Reveals awareness of accent groupings and rhythmic relationships of 2–1 in creating melodies and in developing dance movements.
		Reveals awareness of beat and even-uneven rhythmic patterns in creating accompaniments with percussion instruments.	———————————————→
Harmony		Is gaining facility in improvising ostinati for pentatonic melodies.	———————————————→
Form		Reflects growing awareness of phrase structure in creating melodies and interpretative movements.	Illustrates awareness of same or different phrases in creating melodies, accompaniments, and expressive movements.
Expression	Displays sensitivity to expressive qualities in choice of instruments in improvising sound effects to stories and poems.	Displays sensitivity to expressive qualities in choice of instruments for accompaniments.	———————————————→
			Shows consideration of expressive qualities of words in creating own songs.
Style			

Grade IV	Grade V	Grade VI
Uses voice and melody instruments, including piano, to create own melodies.	→	→
Creates dance movements of increasing complexity and expressiveness.	→	→
→	Creates rhythmic and melodic accompaniments (chants and ostinati) for class songs using a variety of instruments, including the voice.	→
Creates appropriate accompaniments for class songs on autoharp and piano.	→	Creates compositions for orchestral instruments.
Uses knowledge of major, minor, and pentatonic tonalities in creating melodies.	→	→
	Uses knowledge of melodic and rhythmic alteration in creating melodies.	→
		Experiments with other tonal organizations (pentatonic, tone row) in creating compositions.
Uses knowledge of 2-1 and 3-1 rhythmic relationships in creating own compositions and in planning dance patterns.	Displays knowledge of complex rhythmic relationships, including syncopation, in creating own compositions and dance movements.	→
Shows awareness of accent groupings and rhythmic patterns in planning rhythmic, melodic, and harmonic accompaniments for songs.	→	→
→	Uses knowledge of chord structure in creating chants, descants, and harmonic parts for songs.	→
Uses knowledge of intervals and chords in harmonizing own melodies.	→	→
		Experiments with secondary chords and chords built on intervals of fourths and seconds in creating own compositions.
Uses knowledge of two- and three-part forms in creating melodies, accompaniments, and dance patterns.	Makes use of knowledge of rondo and variation forms in creating compositions and in planning dance movements.	Uses knowledge of polyphonic forms in creating dance movements.
→	→	→
→	→	→
	Reflects sensitivity to expressive organization of melody, rhythm, and harmony in own compositions.	→
	Reveals awareness of expressive qualities of major-minor tonalities in creating compositions.	→
		Indicates awareness of need for unity, variety, and climax in own compositions.
Indicates awareness of cultural characteristics in choice of instruments and rhythmic patterns for accompaniments.	Reflects awareness of cultural characteristics in planning accompaniments, dance movements, or own compositions.	Reflects awareness of period characteristics in planning accompaniments, dance movements, or own compositions.

Musical Growth
Through Reading

	Kindergarten–Grade I	Grade II	Grade III
SKILL	Associates line notation and melodic contour lines with musical concepts.	Is acquiring ability to associate symbols of musical notation with musical concepts. Is beginning to use notation as an aid to listening, performing, and creating.	⟶ ⟶ Is developing a functional knowledge of musical symbols and terminology: staff, pitch names, meter signatures, note and rest values, tempo, and so forth.
CONCEPTS *Melody*	Associates line notation and contour lines with melodic direction. Uses number notation in singing and playing melodic fragments.	Identifies melodic direction and step-skip tonal movement in musical notation. ⟶ Identifies same-different tonal patterns in notation.	Identifies scale-line and chord-line patterns within musical context. Uses numbers and/or syllables and letter names in performing and creating. ⟶
Rhythm	Interprets line notation in terms of short-long rhythmic patterns.	Identifies even-uneven rhythmic patterns in notation: ♫ , ♩ ♩ , ♩ ♪ , ♩. ♪	Interprets notation of 2-1 rhythmic relationships: ♩ ♩ = 𝅝 , ♫ = ♩ , ♬ = ♪ Is aware of function of meter signatures.
Harmony			
Form		Recognizes repetition of melodic and rhythmic patterns in notation.	⟶ Can identify like and unlike phrases in notation.
Expression			
Style			

Grade IV	Grade V	Grade VI
Uses notation increasingly as an aid in listening, performing, and creating.	Is gaining independence in using notation as an aid in listening, performing, and creating.	⟶
Is extending his functional knowledge of notation to include key signatures and expressive markings.	⟶	Has functional knowledge of all notational symbols, including bass staff, and of all common expressive markings.
⟶	Can identify all common tonal patterns, including chromatic passages, within designated keys.	⟶
⟶	⟶	⟶
Identifies same-different and sequential tonal patterns in notation.	⟶	⟶
Interprets key signatures to establish tonality.	⟶	⟶
Interprets notation of 3-1 rhythmic relationships (𝅗𝅥 𝅘𝅥 𝅘𝅥. 𝅘𝅥𝅮 𝅘𝅥𝅯) and of syncopation (𝅘𝅥𝅮 𝅘𝅥).	Is acquiring facility in interpreting complex rhythmic patterns in notation.	Reproduces complex rhythmic patterns from notation independently.
Interprets meter signature to establish accent groupings and relationships of note values.	⟶	
Is aware of function of meter signatures.	⟶	Interprets meter signatures, including those symbolizing uncommon meters.
Interprets chord symbols (Roman numerals or letters) used for autoharp or piano accompaniments.	⟶	⟶
Interprets notation of simple two-part harmonization.	⟶	Interprets notation of two- and three-part harmonization.
		Determines harmonic accompaniment from melodic notation.
⟶	Recognizes repetition and variation of melodic and rhythmic patterns in notation.	⟶
Identifies simple two- and three-part forms in notation.	⟶	⟶
	Observes characteristics of rondo, theme and variation forms by following notation.	Observes characteristics of polyphonic and extended homophonic forms by following notation.
Interprets common tempo and dynamic markings present in score.	⟶	Observes all pertinent expressive markings in the score in listening and performing.
		Studies score to discover cues to musical style.

31

Part II
GUIDING CLASSROOM MUSICAL EXPERIENCES

Planning
for Musical
Experiences

Part I dealt with the concepts, skills, and knowledge considered essential for musical growth and emphasized the importance of adjusting musical experiences in the elementary school to the physical, emotional, intellectual, and musical maturational levels of children as they progress from grade to grade. This implies a need for a music program that embodies a planned sequence of experiences.

In the pages that follow, the authors, guided by the objectives and principles discussed in Part I, suggest how musical experiences—listening, singing, playing, moving, creating, and reading—may be organized sequentially to nourish the continuous musical growth of children. Whereas the musical growth charts in Part I were organized to show the development of three facets of musical learning—skills, literature, and concepts—the charts in Part II have been designed to assist the teacher in developing a coordinated classroom program of these musical experiences. The charts introduce the musical selections for each grade.

As the child learns the literature of his musical heritage, he is developing new skills, skills that increase his awareness of the concepts of musical organization. In the selection of music the authors have faced the problem of making deliberate choices of materials from a musical heritage so vast that no music program could possibly embrace it all. This, however, is precisely what every teacher of music must do. Different teachers may choose different materials, but the responsibility for making choices is constant with all. Music has been included which, in the authors' opinion, is worthy of becoming a part of the musical repertoire of all children. This music has also been chosen because it facilitates the teaching of those musical learnings that lead to musical literacy, discrimination, and independence.

The introduction of specific concepts and skills at certain grade levels should also not be considered as unchanging; they may be offered at an earlier or later stage, depending on previous musical experience. Once the scope of a music program has been determined, however, some organization is necessary if adequate coverage and orderly progression toward attainments are to be accomplished. Teachers in other subjects, such as the language arts and social studies, have established learning sequences in the elementary schools. Music education may be organized similarly when based on sound principles of musical growth, recognizing that variations in the sequence will occur with individual groups of children.

The suggestions made for individual songs and instrumental compositions are not to be considered as guides for a single lesson, but are to be incorporated into a whole series of classroom experiences. The teacher should not feel that the concepts are to be taught in the order in which they are discussed for each selection. It is essential to emphasize these important aspects, but in a sequence most suitable to the particular situation.

A recording including a number of songs, as well as listening selections, accompanies this text.[1] The teaching suggestions for the recorded songs introduce a variety of ways in which recordings may be used as a teaching aid.

Single songs or instrumental compositions will be returned to many times during the year. Each time another facet will be explored—a skill perfected or a new one begun, another concept discovered or a familiar one expanded. The teaching suggestions made in the following pages should be viewed with this in mind. We hope, also, that they will be used as guides from which to draw implications for other experiences using other musical materials.

---

[1] This recording may be obtained from the publisher: Holt, Rinehart and Winston, Inc., 383 Madison Avenue, New York, N.Y. 10017

Guiding Musical Growth
in the **Kindergarten**

	Listening	Singing	Playing
SKILL	Begin to develop habits of listening with discrimination.	Strive for improvement of ability to sing on pitch within a limited range. Provide opportunities for all children to sing alone. Give individual assistance to uncertain singers.	Promote experimentation with simple percussion instruments (sticks, drum, triangle, bells).
CONCEPTS *Melody*	Draw attention to melodic movement in terms of up, down, same, higher, and lower.	Sing short melodic patterns within limited ranges to reinforce awareness of melodic movement.	Help the children perceive tonal movement in terms of up, down, and same through playing melody instruments. Associate up-down and high-low with right-left direction when playing bells.
Rhythm	Help the children become aware of beat (pulse) and accent groupings. Present rhythmic patterns in terms of even (tones of equal duration) and uneven (longer and shorter tones). Call attention to short rhythmic phrases as being same or different.	Stress rhythmic accuracy in singing songs.	Use percussion instruments to strengthen feeling for beat, accent, and rhythmic pattern.
Harmony	Guide the children to become aware of other sounds besides the melody within a musical composition.	Provide opportunities for singing with various types of accompaniments.	Encourage playing of contrasting melodic and rhythmic patterns (ostinati) as accompaniments for songs.
Form	Help the children become aware of melodic phrases as musical entities. Refer to melodic and rhythmic phrases as being same-different.	Stress phrasewise singing.	Help the children become conscious of same-different phrases by selecting same-different instruments for accompaniments.
Expression	Help the children to become aware of obvious contrasts in dynamics and tempo and to relate these to musical expressiveness. Guide the children to distinguish differences in tone color, to identify common orchestral instruments, and to categorize these by high-low pitch.	When singing songs, relate possibilities of altering dynamics and tempo to musical expressiveness.	Explore possibilities of associating musical sounds with particular moods when selecting instruments for accompaniments.

Moving	Creating	Reading
Help the children develop a repertoire of fundamental movements: walking, running, skipping, leaping, and galloping.	Guide the children to discover possibilities of using voice, as well as simple instruments, to improvise their own music.	Introduce line notation to show melodic contour and rhythmic pattern, as well as other visual aids to represent musical concepts.
Encourage the children to imitate the teacher in outlining melodic movement with hand signals. Invite children to reflect over-all melodic contour with their bodies as they dance.	Stimulate the children to improvise melodic patterns, using their own voice and simple melodic instruments.	Introduce line notation to show melodic contour.
Use a variety of physical movements (clap, tap, walk, run, and so forth) to emphasize beat, accent, and rhythmic pattern.	Encourage improvisation of rhythmic patterns to suggest familiar sounds and movements.	Utilize line notation to show even and uneven rhythmic patterns.
Encourage the children to show recognition of phrase as an entity by responding with appropriate movements Aid the children to respond with same-different movements as a means for developing perception of same-different phrases.		Employ curved lines to show phrase span. Associate same-different geometric shapes with same-different phrases or sections of a composition.
Encourage free physical movement to depict the expressive qualities of the music.	Experiment with different instruments when adding accompaniments to familiar songs. Explore possibilities of adding sound effects to stories and poems.	

I'M TALL, I'M SMALL

Singing Game

MELODY

Move: Children should have many opportunities to hear the song while performing the actions suggested by the words before they are invited to sing it. To play the game, one child stands in the center of a circle while others sit with eyes closed. On the words "Guess what I am now!" the leader stretches tall, squats down low, or stands in normal position. Children must guess which position he has taken. The child who guesses correctly becomes the new leader.

Listen: Associate the words "tall" and "small" with HIGH and LOW sounds. Work for general discrimination of highness and lowness. As the teacher sings the final phrase, or plays the final tone on the bells, the ending may be changed as shown below. The children should respond with appropriate movements.

Play: Encourage the children to explore various pitch levels on the bells or piano. Help them to discover that HIGH sounds are found at the *right* end of the keyboard and LOW sounds at the *left* end. Later, the children may take turns playing the final phrase of the song on the bells as the singing game is continued.

Sing: When the song is familiar, encourage individual singing. Choose two children, one to sing the "tall" motives and the other to sing the "small." They may sing the last phrase together. Let them decide individually which tone they will end on. If they end on different tones they will produce HARMONY.

TONAL GAMES

Young children may need many opportunities to experiment with their own voices: to listen to themselves and to understand how it "feels" to sing the melody they hear. To give the children such experiences, tonal games should be a regular part of kindergarten activities. Such games may be used many times during the day and may take various forms, such as the following.

1. Sing fragments of familiar songs, making up new words to fit the occasion:

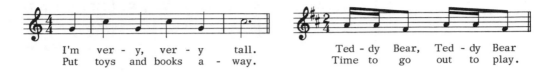

2. Sing greetings and directions, using scale or chord patterns, and inviting the child to echo these:

3. Sing questions to which the child may reply echoing the same tune, but with different words:

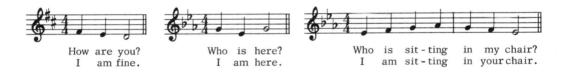

The above tonal groups should be sung in various keys to help the children expand their singing ranges.

THE FARMER IN THE DELL

4. The child takes the nurse . . .
5. The nurse takes the dog . . .
6. The dog takes the cat . . .

7. The cat takes the rat . . .
8. The rat takes the cheese . . .
9. The cheese stands alone . . .

MELODY

Sing: After the song has been learned, various children may sing "Heigh-o, the merry-o" as a solo to encourage individual singing. Transpose the song to various keys to fit the soloist's voice range.

Move: Help the children to develop an awareness of MELODIC ENTITY by planning appropriate movements to fit each complete verse.

RHYTHM

Move: As the children play the singing game, emphasize the UNEVEN rhythm of the melody ♪♩ ♪♩ ♪♩. Experiment with different movements; agree that skipping or galloping seem to fit the uneven rhythm best.

Another day, play or sing the song in this rhythm:

How do we usually move to this song? Does the music now make you want to skip or gallop? (No.) **What kind of movement would fit this music better?** (Walking or running.) Help the children conclude that when music is EVEN, it makes one want to step with even, steady steps; when it is UNEVEN, it makes one want to skip or gallop.

Play: At another time, put the following diagram on the chalkboard:

(even)   —— —— —— —— —— —

(uneven)   —— - —— - —— - —— - —— - —— -

Ask a child to select the appropriate picture as you play or sing one of the versions of the song. Later, point to one of the diagrams and ask a child to play a pattern that "sounds like the picture," even or uneven.

TOODALA

Play-Party Game
Version by Helen Gates

Jauntily

Might - y pret - ty mo - tion, too - da - la,   too - da - la,   too - da - la,

Might - y pret - ty mo - tion, too - da - la,   too - da - la, my   la - dy.

RHYTHM

Move: Talk about all the ways children can move and about the kinds of movements that might be most appropriate for the rhythm of this song.

One child may choose a "pretty motion" which he demonstrates as the class sings the first phrase; the other children imitate him as they sing the second phrase.

Create: Many a verse may be added to this favorite dance song. After the children are very familiar with the melody, allow individuals to sing words spontaneously to fit the RHYTHMIC PATTERN of the first measure, with the entire class answering on the "toodala" refrain. They might sing about the weather or special days ("Mighty rainy days," "Halloween is near"), or about friends or objects in the classroom ("Johnny has a new ball," or "See our pretty pictures"). The teacher may even wish to join in and sing instructions throughout the day ("Now it's time for recess," "Put your books away," and so on).

Play: As the children sing they may change the words of the first measure to "Listen to my drum" (or triangle, sticks, and so forth). One child may answer by playing the RHYTHMIC PATTERN of "toodala" (♩. ♩ ♪) on the appropriate instrument.

TEDDY BEAR

FORM

Move: Guide the children to plan motions for dramatizing this song. Help them plan a new motion for each new two-measure PHRASE. They might be as follows:

Verse 1	*Verse 2*
Turn around once.	Pretend to be climbing stairs.
Lean over, hands on floor.	Fold hands, bow head.
Extend one foot in front.	Reach for light switch.
Shake finger, as if scolding.	Lean head on folded hands.

MELODY

Listen: When the children know the song, play the pattern for "Teddy Bear, Teddy Bear" on the bells or piano. **Listen carefully; how many times do you hear this pattern in the song?** (Four times, at the beginning of each phrase.)

Play: Place bells F♯-G-A on a table; help the children find the pattern for "Teddy Bear." Notice that the pattern moves DOWN and that the middle bell must be omitted in order for the pattern to sound like "Teddy Bear." Ask one child to play the pattern each time it occurs in the song as the class sings.

Sing: After the song has been learned, use it for tone-matching games. Teacher may sing a child's name to the melody for "Teddy Bear," inviting him to answer with words from the song. Sing in different keys so that it will be in the individual child's comfortable singing range.

John -ny Jones, John -ny Jones, Turn a - round.___

HARMONY

Play: Help the children to discover the satisfaction that comes from hearing more than one MELODIC PATTERN at the same time. Place bells A-B-D in that order on a table. As the class sings, one child with good rhythmic coordination may play these bells over and over, beginning with the highest one and moving down, then up:

EXPLORING SOUNDS

The kindergartener's curiosity about his environment and eagerness to explore extends to all facets of his classroom experience. Take advantage of this curiosity to encourage him to discover the potentials of the classroom instruments that he will be using throughout his elementary school music experiences. Examine each instrument; find as many ways as possible to create sound on each; discuss which is the best sound. Help the children to develop a vocabulary to describe the sounds they create.

Tap a drum in different places. How does the sound change? What happens to the sound when something is placed on the drumhead, or when the drum is placed on the floor? Strike the drum with finger tips, open hand, closed hand, with different objects. Compare the sounds of drums of different sizes.

Tap sticks together, near the tips, near the child's hands. What is the difference in sound? Strike a stick on a desk, a table leg, the floor, against a radiator. Discover the differences in sounds of sticks of different sizes.

Hold a triangle by its holder and strike it; hold the top of the triangle and strike again. How is the sound changed? Strike the triangle with different objects: a metal beater, a stick, the rubber tip of a pencil. How does it sound?

Strike a resonator bell with a rubber mallet, a cork mallet, a wooden mallet. Are the sounds the same? Touch the metal bar as the bell is struck. Does it change the sound?

Strum the autoharp. Is one sound heard or many? It may seem like one sound to some children because the tone color of the strings blend together. Play each string separately to help the children realize that the sound they hear is really a combination of many separate sounds. As you strike the autoharp, invite a child to touch the edge lightly, or touch the strings. Discuss the vibrations felt.

Help the children explore the way sound is produced on the piano; if possible, show them the action of the hammers on the strings. Strike a key sharply, then press it gently; press the damper pedal and strike a key. Discover the differences in sounds.

Guide the children to use their instruments to improvise their own "compositions." Use the instruments to add sound effects to the following poems.

MELODY

Help the children become aware of the melodic concept of pitch levels. Find three percussion instruments with HIGH, MIDDLE, and LOW voices; play these at appropriate times as the class chants the poem. The instruments could be played at the end of the line of poetry, or they could be played in the rhythm of the words while the class is speaking.

> Fishes swim in water clear, (low)
> Birds fly up into the air. (high)
> Serpents creep along the ground, (low)
> Boys and girls run round and round. (middle)
>
> Here is a giant who is tall, tall, tall;
> Here is an elf who is small, small, small;
> The elf who is small will try, try, try
> To reach to the giant who is high, high, high.
> —UNKNOWN

EXPRESSION

Find instruments whose sounds help suggest differences in mood of these two winter poems. "Ice" may suggest sounds that are "hard and noisy"; for "Snow," sounds that are "light and soft" might be more suitable.

> ICE
> When it is the winter time
> I run up the street
> And I make the ice laugh
> With my little feet—
> "Crickle, crackle, crickle,
> Creet, creet, creet."
> —DOROTHY ALDES

> SNOW
> The snow fell softly all the night,
> It made a blanket soft and white.
> It covered houses, flowers and ground,
> But did not make a single sound.
> —ALICE WILKINS

HICKORY, DICKORY, DOCK

Music by J. W. Elliot
Words from Mother Goose

Hick-o-ry, dick-o-ry, dock, *(tick, tock)* The mouse ran up the clock; *(tick, tock)* The clock struck one, The mouse ran down, Hick-o-ry, dick-o-ry, dock. *(tick, tock)*

RHYTHM

Move: The children may keep time as they sing by swinging their arms like a pendulum on a clock. Help them to recognize that the pendulum keeps on swinging even when no words are being sung, thus emphasizing the continuity of the steady BEAT.

EXPRESSION

Play: Add "sound effects" to the singing: two wood blocks of different pitches for the ticking of the clock; a GLISSANDO on bells, xylophone, or piano (upward in measure 4, downward in measure 6) to describe the mouse running up and down the clock; and a gong or cymbal on the word "one."

MELODY

Play: The tick-tock of the clock may also be represented by c-c' on the step bells throughout the song:

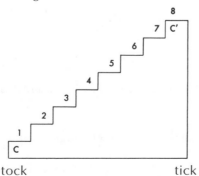

Discuss which is HIGHER or LOWER, the "tick" or the "tock," and play the bells in the correct order.

DAPPLED PONY

Czechoslovakian Folk Melody
Words by Betty Welsbacher

Come, my po - ny, dap - pled po - ny, ride with me to - day.
Run, my po - ny, dap - pled po - ny, take me far a - way.

Find a road that nev - er ends, find a place with lots of friends,

Come, my po - ny, dap - pled po - ny, home at end of day.

RHYTHM

Move: Listen to the music. Invite the children to move about the room imitating the movements of the pony. Draw attention to the different ways they are moving.

Some may trot with the RHYTHM OF THE MELODY (♩♩ ♩♩); others may move more slowly to the RHYTHM OF THE BEAT ♩ ♩). Note that both patterns are EVEN.

Play: Select an instrument which might sound like ponies' hoofs (two up-turned paper cups could be used). **Can you play an even rhythm (♩♩ ♩♩) that sounds like a trotting pony?** After the child has established his own tempo, begin to sing, adjusting your tempo to his so that you are singing one syllable to each eighth note.

Ask a second child to play a pattern for Mother Pony. **Will she take longer or shorter steps?** (Longer.) Help the child play a pattern with longer sounds

(♩ ♩ ♩ ♩). This time, as you match the song tempo to his, sing two syllables to each of his beats.

How would Grandfather Pony move? (With very long steps.) As a third child chooses an instrument and plays an appropriate pattern (𝅗𝅥 𝅗𝅥), sing four syllables to each of his beats.

Late in the year some children may be able to sustain the three patterns independently as an accompaniment while the class sings:

Baby Pony (woodblock)

Mother Pony (high drum)

Grandfather Pony (low drum)

FORM

Move: Help the children to become aware of PHRASES. **Can you find places in the song which suggest that the pony is resting for a moment, or perhaps turning around?** Draw attention to those children who turn at the end of each phrase (on the words "today," "away," and "friends").

Listen: When the music is familiar and all can sense the four phrases, draw attention to SAME and DIFFERENT phrases. Cut four ponies from felt or construction paper; one should be a different color or shape. **Can you put a pony on the feltboard at the beginning of each new phrase? Which pony should be different from the others?** Help the class decide that the third pony should be different because the melody of this phrase sounds different from all the rest.

CHILDREN'S MARCH: "OVER THE HILLS AND FAR AWAY"

Bowmar Orchestral Library, BOL#68   Percy Grainger

RHYTHM

Listen: Play the composition in its entirety for the children. Ask them to close their eyes and imagine that they are moving as they listen. **What kind of movements did you make? Were they always the same? If not, when did they change?** Play the composition again and ask the children to raise their hands if they imagine that they are changing the style of movement.

Move: After the children have "imagined" their movements, invite them to show you how they moved. Notice differences in their responses. Some children may skip or gallop to the UNEVEN rhythm of the melody; others may march or walk to the EVEN rhythm of the beat sounded by the lower instruments in the accompaniment. Draw attention to the different kinds of movement. Discuss the fact that one can hear and feel more than one kind of rhythm at a time.

Guide the children to notice the ritardando (slowing down) at the end of the composition. **Can you show with your bodies that the music is getting SLOWER?**

Read: Put these two diagrams on the chalkboard and ask the children to select the one that matches the rhythm of the melody at the beginning of the music:

⎯⎯ ⎯ ⎯⎯⎯ ⎯ ⎯⎯⎯ ⎯ ⎯⎯⎯ ⎯   (uneven rhythm of melody)
⎯⎯⎯ ⎯⎯⎯⎯ ⎯⎯⎯⎯ ⎯⎯⎯⎯   (even rhythm of beat)

Discuss with the children the differences in the two diagrams.

Play: Point to one of the diagrams and ask a child to play that pattern on a percussion instrument. Later, two children with good rhythmic coordination may be invited to play the two patterns simultaneously on contrasting instruments.

MELODY

Listen: Draw the children's attention to the over-all contour of the first melody that moves gradually upward and down again. Diagram the melodic contour on the chalkboard:

How many times do you hear a melody that moves like this? (Four times.) Help individual children follow the diagram with their hands as they listen to the music.

Put this pattern on the chalkboard:

⎯ ⎯⎯⎯⎯⎯ ⎯ ⎯⎯⎯⎯⎯

Can you find a place in the music that sounds like this? (Beginning of the middle section.)

FORM

Listen: As the children listen, help them to become aware of the design of the music. Listen for the end of the first phrases where the music pauses. Discover that the second phrase is the same, except that it sounds slightly softer. Listen for the contrasting middle section, which is also made up of two similar phrases. Ask the children to listen for the return of the first melody they heard. Some children will recognize that it is slightly altered the last (fourth) time it is heard.

Move: Invite the children to create their own dance to this music. Divide the class into two groups. One group may dance during the opening section and the similar closing section, the other group during the contrasting middle section.

CREOLE LULLABY

Creole Folk Song

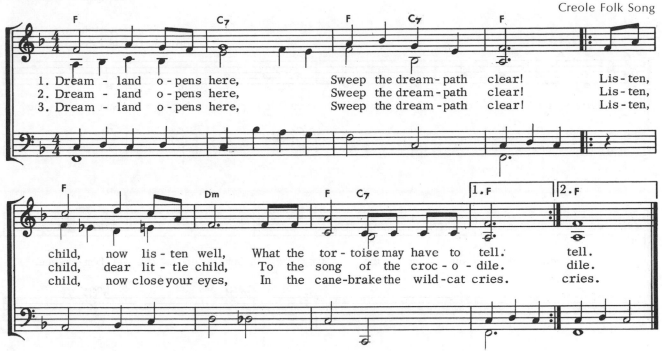

From *Bayou Ballads* by M. Monroe, copyright 1921 by G. Schirmer Inc., New York, N.Y. Used by permission.

EXPRESSION

Listen: Before the children attempt to sing this sustained melody, they should hear it on several different occasions. This would be a good choice to sing or play quietly during their rest period. Draw attention to the easy, sleepy sound of the melody which seldom moves very far up or down. Notice the SLOW tempo of this song. **Is this a good choice for a lullaby?**

Discuss the words. If tortoises, crocodiles, and wildcats are unfamiliar to your children, locate pictures and talk about the animals, where they live, what they eat, and so on. **Can you imagine how a tortoise would move? Would a crocodile move in the same way? What about a wildcat? Do you think the child in the song is afraid of these animals, or finds them pleasant to dream about?**

Play: Add to the dreamlike mood of the melody with an instrumental accompaniment. When the children know the melody, one child may play a bell softly at the beginning of each measure. He may play either the F or C bells.

Sing: When children have learned the melody, discuss the way one should sing a lullaby. **Will you sing with a LOUD voice, or with a SOFT voice? Should the song be FAST or SLOW?**

RHYTHM

Listen: Ask children to listen for the LONG tones in the song. These occur on the words "here," "clear," "well," and "tell."

Sing: As they sing, remind them: **Each of these words must be held a long time.**

FORM

Move: To help children feel the sustained mood of the long phrases, suggest that they move their arm in a slow arc as they sing. Each phrase is four measures long. **Be sure you do not finish your arc too soon! Move your arm slowly and smoothly. Make your voice move smoothly too.**

THE SUN*

Music by William S. Haynie
Words by Louise Fabrice Handcock

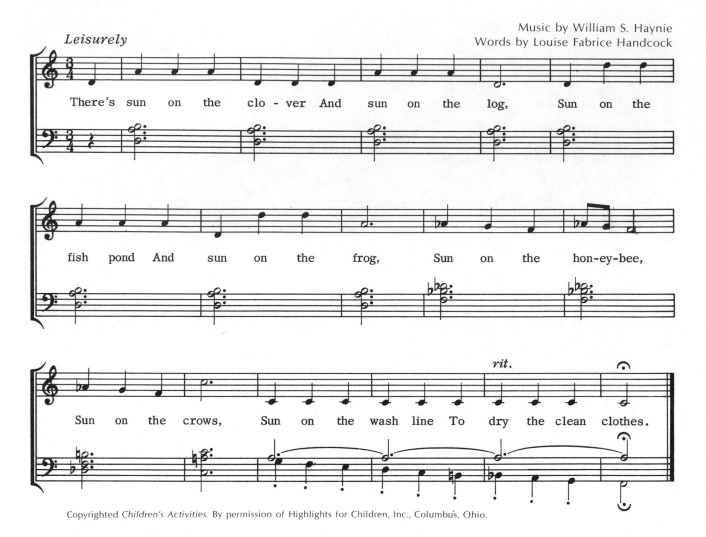

Leisurely

There's sun on the clo-ver And sun on the log, Sun on the fish pond And sun on the frog, Sun on the hon-ey-bee, Sun on the crows, Sun on the wash line To dry the clean clothes.

Copyrighted *Children's Activities.* By permission of Highlights for Children, Inc., Columbus, Ohio.

EXPRESSION

Listen: **Listen to this song and tell me how many different things the sun shines on.** As the children listen and name the eight different things, replay the recording several times until they have been named in order: clover, log, fish pond, frog, honeybee, crows, wash line, clean clothes.

What helps to make this a "sunny" song? Play the recording another time before allowing the children to offer suggestions. They may notice the lilting melody, which bounces back and forth from low to high tones and contributes to the sunny mood. The light sound of the clarinet playing the melody and the sound of the plucked strings also add to the lightness of the expression.

Sing: After the children have heard the recording several times and have discussed the mood and the accompaniment, invite them to sing the song. Do not allow them to sing with the recording; challenge them to sing as much as possible independently. After they have attempted to sing, replay the recording and

*Songs and instrumental selections marked by an asterisk are included in a supplementary recording that is available from the publisher.

locate places where the children had problems. Repeat these steps as often as necessary—listening, then singing without assistance—until the melody is learned.

Play: Choose a "sunny" instrument such as finger cymbals or triangle and ask one child to play each time the word "sun" is sung.

MELODY

Listen: Late in the year, when the children have enjoyed the song many times, help them describe the way the melody moves. Put out five bells, D-E-F-G-A, and play the first phrase for the class. Notice that only the first and last bells in the group are played and that the melody moves back and forth from LOW to HIGH.

Can I play the melody for "sun on the fish pond" with these bells? Guide the children to decide that higher bells are needed. Add the B-C-D bells and play this phrase.

Play the A♭-G-F pattern of "sun on the honeybee." **What is different about this pattern?** Help the children realize that you are now playing bells that are closer together. **We say that this pattern moves by STEPS. The first two patterns moved by SKIP, because we played bells that were far apart.**

Who can tell me how many bells I will need to play "Sun on the wash line to dry the clean clothes"? (Only one.)

Move: Help the children become aware of TONAL DIRECTION by using hand levels to picture the melodic movement.

Read: Put these diagrams on the chalkboard:

(There's sun)   (Sun on the)   (the clean clothes)

Notice the differences between the patterns that sounded with the bells far apart (SKIPS), those that were near together (STEPS), and those that stayed the SAME.

RHYTHM

Move: Help the children sense the rhythm of the melody by clapping lightly on the SHORT tones (♩ , ♫) and slide palms together in a long "swish" when they hear the LONG tones (♩ , ♩.).

HOW D'YE DO, MY PARTNER

With a lilt   Swedish Singing Game

Verse: How d'ye do, my part-ner, How d'ye do to-day?____
Refrain: Tra-la-la-la-la-la, Tra-la-la-la-la-la,

Will you dance in a cir-cle? I will show you the way.
Tra-la-la-la-la-la-la, Tra-la-la-la-la-la.

MELODY

Listen: Sing the complete song for the children. **What kind of song is this?** (A dance song.)

As the children listen again, draw attention to the melodic contour. Phrases 1, 2, and 3 move gradually UP and then DOWN. Phrase 4 begins HIGH and moves down to LOW.

Phrases 1, 2, 3   Phrase 4

Ask the children to show the melodic contour with their hands as you sing the song.

Sing: Invite the class to sing the song without your assistance. Later, sing it as a dialogue with one group singing the first and third phrases and the other group answering by singing the second and fourth phrases.

RHYTHM

Move: Invite individual children to "show the way." Give each child an opportunity to demonstrate his dance for the rest of the class as you play the piano. Call attention to those children whose movements "match the music."

Play the melody in different rhythms as shown in the following music. Ask the class to demonstrate different ways of dancing to each rhythm. Discuss differences in the movements made. Help the children to distinguish between melodies that "march" or "walk" and those that "swing" (in threes). Notice those that are EVEN and those that are UNEVEN.

Var. 1 *Light gallop*

Appropriate movements would be as follows:

Original melody: swaying, sliding, swinging in a circle
   Variation 1: skipping or galloping
   Variation 2: marching or walking briskly
   Variation 3: tiptoe run
   Variation 4: long slide, possibly leaping
               (Compare this slow, uneven rhythm to faster one in
               original.)

FORM

Move: After the children have had opportunities to experiment with each of the different rhythms, the dance should be performed with partners as suggested by
the words in the original version. Invite the children to plan their own dance.
They might begin by the partners standing facing each other. During phrase 1,
the first child should bow or curtsy; the second child may do the same in
return during phrase 2. On phrases 3 and 4 the partners may take hold of each
others' hands and step lightly in a circle. During the refrain each child might
dance alone, returning at the end to bow again to his partner.

MEMORIES OF CHILDHOOD

Bowmar Orchestral Library, BOL #68   Octavio Pinto

EXPRESSION

Pinto composed these little pieces for his wife; they are descriptive of the playtime activities of their two children, Anna Maria and Luiz Octavio. Each of the short compositions is prefaced by a poem, given here in translation. Give the children an opportunity to listen to and enjoy each of the five selections separately, on different occasions. When all the compositions have become familiar, listen to them in succession and observe differences in mood. Guide the children to develop a musical vocabulary with which to discuss what happens in the music to make the differences. Help them talk in terms of melodies that are HIGH or LOW, that move UP or DOWN, that may be SAME or DIFFERENT. Notice rhythms that are EVEN or UNEVEN, that make one want to move steadily as in a march, or smoothly as in a waltz. Discover whether the music is FAST or SLOW, LOUD or SOFT. Notice differences in the SOUNDS of instruments.

RUN, RUN

The garden is full of life. In the sunshine children run about gaily and noisily. Outside on the street, the poor blind man with his hand organ sings his sorrow.

Listen: Play the selection without reading the poem and discuss the children's reaction to it. **Does this seem to be happy or sad music? Does it have the same feeling throughout?** The children will no doubt suggest that it is both happy and sad in different parts.

Discover that there are three parts to the music, the first and the last sounding the SAME. Compare the parts. The first part has a bright melody made up of SHORT tones moving rapidly in an EVEN rhythm; it becomes gradually LOUDER as it moves in an UPWARD direction. The melody of the second part begins HIGH and moves in a DOWNWARD direction; it is more quiet, is made up of longer and shorter tones which produce an UNEVEN, swaying rhythm.

Move: Divide the class into two groups, one to move during the first and third parts, the other to move during the second part. Remind the children that they must move in different ways to reflect the music they hear. Discuss the different ways children choose to show the changing moods.

After the children have given their ideas as to what the mood might suggest, read the poem. They may then wish to dramatize the music, with one child playing the part of the hand-organ man while others play in the garden.

RING-AROUND-THE-ROSY

"Let's play Ring-Around-the-Rosy," says little Anna Maria." Quickly they form a ring, singing and dancing.

Listen: Everyone has played Ring-Around-the-Rosy. Ask the children to describe how the game is played. **Listen to how the music seems to return to the same place over and over, just as we return to the same place when we dance in a circle. Can you hear any place in the music that suggests you "all fall down"?** The children will conclude that this occurs at the end where the music becomes FASTER. Some may also notice the interruption in the rhythmic movement near the middle of the music (the repeated tones).

Move: Invite the children to play the game as they listen. Remind them to move quickly around the ring with small tiptoe steps. If they wish to "fall down"

during the middle part, they will need to be ready to arise quickly so that they can move in a ring again as the music continues.

MARCH, LITTLE SOLDIERS
At the other corner, little Luiz Octavio comes marching by with his men in paper hats carrying wooden guns.

EXPRESSION

Listen: **What kind of music is this? What do you hear that helps you to know?** The children may suggest that this is a march or a parade, because they can hear the sound of a bugle and the steady beat of drums.

FORM

Move: One boy may pretend to be the bugler and announce the INTRODUCTION of the march. The other boys may begin to march as they hear the main melody, which is repeated. Notice the sound of the deep bass drum underlying the second melody. Call attention to the return of the first melody, which is now higher. As the boys march around the room, suggest that they change direction at the beginning of each new section (A, A, B, A).

SLEEPING TIME
The sun falls down in the west. Six times the cuckoo sings in the clock. The little girls sing lullabies; sing that their dollies must go to sleep before the bogeyman comes.

EXPRESSION

Listen: Read the poem to the class. Ask the children to listen for the cuckoo clock; help them count its six strokes.

How do you know that this is a lullaby? (It is soft and quiet, with a rocking-like melody that moves up and down.) The rhythm suggests the swaying of the little girls as they rock their dollies.

Is there a scary section where the dollies may think the bogeyman is coming? (Yes, where the low tones are heard.) **What do the dollies do?** (Begin to cry.) **Then what happens?** (They rock the dollies to sleep again.)

Move: The boys dramatized "March, Little Soldiers." "Sleeping Time" may belong to the girls, who will enjoy rocking their dollies in time to the music. One may "be" the clock and pretend to strike six times. Decide appropriate actions for the "bogeyman" section.

HOBBYHORSE
And now playtime is over and the children come prancing happily home on their wooden hobbyhorses.

Listen: **How does the music tell us that the children are happy to return home?** (The light, rollicking melody.) **Are they going straight home or are they stopping on the way?** (They seem to be slowing down or stopping in certain places in the music.) **How do we know when they finally reach home?** (At the end where the music becomes very FAST.)

Move: **How do these hobbyhorses move? Are they trotting, EVENLY, or are they galloping, UNEVENLY?** Encourage the children to experiment and guide them to decide that trotting (a light, steady, even run) is most appropriate for this music. Listen for changes in the music which might suggest changes in action. Experiment with different movements to decide what might best fit the sound of the music.

Guiding Musical Growth
in the First Grade

	Listening	Singing	Playing
SKILL	Work for improvement in the ability to listen with discrimination.	Work for improvement in ability to sing on pitch within a limited range. Provide opportunities for all children to sing individually. Give special help to uncertain singers.	Encourage experimentation with a variety of percussion instruments (triangle, sticks, bells, and so forth). Help children gain facility in playing instruments by demonstrating proper playing techniques for them.
CONCEPTS *Melody*	Draw attention to melodic movement in terms of up, down, same, step, skip, high, and low.	Emphasize melodic movement through the singing of tonal patterns.	Help children perceive tonal movement in terms of up, down, same, step, skip through playing melody instruments. Stress association of high-low concepts with right-left direction in playing bells and piano.
Rhythm	Guide children to become aware of differences in over-all rhythmic movement: 1. Identify beat and rhythmic pattern. 2. Identify rhythmic patterns as even and uneven (made up of the same, longer, or shorter tones).	Strive for rhythmic accuracy in reproducing melodies.	Use a variety of percussion instruments to help children become conscious of beat and rhythmic pattern.
Harmony	Stress presence of multiple sounds by calling attention to melody and accompaniment.	Provide opportunities to sing with accompaniment.	Provide experiences in creating multiple sounds through playing simple melodic and rhythmic accompaniments.
Form	Help children to become aware of melodic and rhythmic phrases as same-different and to recognize sections of a composition as being same, different, or similar.	Stress singing by phrase.	Help children become conscious of same-different phrases by associating them with same-different instruments.
Expression	Emphasize the relationship of obvious changes in tempo and dynamics to musical expressiveness. Help children identify common orchestral instruments by tone color and as belonging to high-low categories.	Work for expressive singing by emphasizing appropriate tone quality, tempo, and dynamics.	Provide opportunities to explore the expressive possibilities of instruments of varying tone qualities, singly and in combination.

Moving	Creating	Reading
Provide opportunities for interpreting music through dramatization and impersonation. Help children gain control of fundamental movements (walk, run, skip, and so on) by providing many opportunities for physical response to music.	Stimulate children to create rhythmic and melodic patterns using their own voices and simple instruments.	Use line notation to represent familiar melodic and rhythmic patterns, in order to help children associate visual symbols with musical concepts. Introduce staff notation when children have functional use of line notation.
Encourage children to imitate teacher in outlining melodic movement with hand levels. Guide children to reveal awareness of melodic contour in their body movements.	Help children reinforce their understanding of melodic movement by improvising melodies.	Use melodic contour lines and line notation to represent melodic direction. Introduce numbers as a means of identifying melodic patterns.
Emphasize beat and rhythmic pattern by using a variety of physical responses (tap, clap, march, run, and so forth). Encourage children to indicate their recognition of even-uneven rhythmic patterns by moving in appropriate ways.	Encourage children to use a variety of rhythmic patterns in their improvisations.	Use line notation to help children gain concepts of rhythmic patterns made up of longer and shorter tones.
	Help children to improvise accompaniments for pentatonic melodies.	
Aid children to respond with same or different body movements as a means of developing perception of same-different phrases.		Aid children to observe same-different phrases in notation.
Encourage free physical, spontaneous response to the expressive qualities of music.	Encourage children to experiment with different instruments in their improvisations and in creating accompaniments.	

SEESAW, MARGERY DAW*

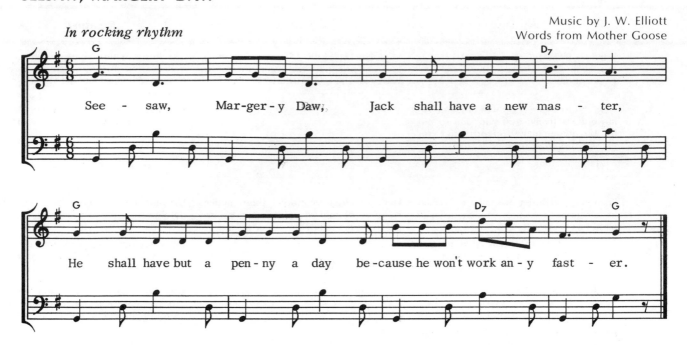

Music by J. W. Elliott
Words from Mother Goose

In rocking rhythm

See - saw, Mar-ger-y Daw; Jack shall have a new mas - ter,

He shall have but a pen - ny a day be-cause he won't work an - y fast - er.

MELODY

Listen: **Have you ever ridden on a seesaw? How did it move? Can you show me with your arms? Can you hear a pattern in the music that goes up and down, back and forth, just like you move on the seesaw?**

After listening to the song, guide the children to realize that the melody for the words "Seesaw, Margery Daw" moves UP and DOWN, back and forth. To help them recognize the up–down movement, from high to low, demonstrate on the stepbells.

Do you hear another place in the music that goes up and down, from high to low? ("He shall have but a penny a day.") Some children may notice that the pattern is also heard in the instrumental introduction on the recording, played by the string quartet.

Sing: After the children have heard the song several times and have discussed the words and the melodic contour, ask them to sing the song without assistance. Play the recording again. **Did you sing the melody just like it sounds on the record?** Help the children identify any errors made; repeat these steps until they can sing the complete song accurately. *Do not sing* with them, for the children will not become independent singers if your stronger voice constantly acts as a "crutch."

Play: On another day, place resonator bells D-E-F♯-G in order. **When you ride a seesaw, do you move a long way from high to low, or do you move just a short distance?** (A long way.) **Can you find bells that are far apart and play a pattern that moves up and down, from high to low, like the seesaw?** Help the children decide that they will need the two bells that are farthest apart, G and D. Notice that some bells must be skipped over in order to make the pattern sound like the up–down movement of the seesaw.

HARMONY

Listen: Draw attention to the repeated up-down pattern played by the stringed instruments in the accompaniment to the melody.

Play: As the children sing the song, invite one child to play the G-D pattern on the bells, over and over. You will notice that the piano accompaniment changes in the fourth, seventh, and eighth measures. However, the repeated bell pattern is acceptable, even though it produces a dissonance on the first beat of the eighth measure.

RHYTHM

Play: Use two wood blocks of different pitches to be played on the ACCENTED BEATS throughout the song. Give one to each of two children; help them decide which player (high or low) should begin the pattern. Stress the importance of playing a steady, even rhythm.

high low   high low

Move: Other children may show their awareness of the underlying pulse by imitating the motion of the seesaw with their arms as *they sing*.

WHO WILL COME WITH ME?

Playfully   American Folk Song

1. Who will come with me, the jol - ly, jol - ly ro - ver?
2. Who will skip with me, the jol - ly, jol - ly ro - ver?

Who will come with me, the jol - ly, jol - ly ro - ver, } And
Who will skip with me, the jol - ly, jol - ly ro - ver, }

see,_____ and see,_____ and see what we can see?_____

RHYTHM

Move: Sing or play the first verse of the song for the children. **What would be a good way to move when you went with the jolly rover? Will you march or skip?** Sing the song again while the children experiment. Some may sense the UNEVEN rhythm of the melody, and skip; others may feel the EVEN rhythm of the beat, and walk. Both responses are correct. Draw attention to the two ways of moving and discuss the differences.

Sing the second verse of the song and invite the children to skip or gallop in response to the UNEVEN rhythm of the melody.

Improvise a third verse in an EVEN rhythm and ask the children to respond with appropriate movement.

Who will walk with me,   the jol - ly, jol - ly   ro - ver?

Read: Later in the year, return to the song. **I can show the rhythm of a song in a picture.**

(Even)   —— —— —— —— —— —— —— ——

(Uneven) —— — —— — —— — —— — ——

Give the children time to discuss the differences they observe in the two diagrams; in one all the lines are the SAME, in the other the lines are LONGER and SHORTER.

Which picture shows the rhythm of a song which is EVEN? How would you move to an even rhythm? (Walk or run.) **Which picture shows the rhythm of a song which is UNEVEN? How would you move to this?** (Skip or gallop.)

Play: Give individual children an opportunity to reveal their understanding of the line notation by asking them to play appropriate patterns on the drum or sticks as the teacher, or a child, points to one of the pictures.

FORM

Sing: Choose one child to be the rover. He may stand in front of someone and sing the first PHRASE, "Who will come with me, the jolly, jolly rover?" The person he has chosen answers with the second phrase. All may sing the last phrase as they skip around the room.

Listen: **Count the number of phrases that were sung.** (Three.) **Do any phrases sound nearly alike?** (One and two.) **Which phrase has a melody of its own?** (Three.)

HEY, BETTY MARTIN

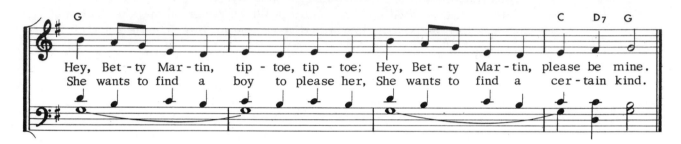

EXPRESSION

Play: **What should "tiptoe" music sound like? Should it be soft or loud?** Select instruments that have a "tiptoe" sound (finger cymbals or rhythm sticks) with which to accompany the singing.

RHYTHM

Listen: Discover the difference between the two RHYTHMIC PATTERNS ♩ ♩ ♩ ♩ and

♩ ♩ ♩ **Which pattern has a LONG sound at the end?**

Move: Encourage the children to match the rhythmic patterns as they tiptoe:

step   step   step   step   step   step   wait

MELODY

Read: Help the children visualize the DOWNWARD-moving melodic contour by making use of hand levels and line notation:

Hey,

Bet-

ty

Mar-

tin

FORM

Listen: Help the children begin to develop an awareness of melodic MOTIVE. **Which melody patterns sound the SAME?** ("Hey, Betty Martin, tiptoe, tiptoe.")

Move: Plan a dance that fits the form, using similar movements for patterns that are the SAME, contrasting movements for patterns that are DIFFERENT.

WHO'S THAT TAPPING AT THE WINDOW?

Slowly

American Folk Song

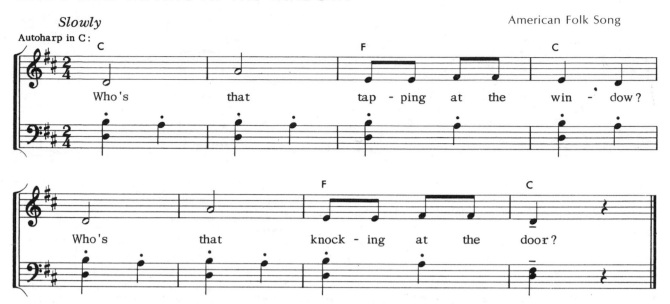

Reprinted by permission of the publishers from *On the Trail of Negro Folk-Songs* by Dorothy Scarborough. Cambridge, Mass.: Harvard University Press, copyright 1925, by The Harvard University Press; 1953 by Mary McDaniel Parker.

RHYTHM

Listen: Clap one of these RHYTHMIC PATTERNS: ♩♩♩♩ ♩ ♩ or ♩♩♩♩ ♩. Ask the children to listen to the song and decide which pattern you had clapped. Notice that the first pattern has six separate sounds; the second has only five.

Describe the sound of the patterns using the terms SHORT and LONG:
S S S S L L   and   S S S S L
Discover that the song begins with a pattern that sounds

LO-ONG   LO-ONG (♩   ♩)

Play: Perform the song as a dialogue. One child may play the beginning pattern on a drum; two others answer in turn, playing the appropriate pattern on sticks and wood block.

MELODY

Play: When the song is familiar, help the children explore STEPS and SKIPS. Place bells D-E-F♯-G-A in order; invite the children to experiment until they can find the pattern for "Who's that" (D-A). Help them notice that they played bells that were far apart. **This pattern moves with a SKIP because we had to "skip" some bells.**

Listen: The teacher should play the melody for "tapping at the window" (E-F♯-E-D). Guide the children to realize that now the bells that were played are very near to each other. **This pattern moves by STEPS.**

Read: As the children sing the song, encourage them to imitate the melodic movement with hand levels, thus showing their understanding of skips and steps.

SLEEP, BABY, SLEEP

Andante   German Folk Song

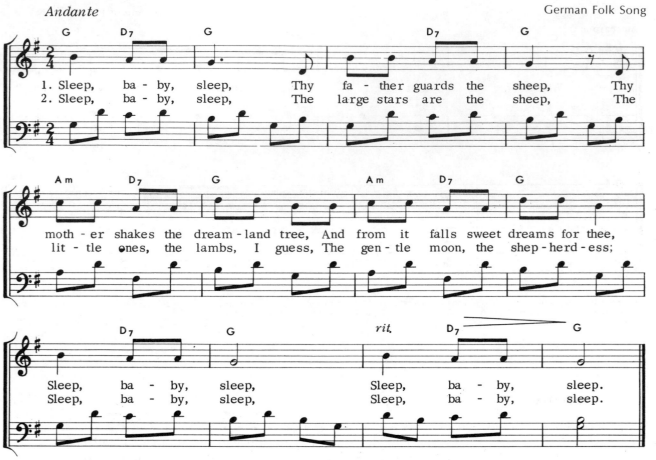

1. Sleep, ba-by, sleep, Thy fa-ther guards the sheep, Thy
2. Sleep, ba-by, sleep, The large stars are the sheep, The

moth-er shakes the dream-land tree, And from it falls sweet dreams for thee,
lit-tle ones, the lambs, I guess, The gen-tle moon, the shep-herd-ess;

Sleep, ba-by, sleep,   Sleep, ba-by, sleep.
Sleep, ba-by, sleep,   Sleep, ba-by, sleep.

EXPRESSION

Sing: The children will quickly conclude that this lovely melody should be sung smoothly and quietly, with as beautiful a tone as they can produce. They may also decide that the song should move more SLOWLY and SOFTLY at the end as the "baby" falls asleep.

Move: By pretending to "rock" their baby, slowly and gently, the children will be helped to become sensitive to the mood of this song and to emphasize the flowing line of the melody.

Listen: Compare the mood of this song with that of the "Cradle Song," which follows. **What things make both of these create the mood of a lullaby?**

FORM

Play: Plan an INTRODUCTION and a CODA using the melodic fragment for "Sleep, baby, sleep."

| G | A | B |

Down

It may be played twice at the beginning and twice at the end. Talk about how the bells must be played to maintain the mood of the song.

CRADLE SONG

from "Children's Games" by Georges Bizet

Adventures in Music, Grade 1

EXPRESSION

Listen: Enjoy this restful, gentle music on several different days. You may wish to play it for the children during rest periods without comment. When they are familiar with the composition, talk about the things they have heard in the music.

What kind of music is this? (Lullaby.) **What helps you to know?** Guide the children to notice the rocking motion of the melody, which moves in an UNEVEN rhythm. The SOFT sounds of the instruments, the many repetitions of the SAME melody, and the moderate TEMPO (speed) also contribute to the quiet, sleepy mood.

As the children listen on different days, direct their attention to the instruments. During the first section the melody is played by the VIOLINS; the second section begins with the CLARINET followed by the FLUTE; the third section begins with the violins again. Show the children pictures of the violin, clarinet, and flute. Help them associate the sound of each with its picture.

Move: Invite the children to mirror the swaying rhythm as they "rock" their babies, or move quietly around the room. Some children may show their awareness of the CONTOUR of the melodic line (down–up–down) with their hands and bodies as they move.

MELODY

Listen: Draw attention to the main melody:

How many times do you hear this melody in the music? (Six.) Discuss the fact that although the melody is played sometimes HIGH and sometimes LOW, it is always the SAME melody.

Play: Place the following bells in order: F♯-G♯-A♯-B-C♯-D♯. Help the children find the first pattern of the melody. They must begin on the white bell (B), play down by steps, then skip back to the white bell and move up by steps.

FORM

Listen: Decide that there are three main SECTIONS in this composition. (The last section is shorter than the first two, ending with viola and flute coda based on a segment of the main melody.) **How do you know when the first part of the music comes to an end?** Guide the children to observe that the music slows down toward the end of each section and pauses on a LONG tone.

Help the children notice that each new section begins with a different instrument. Guide them also to hear the addition of the high melody (clarinet) at the beginning of the third section.

Move: Encourage the children to show their recognition of sections by their movements; divide the class into groups, one to move during each section.

PUSSYCAT, PUSSYCAT

Andantino

Music by J. W. Elliot
Words from Mother Goose

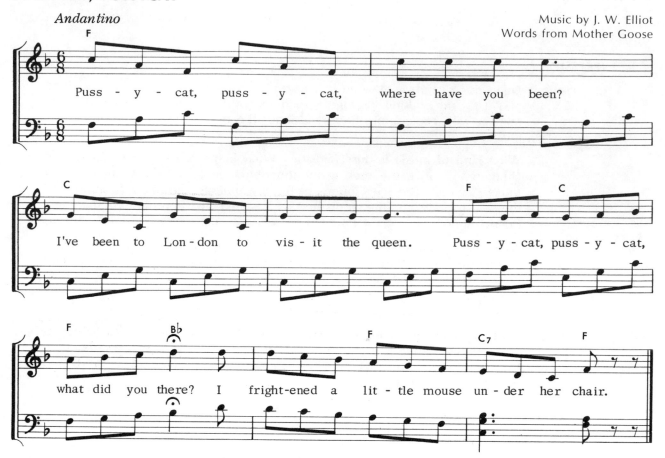

MELODY

Listen: After the children have heard the song and discussed the words, ask them to locate patterns where the melody (1) moves DOWN by SKIPS, (2) moves DOWN by STEPS, (3) stays in the SAME place, and (4) moves UP by STEPS. As they offer their answers, help them check these by observing the bells as you play the patterns they suggest.

Read: Introduce the idea that one can draw a picture of a melody pattern. Put the following diagrams on the chalkboard. Ask the children to select the appropriate picture for each melodic pattern.

(Pussycat)   (Where have you been?)   (What did you there?)

Play: Two groups of three children may play the melody of the first two phrases on the resonator bells:

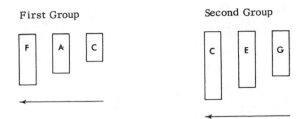

First Group   Second Group

Some children may realize that the two TONAL PATTERNS are the SAME, except that the second pattern is LOWER than the first.

FORM

Sing: Divide the class into two groups to sing the questions and answers alternately, thereby helping them to develop awareness of PHRASE structure. This is also a good song to help expand children's ranges. On some occasions choose one child to sing the answers as a solo.

DANCE IN THE CIRCLE

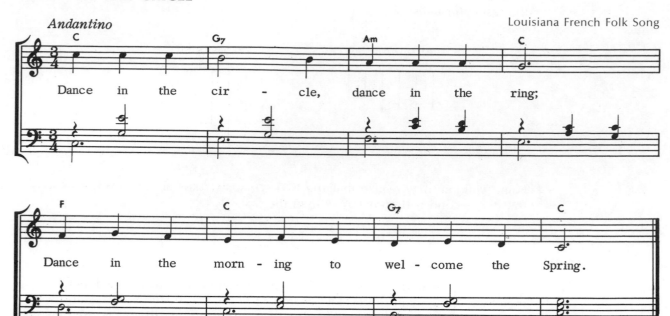

Andantino   Louisiana French Folk Song

Dance in the cir - cle, dance in the ring;

Dance in the morn - ing to wel - come the Spring.

RHYTHM

Move: After the children have sung the song, invite them to improvise their own dance. They may respond with swaying, sliding, or swinging motions reflecting the waltzlike rhythm. Draw attention to the different movements and discuss their appropriateness.

Play: To help the children become more sensitive to the ACCENT GROUPING, invite one child to play a drum on the HEAVY beats.

MELODY

Read: Ask the children to help you make a picture of the way the melody moves. (In these activities stress the general melodic contour; do not be concerned with the back-and-forth movement in measures 5, 6, and 7.) Draw a staircase on the flannel board and give the children felt disks to place on the board. As you sing, help them place the disks on appropriate steps. Discover that the first disk must go at the top of the stairs and that each new one must be placed on the next lower step.

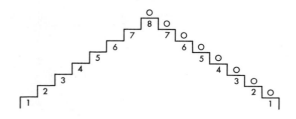

Sing: **How many steps did we have in our melody?** (Eight.) **Can you sing the numbers as you count the steps? Let's call the lowest step number "1."** Write the numbers on the steps as the class sings up the scale.

How would we have to sing the numbers to make the melody sound like "Dance in the Circle"? (Backwards.) **Can you begin on the highest step and sing down from eight to one?** Point to the numbers as the children sing.

Play: Give one bell, C-D-E-F-G-A-B-C, to each of eight children. As the class sings, guide them to play the outline of the melody, sounding the appropriate bell on the first beat of each measure.

Reinforce the use of numbers by applying them to familiar tonal patterns. Write the numbers on the chalkboard; place the bells in order and give the children an opportunity to find the corresponding correct bells.

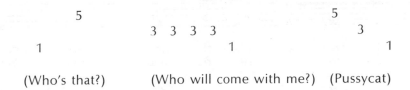

5							5	
					3 3 3 3			3
1						1		1

(Who's that?)   (Who will come with me?)   (Pussycat)

HA, HA, THIS-A-WAY

Playfully   American Folk Song

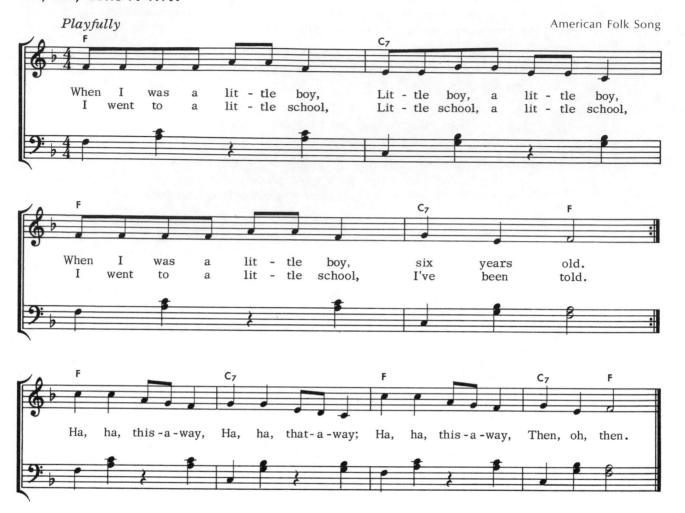

RHYTHM

Move: As some children sing this song, others may move around the room as though they were going to school. During the refrain, ask those that are moving to show different ways to move, as suggested by the words "This-a-way, that-a-way." They may walk, run on tiptoe, take long steps, move backwards, move to the side, and so forth.

Read: Show in line notation on the chalkboard some of the patterns that the children have stepped:

> (walk with beat)   ____ ___   ____ ___
>
> (step with accent)   _____   _____
>
> (run on tiptoe)   _ _ _ _   _ _ _ _

Discuss differences in the patterns in terms of LONGER, SHORTER, and SAME.

Later in the year, introduce the idea that the patterns of rhythm which they stepped and saw in line notation can also be shown with NOTES. Place appropriate notation patterns on the chalkboard opposite the line notation they have stepped:

Discuss the differences children observe in the three notational pictures.

The rhythms that we sing can be shown with lines and with notes, also. Place this pattern — — —— on the chalkboard; chant it: short–short–long. Then show the pattern with notes: ♩ ♩ 𝅗𝅥 Sing the song again and help the children discover that this is the pattern of the words "six years old."

Return to familiar songs and guide the children to determine the line notation for distinctive rhythm patterns. Then help them change the line notation to traditional notation:

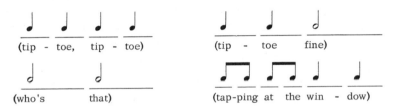

Play: Put the three stepping patterns for "Ha, Ha, This-a-way" in notation on the chalkboard. Invite a child to choose an instrument for one of the patterns and play the same as an accompaniment while the class sings. Later, some first graders may be able to play two or all three patterns together as an accompaniment. Sticks may be appropriate for the eighth-note pattern, a drum for the quarter-note pattern, and finger cymbals for the half-note pattern.

FORM

Move: Guide the children to sense that the song is made up of three PHRASES. (There is a LONG tone at the end of each phrase.) Ask them to show the phrase structure as they move by changing direction at the beginning of each phrase.

Listen: Help the children realize that phrases may be made up of several PATTERNS (motives). **Listen to the first phrase. How many times do you hear this pattern?** (Teacher claps: ♫ ♫ ♫ ♩) When the children have decided that it is heard three times, the teacher should clap the three patterns and ask the children to complete the phrase. (They should clap: ♩ ♩ 𝅗𝅥.) **This phrase has four patterns; three are the SAME, one is DIFFERENT.**

How many patterns can you hear in the last phrase? How many are the same? The children should conclude that there are four patterns: Three that are the same (♩ ♩ ♫ ♩) and one that is different (♩ ♩ 𝅗𝅥).

PARADE*

RCA Victor, LM2080   Morton Gould

"Parade" is a composition for percussion instruments: two snare drums (one large and one small), two bass drums (one large and one small), cymbals, and a marching machine that simulates sounds of marching feet.

EXPRESSION

Listen: Introduce the composition without mentioning its title. Ask the children to tell what the music suggests; they may decide that it sounds like a march or a parade.

As the children listen again, focus their listening. **Are the instruments playing a MELODY that you can sing? Are they making MUSIC?** Help the children conclude that, although there is no melody that can be sung, this is still music because there is RHYTHM.

Draw attention to the fact that there is a kind of "melody" because some drums make HIGH sounds and some make LOW sounds. If possible, bring drums of different sizes into the classroom; experiment to discover that size of drum helps determine whether its sound will be high or low. The smaller the drum is the higher it sounds, and vice versa.

Later, help the children identify the specific instruments that are included in this composition. Compare the deep, sustained sound of the BASS DRUM with the crisp, rattling sound of the SNARE DRUMS. Ask the children to think of words to describe the sound of the CYMBALS. Draw attention to the marching machine, which is used in this composition for special effects.

Invite a high school drummer to come to class and show the children the snare drum. Ask him to demonstrate the difference in the sound of the drum when the snares are attached and when they are released.

To be sure that the children have associated the sound of each instrument with its appropriate name, divide the class into four groups and ask the children to show their recognition in the following manner: The first group of children should raise their hands when they first hear the bass drum; the second group may indicate when the snare drum begins to play; the third group identifies the marching machine; and the fourth group may indicate the entrance of the cymbals.

On another day, play the composition again and draw attention to other aspects of the music. **As you listen to the music, imagine your parade. Does it begin near to you or far away? When is it nearest to you? What happens at the end? How do you know?** Decide that the parade begins far away, passes by close, and then disappears in the distance, because the music begins SOFTLY, becomes LOUDER, and then becomes SOFT again.

Move: Divide the class to form two "parades" starting from opposite ends of the room. Help the children plan their marching so that they will meet and pass during the loudest part of the music and be far apart when the music ends.

IMPROVISING WITH PERCUSSION INSTRUMENTS

Discuss: Encourage the children to talk about the different things they have heard in music which help to make it interesting. Replay "Parade" and make a list of the sounds that helped create the mood of a parade. Guide the children to include in their list such musical ideas as (1) changes between LOUD and SOFT, (2) differences between SLOW and FAST, (3) contrasts in the sounds (TONE COLORS) of instruments, (4) differences in RHYTHM PATTERNS, and (5) combinations of HIGH and LOW sounds.

Invite the children to bring something to school that they think makes an interesting sound. Take turns letting each child produce a sound on his instrument; discuss the quality of each. Notice that some sounds last a long time and gradually die away, while other sounds are very short. Help the children think of words to describe sounds: clanging, tapping, clicking, booming, scraping, ringing, and so forth. Group the instruments by quality of sound. With teacher as "director," signal one group after another to play in "unison." Discuss the interesting sounds that result from the combinations of instruments.

Group the sound-makers into HIGH and LOW divisions and experiment again with combinations by having the groups play one after the other. Invite each child to experiment until he can play LOUD and SOFT on his instrument. Explore possibilities of combinations of loud and soft with high and low.

Create: Invite individual children to improvise interesting RHYTHM PATTERNS. At this age the patterns are likely to be somewhat erratic and nonmetric. Do not destroy the child's imagination by trying to force the patterns into traditional metric groupings. However, do help him to realize the importance of remembering his pattern; encourage him to repeat the pattern he has developed several times. Some interesting patterns might be charted in line notation. When several patterns have been "notated," help the class to play them, one after another, as a "percussion composition." Try the patterns in different sequences; play the same pattern on different instruments; discuss the differences that occur.

On another day, divide the class into groups of four or five children. Allow each group to take turns improvising a composition for the class. Guide the members of the groups to select instruments of contrasting tone color and pitch level. The children may use the sound-makers they brought from home or select percussion instruments from those available in the classroom. (At first, avoid melody instruments such as the bells.) One child in each group may be selected as the "director." He points to one child, who begins playing a rhythm of his choice; as he points to other children in turn, they also begin to play. Guide the children to suggest ways that the director may indicate other ideas, also, such as when he wishes one child to cease playing or whether he wants the instrumentalist to play softly or loudly, fast or slow.

If possible, tape the performances so that the children can listen to their own compositions. Discuss ways to improve the performances. **Did all of the children play too loudly? Were the instruments too similar in sound? Perhaps Mary can play a pattern that is different from everyone else's? The composition is too long, too short. Everyone played all the time; it would be more interesting if Johnny was quiet for awhile and then started again with a new rhythm.** Suggestions such as these may emerge from the discussion.

Variations on the activities suggested should often be included in music time. Give different children opportunities to be "director." On some occasions the class may wish to develop compositions to match a descriptive title such as "A Walk in the Park," "The Playground," or "Night Time." At another time one child might improvise rhythm patterns while other children develop movements to match the sounds they hear.

MY PONY

Music by C. G. Hering
Words by Carl Hahn

Moderato

Trot, trot, trot! Trot, my po - ny, trot! Where it's smooth and

where it's ston - y, Trot a - long, my lit - tle po - ny.

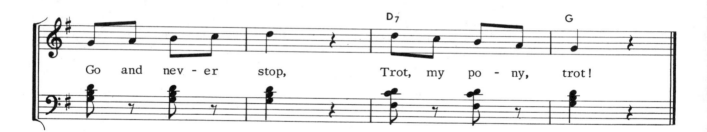

Go and nev - er stop, Trot, my po - ny, trot!

MELODY

Listen: **Can you tell me if the melody is moving UP or DOWN at the beginning of the song—at the end of the song?**

Play: As the children find the tunes for "Trot, trot, trot," and "Go and never stop," on the step bells, help them to conclude that tunes may move by SKIPS or by STEPS. As they play the tune for "Go and never stop," count the bells, then sing this pattern with numbers: 1-2-3-4-5.

To dramatize the difference between this pattern, which STEPS, and the pattern of "Trot, trot, trot," which SKIPS, give resonator bells to five children and have those who are playing bells 2 and 4 squat down as the others play 1-3-5. Later, they may discover that the tune for "Trot, my pony, trot," moves in the opposite direction of "Go and never stop,": 5-4-3-2-1.

Read: Show MELODIC DIRECTION in line notation on the chalkboard. Ask the children to determine the numbers and add them to the picture:

$$\frac{5}{trot} \qquad \frac{5}{Trot}$$
$$\frac{4}{my}$$
$$\frac{3}{trot} \qquad\qquad \frac{3}{po-}$$
$$\frac{2}{ny}$$
$$\frac{1}{Trot} \qquad\qquad\qquad \frac{1}{trot}$$

Later, put the notation for the first phrase on the chalkboard. Review with the children how the melody moves in steps and skips.

Observe the notation and guide them to make observations about this new picture of the melody. **What in the picture might have told you when the melody would skip and when it would step?**

Discuss the STAFF, observing that it consists of LINES and SPACES. Stress the fact that notes appear *on* the lines and *in* the spaces.

Draw a staff on the flannel board and cut out a number of felt notes. Give the children opportunities to place notes on the lines as well as in the spaces.

Refer to the notation above. Discuss the fact that melodies that step have notes on both lines and spaces; melodies that skip omit some lines or spaces. Place a pattern on the feltboard and ask the children to tell you if it skips or steps. Play the pattern on the bells and ask the children to decide if their answer was correct.

FORM

Move: Draw attention to the three PHRASES of this song by helping the children plan their movements to reflect the phrase structure: trotting forward on the first phrase, in the opposite direction on the second phrase, and returning to the original direction on the third phrase.

SHOHEEN SHO

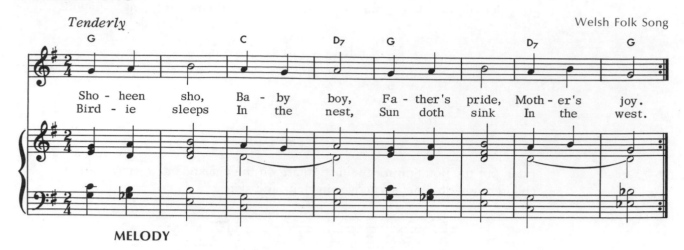

Tenderly   Welsh Folk Song

Sho - heen   sho,   Ba - by   boy,   Fa - ther's pride,   Moth - er's   joy.
Bird - ie   sleeps   In the   nest,   Sun doth   sink   In the   west.

MELODY

Read: Put the line notation for the complete song on the chalkboard:

Discuss the picture; notice the direction of each short, three-tone pattern. **The first pattern moves 1-2-3. Can you decide the numbers for the rest of the melody?** Write them above the lines as the children determine them: 1-2-3, 2-1-2, 1-2-3, 2-3-1. Notice that the entire song moves by steps except for the last tone, which skips.

Play: Place the bells G-A-B in order and give different children the opportunity to play the complete melody. Then help the class sing as someone plays the bells.

Read: On another day, place the staff notation for the song on the chalkboard without words. Ask the children to study the notation; look for steps and skips and determine the numbers. **Who thinks they know this melody?**

Sing: Sing the melody with numbers following the notation. When the children discover the title, sing the song with words.

RHYTHM

Read: Study the line notation and chant the RHYTHM OF THE MELODY:
                        S S L   S S L.   S S L   S S L

Put the rhythmic notation on the chalkboard:

Notice the similarity of the four RHYTHMIC PATTERNS. Chant the rhythm again, using "short" and "long."

EXPRESSION

Discuss: Ask the children to decide what type of song this is. (Lullaby.) Compare the mood of this song with that of others they know, such as "My Pony" and "Pussycat, Pussycat."

Sing: Talk about the kind of voice one should use to express the mood of a lullaby. **Can you sing this song softly and smoothly so that it might put the baby to sleep?**

TWILIGHT*

Quietly

Words and music by A. Giron

Soft - ly the twi - light ends an - oth - er day.

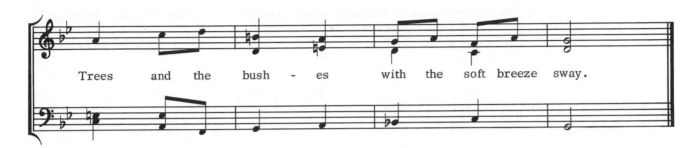

Trees and the bush - es with the soft breeze sway.

EXPRESSION

Listen: Play the recording of this song several times for the children on different occasions so that they may enjoy the contemporary flavor of this music.

Draw attention to the instrumental introduction. The melody is played by an English horn, while the accompaniment is played on the HARP. Talk about how the soft sounds of these instruments help to sustain the quiet mood of the song.

Discuss the meaning of the word "twilight." Ask the children to describe things they have noticed at the end of the day such as the setting of the sun in the west, the lengthening of shadows, and so on.

Sing: When the children have listened carefully on several days, ask them to sing the melody softly. **Did your melody sound exactly the same as the melody on the record?** Help the children learn to evaluate their own performances and to identify their own errors. When the melody is familiar, talk about the tone of voice that should be used to sing this twilight song.

Create: Read the following poems about different times of day. Talk about the different moods suggested by each. Some classes may want to make up a melody for one of the poems (see suggestions on page 279). Other classes may wish to create their own poems about their favorite time of day.

SINGING-TIME

I wake in the morning early
And always, the very first thing,
I poke out my head and I sit up in bed
and I sing and I sing and I sing.
—ROSE FYLEMAN

From *The Fairy Green* by Rose Fyleman, Copyright 1923, by Doubleday & Co., Inc.

THE FIREFLY LIGHTS HIS LAMP
Although the night is damp,
The little firefly ventures out,
And slowly lights his lamp.
—UNKNOWN (Japanese)

Play: The children may add an accompaniment to "Twilight." Finger cymbals played softly will add to the mood of the song. Play on the first beat of each two-measure motive.

FORM

Play: The song is made up of four two-measure motives. The first, second, and fourth motives are similar; the third is different. To help the children become sensitive to the structure of the song, give one child the D-F-G bells. He may play during the similar motives as the class sings. A second child may play the A-B-C bells during the third motive.

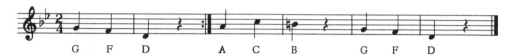

POOR BIRD*

Japanese Singing Game

Poor bird, you are so sad,   Sit-ting in your bam-boo cage.

Will you sing a song for___ me,   If I come and set you free?

All to-geth-er, now fall down.   Who's be-hind you? Can you guess?

EXPRESSION

Listen: Sing the song with the accompaniment, or play the recording, and invite the children to discuss the music. Draw attention to the different sounds in the accompaniment on the recording. It is played by a recorder (an ancient wooden flutelike instrument), a koto (a Japanese stringed instrument), and a flute.

This is a Japanese children's singing game. Explain the way the game is played; ask the children to think of games they play which are similar. Talk about the interesting fact that boys and girls all over the world enjoy doing the same things such as singing songs and playing games.

FORM

Listen: As the children listen again to the recording, discover that the song is made up of six PATTERNS (each two measures long) that are quite similar.

Play: To help show the design of the song, one child may play an A-bell at the beginning of each pattern.

Move: The class will enjoy playing the game as they sing. All stand in a circle except one child, who is "it"; he sits in the center with eyes closed. As the class walks around the circle singing, one player (designated by the teacher) goes quickly to the center and stands behind the seated player. On the "all together, now fall down" children in the circle drop down. The player who has gone to the center sings, "Who's behind you, can you guess?" When the player who is "it" guesses right, he returns to the circle and the second player remains in the center.

RHYTHM

Play: Add an accompaniment with percussion instruments to help children feel ACCENT. Give one instrument to each of four children. They should play in turn, one on each HEAVY beat: (1) drum with soft beater, (2) wood block, (3) triangle, (4) finger cymbals. Notice that this complete pattern is repeated three times.

HARMONY

Play: To help the children become sensitive to MULTIPLE SOUNDS, a child with good muscular coordination may play an accompaniment on the piano. Help him find A and E on the keyboard. Using the index fingers of both hands, he may play one or both of these tones at the beginning of each pattern:

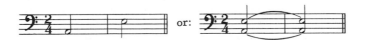

Create: This melody is based on the pentatonic scale, which has no half steps. Therefore any combination of tones from this scale combined with the melody will be satisfying. Place bells G-A-B-D-E in order. Invite one child to improvise a pattern on these bells as the class sings. The child may pretend that he is imitating the sound of a bird song. Discuss ways of improving the pattern, such as varying the number of tones used, changing the rhythm, and so forth.

INTRODUCTION AND ROYAL MARCH OF THE LION

From "Carnival of Animals" by Camille Saint-Saëns

Bowmar Orchestral Library, BOL #51

FORM

Listen: **This composition is in two parts, beginning with an INTRODUCTION. An introduction is the part of the music that says, "Get ready! Something is going to happen! Can you tell by the sound of the music when the introduction is completed?** (After the first GLISSANDO on the piano.)

MELODY

Sing: Learn to sing the main theme:

Suggest that the children hum this melody with the record each time they hear it.

Listen: **How many times in a row do you hear this same tune (nearly the same) repeated?** (Four times.)

What happened to this tune the last time it was played? (It was much HIGHER.)

EXPRESSION

Discuss: After the music has become familiar, discuss what it is describing.

This music is supposed to be describing an animal. Would this animal be large or small? Would it be a jungle animal or a family pet? How would the animal move? What kind of voice would he have?

Encourage the children to give their answers to questions such as these and to give reasons for thinking as they do. ("It is a big animal because the music has a 'big' sound." "It would be a jungle animal because the music is low and sounds sort of scary." "This animal would have a big, low voice because the part the piano plays sounds like an animal growling.")

After the children have made their suggestions, explain that the composer is trying to describe a lion. **The lion is a proud animal; he is "King of the Beasts." The composer tried to make the music sound proud by using a "fanfare" introduction which announces, "Here comes the King!" Then he describes the lion padding around slowly on his big paws, stopping now and then to growl at something.**

Listen: **Listen again to the music. Can you imagine a big lion as you listen? What makes the "growling" sound?** (The piano.) **Can you count the number of growls?**

Move: Let the children dramatize the music. Some may pretend to be the guards announcing the entrance of the King. One child may be the Lion King. He might be followed by a whole line of Lion Princes.

How will the lions move? Can the lions show that they are growling by tossing their heads at the proper time?

Guiding Musical Growth
in the **Second Grade**

	Listening	Singing	Playing
SKILL	Work for improvement in ability to listen with discrimination.	Help each individual expand his singing range.	Provide opportunities for continuing experimentation with a variety of simple rhythm and melody instruments.
		Encourage the children to sing individually.	Encourage exploration at the piano keyboard.
CONCEPTS *Melody*	Identify melodic movement as moving by steps (scale-line) or skips.	Help increase understanding of melodic movement by singing tonal patterns with numbers and/or syllables.	Help the children expand their awareness of melodic movement through playing melodic fragments on pitched instruments.
	Guide children to sense general differences in major and minor qualities.		Associate number relationships with pitch relationships on melody instruments.
Rhythm	Call attention to different accent groupings as moving in twos and threes.	Stress the importance of singing with strong rhythmic feeling, reproducing rhythmic patterns clearly and accurately.	Strengthen awareness of rhythmic pattern by adding repetitious patterns as accompaniments.
	Stress differences in rhythmic pattern as made up of same, longer, or shorter tones.		Provide situations where the children may initiate beat or rhythmic patterns on percussion instruments.
Harmony	Invite the children to help determine needed chord changes in song accompaniments.	Include simple rounds and chants in repertoire to develop sensitivity to multiple sounds.	Provide experiences with multiple sounds through playing simple melodic and rhythmic accompaniments.
	Help the children to become aware of multiple sounds (harmonic and rhythmic).		
Form	Encourage the children to identify phrases as the same or different melodically and rhythmically.	Emphasize the importance of singing complete phrases.	Help the children to add introductions and codas based on melodic or rhythmic patterns drawn from the song.
	Make the children aware of repetition and contrast of sections in short compositions.		Direct attention to phrase structure when planning accompaniments.
Expression	Draw attention to the use of varying instrumental tone qualities as a means of musical expressiveness.	Suggest variations in dynamics to give expressiveness to songs the children sing.	Guide the children to select instruments for accompaniments that are expressively appropriate.
	Help the children to identify tempo and dynamic changes and their contribution to musical expressiveness.		
	Discuss distinctive tone qualities of common instruments.		

Moving	Creating	Reading
Give the children ample opportunity to use their vocabulary of fundamental movements in various types of musical situations: singing games, simple folk dances, free interpretation.	Set up situations conducive to the creation of original melodies or accompaniments. Provide opportunities for creative physical response to music.	Help the children learn to associate musical notation with familiar musical concepts. Furnish experiences in which the use of notation is a meaningful adjunct to performing, creating, or listening.
Encourage the children to indicate melodic contour with hand and body movements.	Call attention to possibilities of using step and skip movement when creating melodies.	Draw children's attention to melodic direction and step-skip movement in musical notation. Help the children to use aural awareness of melodic movement in reproducing melodies from notation, using numbers and/or syllables.
Select music of varying accent groupings and rhythmic patterns to which the children may respond. Reinforce awareness of beat, accent, and pattern by clapping, tapping, stepping, and so forth. Provide opportunities for the children to improvise movements for various types of music.	Guide the children in creating accompaniments based on their increasing awareness of beat and rhythmic pattern.	Aid children to recognize and reproduce even-uneven patterns in notation. Provide opportunities for using quarter, eighth, and half notes to represent rhythmic relationships.
	Encourage improvisation of ostinato patterns for pentatonic songs.	
Help the children plan dance movements that reflect same-different forms of music heard.	Draw attention to the importance of phrase in creating songs and accompaniments.	Guide the children to observe repeated melodic and rhythmic patterns in notation.
Encourage free spontaneous physical response to the expressive qualities of music.	Suggest consideration of expressive qualities of words in creating original songs. Provide opportunities for experimentation with many kinds of instrumental sounds.	

THE ANGEL BAND*

South Carolina Folk Song

Moderato

"The Angel Band" from *36 South Carolina Spirituals* by Carl Diton, copyright 1930, 1957, by G. Schirmer, Inc., New York, N.Y. Used by permission.

RHYTHM

Listen: Listen to the instrumental introduction to this song and notice the sound of the wood block. **How does the pattern for the wood block sound?** (Short-short-long.) **How many times do you hear this pattern?** (Nine times.) **Can you clap it?**

Listen to the children sing. Can you hear a pattern that sounds like this? ♫ ♫ ♩ (Teacher claps.) **Can you describe its sound?** (Short-short-short-short-long.) **Can you clap it?**

Read: Put the notation for the two patterns on the chalkboard. Compare the patterns and discuss the differences in the way the two pictures look.

♫ ♩   and   ♫ ♫ ♩

Play: Children will enjoy choosing nine different instruments to play as they count the angels. Remind them that they must play with the ACCENT.

MELODY

Read: Put these patterns on the chalkboard:

— —
— — — — — —
— — —
—
—

(There was one)   (Wasn't that a band?)   (Sunday morning soon)

Discuss the way each pattern will sound: UP or DOWN, STEP or SKIP. Ask the children to listen as they sing and find the word patterns for each. Invite the children to look at the notation. **Notice the way the picture helps us to know how the melody moves.**

Sing: After the children know the song, Part I may be sung in the following manner: Divide the class into nine groups, each singing about one angel and all joining on the last phrase. Stress that each "angel pattern" must "match." **Are you all singing the same tones? Listen to each other carefully.**

HARMONY

Listen: Ask the children to listen to the recording. **How many instruments do you hear?** (Four.) The children will recognize the sounds of the wood block and bells, but may have difficulty identifying the xylophone and marimba. If these are not available for demonstration, show pictures of them and discuss their tone colors.

The xylophone plays the melody. Which instrument plays a pattern of long tones HIGHER than the melody? (Bells.) **Listen for the marimba playing a repeated pattern that is LOWER than the melody.**

Play: Help the children play the patterns they have identified in the accompaniment to the singing.

This is a pentatonic melody, so any combination of the tones G-A-B-D-E can be used for the accompaniment. The children will enjoy experimenting with these tones to make up patterns of their own.

THREE PIRATES

Sprightly

Old English Sea Chanty

Three pi - rates came to Lon - don Town, Yo - ho!_____ Yo - ho!_____ Three

pi - rates came to Lon - don Town, Yo - ho!_____ Yo - ho!_____ Three

pi - rates came to Lon - don Town, To see the King put on his crown, Yo -

ho, you lub - bers! Yo - ho, you lub - bers! Yo - ho! Yo - ho! Yo - ho!

RHYTHM

Read: Place two patterns of line notation on the chalkboard. Ask the children to decide how each will sound, even or uneven.

— — — — — —   – — – — – — – —

Tap each pattern and discuss the differences in sound and in picture. Notice that in the EVEN pattern the lines are the SAME, while in the UNEVEN pattern the lines keep changing.

Look at the music for "Three Pirates." **Which of the line pictures matches the notes of this song? How will it sound?** (Uneven.) **How do you know?** (The notes keep changing.)

A rhythm that moves evenly is made up of notes that all look alike:

♩ ♩ ♩ ♩   or   ♪ ♪ ♪ ♪

Uneven rhythms are made up of different kinds of notes:

♪♩ ♪♩   or   ♩ ♪♩ ♪

FORM

Listen: Discuss the meaning of PHRASE. **A phrase is a musical idea; sometimes you can tell when a phrase ends because the music seems to rest, or pause, for a moment. Can you hear phrase endings in this music which seem to pause?** Sing or play the song for the children and guide them to hear the sustained "Yo-ho!" at the end of the first, second, and fourth phrases. **The end of the third phrase comes on the word "crown." It does not pause here, but the music that follows is a different musical idea, so we know that a new phrase has begun.** Discuss the melodic and rhythmic differences between the third and fourth phrases.

Move: Choose three children to be the pirates "coming to London town." Ask them to show when each new phrase begins as they march around the room. They should turn a corner at the end of each phrase.

MELODY

Read: Ask the children to look at the melody in their books. **How does the melody move on the word "Yo-ho!" at the end of the first and second phrases?** (Up by skip.) **Will the melody sound the same both times?** (No, it will be higher on the second phrase.) **When will you sing the lowest "Yo-ho!"?** (At the end of the song.)

Sing: Invite the children to listen to you as you sing. They may join in on the "Yo-ho!" pattern each time it occurs. When they have sung these correctly, invite them to sing the first verse without assistance.

JINGLE AT THE WINDOWS

MELODY

Read: This song is made up of several melodic fragments:

Before the song is learned, place these on the board. As the teacher sings, the children watch to see if they can hear them in the song. Next, have the children locate these fragments in their books. Discuss each pattern in terms of UP, DOWN, SAME, STEP, and SKIP.

RHYTHM

Listen: As the children learn this song by listening to the teacher or to a recording, with books closed, ask them to decide how it moves. **Does it move in "twos" or "threes"? Clap the underlying beat as you listen.** (It moves in twos.)

Do you hear any rhythmic patterns in the melody that are repeated? (Two.)
Can you clap these?

Read: As the children clap, picture these two patterns in line notation on the blackboard:

— — — —   — — —————

—— —— —— ——   — — —————

What words go with the first pattern? ("Pass one window, tideo.") **What
words go with the second pattern?** ("Jingle at the window, tideo.")

Next, help the children notate these rhythm patterns. Discover that the notes

for "Pass one window" must all be alike: ♩ ♩ ♩ ♩. **We call this note (♩) a
QUARTER NOTE. What word will need a different kind of note?** (Last syllable

of "tideo.") **This new note (♩) we call a HALF NOTE. What will we need to
show the rhythm of "jingle at the"?** (Short notes.) **These short notes**

(♫ ♫) **are called EIGHTH NOTES.**

Follow up the notation of the rhythms in this song with the notation of word
rhythms. **How would you notate your own name, objects in the room, days
of the week, and so forth?**

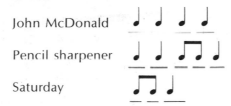

John McDonald

Pencil sharpener

Saturday

Encourage the children to write patterns to which others may clap, or that can
be played on the drum.

Notate the rhythm of familiar songs on the board for a "tune a day" game.
Who can be the first to guess what song this is?

Move: After the song has been learned, play the following singing game (or allow the
children to create their own dance).

Formation: Form a single circle, with boys and girls alternating, and have
each child place his left hand on the left shoulder of the person
in front.

Measures 1–8   The children move around the circle clockwise
in time to the music.

Measures 9–12   Each boy swings the girl standing behind him,
after linking his left arm with hers, and places
her in front of him in the circle.

Measures 13–16   Each boy swings the next girl standing behind
him, after linking his right arm with hers, and
places her in front of him in the circle.

The game may continue until the boys and girls are in their original positions.
As the children play the game they must be careful to move with the music,
stepping in time to the BEAT.

LAVENDER'S BLUE

Allegretto

Autoharp in C:

Traditional

1. Lav - en - der's blue, dil - ly, dil - ly, lav - en - der's green,
2. Call up your men, dil - ly, dil - ly, set them to work,

When I am King, dil - ly, dil - ly, you shall be Queen;
Some with a rake, dil - ly, dil - ly, some with a fork;

Who told you so? dil - ly, dil - ly, who told you so?
Some to make hay, dil - ly, dil - ly, some to thresh corn,

'Twas mine own heart, dil - ly, dil - ly, that told me so.
While you and I, dil - ly, dil - ly, keep our - selves warm.

MELODY

Listen: After the children have learned the melody by listening, ask them to listen to themselves as they sing. **Find places where the melody moves DOWN by STEPS. Can you hear a place where the melody makes a big SKIP UP? Makes a big SKIP DOWN? Can you find a pattern in the music where the melody moves all the way down by steps from HIGH to LOW?** (" 'Twas mine own heart, dilly, dilly.")

Play: The children may play the scale pattern of " 'Twas mine own heart, dilly, dilly" on the bells. **How many bells will you need for this pattern?** (Eight.) Hand one bell to each of eight children (D-E-F♯-G-A-B-C♯-D) in scrambled order. To help the class develop the scale concept, guide them to put the bells in the proper sequence from high to low until their pattern sounds like the tune for "'Twas mine own heart, dilly, dilly." Play the pattern from high to low and from low to high. **We call this pattern of eight tones that move up or down by steps a SCALE.**

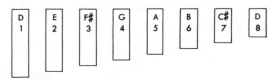

Which bells will play "dilly, dilly" in the first phrase? (4-3-2-1.) **Which ones will play "lavender's green"?** (8-7-6-5.)

Read: Notate the scale on the chalkboard. Mention that this is a "picture" of the scale and discuss the fact that there is a note on each line and each space.

Help the children begin to realize that a note on the staff relates to a specific bell that is distinguished by a letter. If some child should ask about the sharp (♯) which follows the letter names of F and C, explain that a SHARP tells you to make the tone a little HIGHER. Play the D scale, using F and C natural to help the children hear the differences.

Notate the scale in other keys (F, C), helping the children to find the similarities and differences in the "picture." Arrange the bells in correct order to play each new scale.

Sing: Sing the scale with numbers. If syllable names are to be used as a means of music reading, then suggest to the children that there are other names that may be used instead of numbers. The teacher sings:

do	*re*	*mi*	*fa*	*so*	*la*	*ti*	*do*
1	2	3	4	5	6	7	8

We call these SYLLABLES. Help the children learn to sing the scale, ascending and descending, with syllables.

Write melodic patterns with numbers or syllables on the chalkboard and have the children practice playing and singing them.

RHYTHM

Move: Help the children feel the rhythmic flow and ACCENT GROUPING by encouraging them to plan simple movements to this traditional tune (swaying, sliding, and so forth). Discover that this song moves in THREES.

Sing: A lilting voice, accenting the first beat slightly, is needed for this song.

BALLET OF THE SYLPHS

Adventures in Music, Grade 1.   From "The Damnation of Faust" by Hector Berlioz

RHYTHM

Listen: **How does this music seem to move? Is it smooth or is it jerky? Does it move the same way all the time?**

Move: **How do you think you should move to this music?** The children may suggest sliding, swaying, tiptoeing, and so on. To help them feel the ACCENT GROUPING, 1–2–3, encourage them to sway from side to side, or to move about the room with sliding steps (one step to the measure).

EXPRESSION

Discuss: **Does this seem to be funny, happy, or sad music?** The children may suggest that it is sad because it is rather quiet and slow-moving. Discuss the possibility of having "quiet-happy" music.

Listen: **Is this music mostly SOFT or mostly LOUD? Are there any places in the music that sound LOUDER than others?**

Help the children identify the VIOLIN as the main instrument in this orchestration. They may also be able to identify the HARP at the end.

FORM

Listen: Help the children discover that the opening melody is repeated at the end.

Can you find anything different about the melody at the end? (It is LOWER.) **Find the part in the music that sounds DIFFERENT from all the rest.**

How is it different? (The melody is changed and the rhythmic pattern is not as smoothly flowing.)

Move: Suggest that children move their arms in wide arcs above their heads to show the PHRASE pattern. (For this activity consider a phrase as being eight measures long.)

Create: Encourage the children to develop their own dance interpretation to this music. Discuss ways that they may show the phrase structure in their movements. (Change direction.) Suggest that they indicate the "different" middle section with "different" movements.

LITTLE TOM TINKER

Traditional Round

Lit-tle Tom Tin-ker got burned with a clink-er and he be-gan to cry.____

Ma!_____ Ma!_____ What a poor fel-low am I._____

RHYTHM

Read: Ask the children to find patterns of notes that will sound EVEN and patterns that will sound UNEVEN. **How do you suppose the note pattern for "Ma! Ma!" will sound? Will it be even or uneven?** After the children have made suggestions and given reasons, chant the entire poem for them. Decide whether or not they were correct; then ask the class to chant the words.

Play: Help the children to increase their awareness of beat and rhythmic pattern.

One child may play the accented beats (♩. ♩.) while another plays the rhythmic patterns. Discuss the fact that the BEAT is steady and even, but that the RHYTHMIC PATTERN may be either even or uneven.

MELODY

Read: Review what children recall about how melodies move: They may move up or down or stay the same; they may move by steps or by skips. Discuss ways we can show how melodies move in line notation or with notes. Put a staff on the chalkboard or flannel board. Discuss the fact that the STAFF includes LINES and SPACES; both are important. When melody patterns stay the same, all the notes are on the same line or in the same space; when they move by steps the notes will be placed in order from line to space to line, and so forth; when they move by skips some lines or spaces are omitted. Allow the children to take turns putting notes *on* lines and *in* spaces. Ask them to show patterns that step, skip, or stay the same. Play the patterns they have made and have the class decide if they followed directions correctly.

Look at the notes for "Little Tom Tinker." Where will the melody stay the same? Where will it skip up? Skip down? Step down?

This melody begins on 1. Can you count lines and spaces and decide the numbers for the entire melody? As the children decide, write the numbers on the chalkboard:

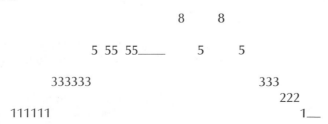

```
                              8       8

                   5 55 55____      5      5

                333333                   333
                                         222
         111111                          1__
```

Sing: Help the children sing the melody with numbers; then invite them to sing it with words.

Play: Place the bells in order: D-E-F#-G-A-B-C#-D. Encourage the children to experiment in finding various melodic patterns (1–3–5; 8–5–3; 3–2–1). Some of the children may be able to play the entire melody.

HARMONY

Play: One child may play the pattern for "Ma! Ma!" over and over as the class sings the song.

Sing: When the children know the song well, some may sing the "Ma! Ma!" pattern while others sing the melody. Later in the year, help the class sing the song as a two-part round.

GO TELL AUNT RHODIE

Slowly   American Folk Song

1.   Go   tell   Aunt   Rho - die,____   Go   tell   Aunt   Rho   -   die,____
2. The   one   she's   been   sav - ing,   The   one   she's   been   sav   -   ing,   The

Go   tell   Aunt   Rho - die,   The   old   gray   goose   is   dead.
one   she's   been   sav   -   ing   To   make   a   feath - er   bed.

3. She died in the mill pond,   4. The goslings are crying.
   Standing on her head.   The old gray goose is dead.

5. The gander is weeping
   The old gray goose is dead.

EXPRESSION

Sing: **Since this is a story, it is very important that we sing with very good diction.** Decide whether this song should be sung quickly or slowly, smoothly or bouncily. **How can you show with your voice the sadness of the goslings and the gander?** Compare the mood of this song with that of "Lavender's Blue."

Play: As you play this song, emphasize the sadness of the last two verses by changing the key from G major to G minor. To do this, merely change all B's to B flats.

RHYTHM

Move: Show the rhythm of the melody by rubbing palms together on the sustained quarter notes and tapping on the eighth notes. To help the children to become aware of the relation of BEAT to RHYTHMIC PATTERN have half of the class clap the beat while the other half claps the rhythm of the melody:

Rhythm of melody:

Rhythm of the beat:

Listen: **Find the words where the melody rhythm moves with the beat. Words where it moves with tones that are shorter than the beat. Is there any word that is longer than the beat?** (Dead.)

MELODY

Listen: **Does this melody move mostly by STEPS or by SKIPS?** (Steps.) **Can you listen well enough to tell when the melody gets home to 1 (do)?** (The end of each phrase.)

Read: **Look at the notes for "Go Tell Aunt Rhodie." How many bells will we need to play the entire melody?** (Five.) **On which line of the staff is the home tone 1 (do)?** (Second line.) **The name of the bell for this tone is G; can you find the rest of the bells needed to play the melody?** Help the children find the G-A-B-C-D bells and place them in order.

Play: Many of the children will be able to play this tune on the bells; some may be able to play it on the piano as well.

The children should also be encouraged to transpose this melody to other keys (C, F). Teacher might suggest the bell for the home tone and let the children experiment to find the remaining bells.

HARMONY

Listen: This song is very pleasing when sung with autoharp accompaniment. The children may help to decide when a new chord is needed.

Play: Invite one child to stroke the autoharp strings on the accented beats while the teacher manipulates the chord buttons.

RAIN SONG*

Music by Irving Lowens
Words by an anon. seven-year-old

From *We Sing of Life*. Used by permission of The American Ethical Union and Irving Lowens.

EXPRESSION

Listen: These are wonderful words; the children will want to talk about the kind of rain that might make them feel as these words describe. **What kind of accompaniment would you use for a song like this? Listen to the recording; does it help to create a mood that is described in the words?**

FORM

Listen: **As you listen to the recording, what is the first thing you hear?** (A melody played by bells.) **Is this a part of the song?** Help the children decide that it is not the main part of the song. **This bell melody tells us that the song is about to begin. We call it an INTRODUCTION. What ends the song?** (Bells and piano.) You may wish to give the children the term CODA to describe this section.

HARMONY

Listen: **How does the bell melody of the introduction move?** (Downward.) **How many times do you hear it?** (Four.)

Play: Place the bells in order and help the children find the pattern they hear in the introduction.

Play the pattern once as an introduction; then play it twice while the class sings. At the end of the song, the bells will continue for one measure after the singers stop.

Some children may be able to play this repetitious pattern as a piano accompaniment:

MELODY

Listen: This song is in a MINOR key. Help the children become aware of the minor quality by comparing the way it sounds as learned and the way it would sound if sung in a MAJOR key. This can be done easily by simply changing all E flats to E.

CAN YOU PLAY THIS?

As the children are introduced to notation, help them expand their understanding by giving them time to work individually with bells and percussion instruments. Make up patterns for them to learn to play. Put the patterns, with instructions, on charts that the children can take to a quiet corner of the room to practice individually. Provide time for them to work by themselves during the day. When a child can play a pattern, invite him to perform it for the class. Following are some examples:

Play a Rhythm

Can you play this rhythm pattern? It uses LONG (♩) and SHORT (♪) notes.

Play the pattern on a drum. It should sound like this:

— — — — — — — — — — — — — —

When you can play this pattern, make up a new one to end with.

Play a Melody

Can you play this melody? You will need these bells: G-A-B-C-D-E. Start with the B bell.

When you can play this melody, make up a new one to end your song. Now play this melody using the G-A-B♭-C-D-E♭ bells.

What was different about the melody this time?

When you can play this melody, make up a new one to end your song.

CAN YOU WRITE THIS?

Children should also have experience in notating rhythmic and melodic patterns so that they may be able to notate their original compositions. The following suggest some possibilities for practice in writing music.

Write a Rhythm Pattern

Can you write this rhythm in notes? Use the HALF NOTE (𝅗𝅥) for LONG tones and QUARTER NOTES (𝅘𝅥) for SHORT tones:

— — —— — —— —— —— —— —— — —— —— —— ——

How would this look if you used QUARTER NOTES (𝅘𝅥) for LONG tones and EIGHTH NOTES (𝅘𝅥𝅮) for SHORT tones?

Write a rhythm pattern of your own, using QUARTER NOTES and HALF NOTES. Practice your pattern and play it for the class.

Write a Melody

The numbers and letters for a melody are written below the staff. Can you put the notes on the right line or space? Can you play the melody pattern? What song does each pattern come from?

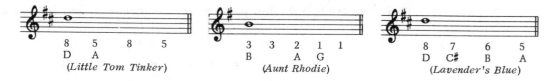

```
8   5   8   5          3  3  2  1  1          8   7   6   5
D   A                  B     A  G             D   C♯  B   A
(Little Tom Tinker)       (Aunt Rhodie)          (Lavender's Blue)
```

Write a melody pattern of your own. Begin on the first space and call it "1". Write the notes on the staff. Write the numbers of your melody below the staff. Play it on the bells.

COMPOSE A MUSICAL STORY

Help the children to become sensitive to the expressive properties of musical elements such as rhythm, melody, dynamics, and tone color by creating their own musical story. You may wish to introduce a recording of "Peter and the Wolf" by Prokofiev before suggesting that the children develop their own story. As the class listens to this composition, call attention to the way the composer uses musical elements to describe his characters: the happy, carefree tune played by the strings which represents Peter; the sly tune played by the clarinet representing the Cat; the low, jerky tune played by the bassoon belonging to Grandfather; and so forth. Notice, also, that the same theme is repeated each time the character is mentioned in the story.

Any fairy tale, such as "The Three Bears," "The Three Little Pigs," or the "Three Billy Goats Gruff," can be used as the basis for the children's improvisation. Review the chosen story with the children; list the characters and discuss each. For example, in "Three Billy Goats Gruff," there are four characters: Big Billy Goat, Middle-sized Billy Goat, Little Billy Goat, and the big, ugly Troll. As the children talk about the characters, guide them to discuss such questions as **What is the size of each character? Big? Little? What kind of voice would each have? High? Low? Loud? Soft? How would each character move? Slowly? Quickly?**

After each character has been discussed, ask the children to select instruments that would be suitable for each, taking the musical characteristics into consideration. Finger cymbals or high-pitched rhythm sticks would be appropriate for Little Billy Goat because he is small and his voice is high. Perhaps a wood block might be appropriate for Middle-sized Billy Goat, and a drum could represent Big Billy Goat. For the Troll, a deep-voiced drum or large cymbal might be suitable.

When the instruments have been chosen, invite individual children to experiment and improvise different rhythm patterns for each character. They may conclude that Little Billy Goat should move quickly (♫ ♫); that Middle-sized Billy Goat should move more slowly (♩ ♩ ♩ ♩); and that Big Billy Goat should move very slowly (𝅗𝅥 𝅗𝅥). The Troll might have a slow, uneven pattern (𝅗𝅥 ♩ 𝅗𝅥 ♩) because he is so big and clumsy.

After the instruments have been selected and the rhythm patterns determined, the teacher or a child may tell the story. Whenever a character is mentioned, one child should play the pattern chosen to represent that character. This musical activity may be combined with dramatization of the story.

The children may then wish to compose songs for each character to sing. Words such as these might be sung by each of the three Billy Goats:

> Trip, trap, trip, trap,
> I'm off to find green grass.

The melody might be the same for all three goats; however, it should be sung at a different pitch level for each. For example:

Little   Middle-sized   Big

The Troll might sing: Someone's tripping over my bridge,
                       I'm going to gobble him up!

HAUL AWAY, JOE

FORM

Read: **This song has an interesting design. Look at the song carefully. What do you see at the beginning of each PHRASE?** Help the children realize that each phrase begins with a PATTERN (motive) that will sound exactly the SAME. **Can you find any other pattern that will sound the same?** (The second half of phrases 1 and 3.)

Sing: When the children know the song well, help them to become aware of the motivic structure of this song by singing it as a dialogue song. One child may be chosen to be the leader; the class sings the "Away, haul away" motive at the beginning of each phrase, and the leader answers.

MELODY

Read: **Look at the pattern for "Away, haul away." How many DIFFERENT tones are used?** (Two.) **Which bells would we need to play these tones?** To help the children decide, put the C scale on the chalkboard with letter names and numbers:

$$
\begin{array}{cccccccc}
1 & 2 & 3 & 4 & 5 & 6 & 7 & 8 \\
C & D & E & F & G & A & B & C
\end{array}
$$

The two bells needed are C and G, and their numbers would be 8 and 5. Write the numbers, with the line notation for the rhythm below, on the chalkboard:

$$5 \quad 8 \qquad 8 \quad 8 \quad 5$$

Sing: **Can you sing this pattern with numbers? With words?** After the children have learned to sing this pattern, sing the entire song, with the children singing the pattern each time it occurs, and the teacher singing the remainder of the song. Then challenge the class to sing the entire melody alone.

EXPRESSION

Discuss: **Who do you think first sang this work song?** (Sailors.) **What might the sailors have been hauling?** (Perhaps the anchor.) **Often, as the sailors worked, one man would sing to help pass the time and make the work easier. He would make up new verses to keep the sailors interested and happy. The men would join in on the repeated parts of the song.**

Create: When the children have learned the song and have sung it as a dialogue, suggest that they make up new verses for their leader to sing. Guide their ideas for verse content. **Where might the sailors be going?** ("We'll go to California.") **What might they be hauling?** ("We're hauling grapes and apples.")

RHYTHM

Move: The children may pretend that they are hauling the anchor as they sing. **Be sure to pull on the ACCENTED BEATS.**

back forward   back forward

BYE'M BYE

Quietly

Texas Folk Song

MELODY

Read: Much of this song can be learned by the children from the notation. **Look at the melody for the first phrase. It uses only two tones: 8 (do) and 5 (so). We can sing the pattern 8 (do)-5 (so) because we know what it sounds like. Now you can sing "Bye'm bye, bye'm bye" as you look at the notation.**

What will you do when you sing "Stars shining?" (Stay in the same place.)

In the next phrase, can you find a melodic pattern that makes this part easy to learn? Help the children to realize that they can sing the same pattern (3-4-5 or *mi-fa-so*) for every "number."

What will you have to do when you sing "Oh, my"? Jump all the way from 8 (*do*) to 1 (*do*). Sing this with numbers or syllables, and then, with words.

Can you sing "Bye'm bye, bye'm bye," in the last phrase without my help? Of course, you can—because it "steps right up the stairs."

Now, go back to the beginning and see if you can sing the song all the way through. (Teacher listens.) **Where did you have trouble?** Listen while Teacher sings that part.

Play: Place the C scale bells in order: C-D-E-F-G-A-B-C. Ask the children to find the big skip for the words "Oh My!" Draw attention to the fact that the letter names on the two bells are the same. **Since the letter names are the same, we could call them by the same number name. So, let us call the high-C bell "high 1" instead of "8."** (If syllables are used, the eighth tone would be named "high *do*.")

To help the children grasp the reason for the repeated names, play slowly up and down the scale. Discuss the fact that the scale sounds completed, "at home," when you reach either the high- or the low-C bell. As one child plays the bells, practice singing up and down the scale, emphasizing that one must sing 1 (for "home") at both ends of the scale pattern:

1 2 3 4 5 6 7 1'   1' 7 6 5 4 3 2 1

EXPRESSION

Listen: **As we sang, how many stars did we count? Are there only five stars in the sky? Why, do you suppose the counting stopped?** (Because there are just too many stars to count.)

Play: The children may wish to pick some "starlike" instruments to accompany this song—finger cymbals or triangle, perhaps; the G bell also might sound pleasing.

Another day, place the bells in this order:

One child may play the descending pattern as the class sings. Start with the words "Stars shining" and end with "number five." Play on the accented beats of each measure.

RHYTHM

Read: Put these notes on the chalkboard: ♪♪♩. **How will this pattern sound?** (Short-short-long.) **How many times can you find this pattern?** (Five.) **The first pattern in the song (♩ ♩.) will sound long-lo-ong. Notice that the second note has a "dot" after it. We call this note a DOTTED HALF NOTE. The half note is lo-ong and the dot tells us to hold the tone even longer. How many dotted half notes can you find in this song?** (Five.)

Play: This song may be accompanied by appropriate percussion instruments playing RHYTHMIC PATTERNS such as ♩ ♪♪ ♩ ♪♪ throughout the song. Allow the children to experiment until they find an expressive rhythmic accompaniment to fit the mood of the song. (One possibility is to play different instruments in turn as the stars are counted.)

JUMBO'S LULLABY AND GOLLIWOG'S CAKEWALK

Bowmar Orchestral Library, BOL #63.   From "Children's Corner Suite" by Claude Debussy

The two compositions included in this lesson are from a suite that Debussy wrote for his daughter. When each selection has been studied separately, play the two in succession and ask the children to compare the contrasting moods. Guide them to use a musical vocabulary in discussing the compositions: Notice melodies that are HIGH or LOW, that move UP or DOWN by STEPS or by SKIPS, that move in EVEN or UNEVEN rhythms. Notice how the composer uses changes in LOUDS and SOFTS, in TEMPO (speed) and in INSTRUMENTATION (tone color).

The suite was originally written for piano. You might secure a piano recording of the suite and allow the children to compare the two versions.

JUMBO'S LULLABY

EXPRESSION

Listen: **The title of this music is "Jumbo's Lullaby." Jumbo is an elephant. Listen and decide why this is a good title for it. What suggests a lullaby? Could it be called "Kitty's Lullaby?"** Play the complete composition and invite the children to share their ideas. The low, rather lumbering melody at the beginning suggests a large animal rather than a small one. The "rocking" motion of the melody, with its repeated down-up melodic pattern, helps to suggest the movement of a cradle. The slow tempo and the soft sounds produced by gentle-sounding instruments, such as the strings and the flute, contribute to the lullaby mood.

As the children become familiar with the music, teach them the names and show pictures of the instruments heard. The melody is introduced by the STRING BASS, which is the biggest- and lowest-sounding member of the string family. Later the same melody is played by a FRENCH HORN joined by an OBOE. Near the end the FLUTE and VIOLIN play Jumbo's tune; this time it is much higher.

FORM

Listen: Play the first melody several times until it is well enough known that the children will be able to identify its repetitions:

Listen carefully, how many times do you hear this melody? (Three times.)

The middle section of the composition is made up of short melodic patterns tossed from one instrument to another. Some children may be able to distinguish a pattern, repeated many times, which moves down by steps:

Toward the end, listen for the combination of this pattern and the first melody.

GOLLIWOG'S CAKEWALK

EXPRESSION

Move: **Can you decide what kind of character might be dancing to this music? How would he move? Would he always move in the same way?** After the children have listened to the entire composition, the children may suggest characters such as a clown, a monkey, a mechanical doll, and so forth. Give each child an opportunity to improvise appropriate movements for his character. Decide that the middle section of the music suggests contrasting movements.

Listen: When all children have had an opportunity to express their ideas, talk about Debussy's title for this composition. A golliwog is an awkward, humorous doll. A cakewalk is a kind of strutting dance. People once held dance contests and gave cakes as prizes for the winners, and thus the dances became known as "cakewalks."

FORM

Listen: **How many sections are there in this music?** (Three.) **Are they the same, or are they different?** (The first and last sections are the same, the second is different.) Discuss the differences between sections. The melody of the first section begins high and gradually moves downward in an uneven rhythm. The melody of the second section is in two parts: The first is a smoothly flowing low pattern; the second, a high pattern of short separated tones.

RHYTHM

Read: Place the two rhythm patterns on the chalkboard:

_ _ _ _ _ _ _ _ _   (first section)
_ _ ___ _ _ ___   (second section)

Ask one child to point to the appropriate pattern as each is heard in the composition.

LONE STAR TRAIL

A fast canter

American Cowboy Song

1. I start-ed on the trail on June twen-ty
2. I get up in the morn be-fore the day-
3. It's ba-con and it's beans al-most ev-'ry

third, I been punch-in' Tex-as cat-tle on the Lone Star
light, And be-fore I go to sleep the moon is shin-ing
day, But I would-n't mind a change if it was prai-rie

Refrain

Trail;   Sing-in' Ki yi yip-py, yip-py yay, yip-py
bright.
hay.

yay! Sing-in' Ki yi yip-py, yip-py yay! ____

MELODY

Listen: Sing the refrain for the class. **Can you hear a place where the melody moves DOWN by STEPS?** (At the end.) **Moves UP by SKIPS?** ("Singin' Ki yi.") **Moves DOWN with a big SKIP?** ("yippy.")

Help the children to determine the numbers for the first two patterns: 5-4-3-2-1 and 1-3-5-5.

Play: Place the G-A-B-C-D bells in order and guide the children to play the two patterns.

Can you play the big skip down? The children will realize that they have no bell that is low enough for this. Add one bell at a time, F♯,-E-D, until the correct one is reached. When the children hear the desired pattern, draw attention to the letter name of the two bells. Notice that both are called D. Remind them of their discovery when studying "Bye'm Bye." **Bells with the same letter name must be called by the same number name (syllable). These will be called "high 5 (so)" and "low 5 (so)."**

Read: Place the notation for the three patterns on the chalkboard:

Help the children write numbers (syllables) under each pattern. Practice singing each pattern, then look at the notation for the entire song. Discover that only these tones are used. Challenge the children to sing the entire song with numbers (syllables).

RHYTHM

Create: After the children know the song well, have them make a list of all the things that cowboys do: riding horses, roping cows, shooting guns; or of things that remind them of cowboys: jangling spurs, chuck wagons, lassos.

Chant each word pattern, clap the rhythm, and determine the rhythmic notation for each pattern. Some examples of rhythmic notation follow.

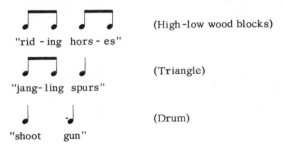

Play: Select a percussion instrument for each of the patterns created. Use the patterns to accompany the song, combining as many as the children can play independently.

EXPRESSION

Play: Suggest that the children might develop an introduction describing the approach of the cowboy: The wood blocks could start SOFTLY as though he were far away; as he comes closer the sound CRESCENDOS with the addition of the drum and the triangle.

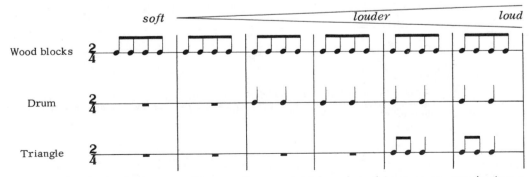

At the end of the song these patterns might be played in reverse, producing a DECRESCENDO as the cowboy rides off into the distance.

ALL THE PRETTY LITTLE HORSES

Tranquil

American Folk Song

Hush - a - by, don't you cry, Go to sleep-y, lit - tle ba - by.

When you wake, you shall have All the pret-ty lit-tle hor-ses:

Blacks and bays, dap-ples and grays, Coach and six-a lit-tle hor-ses.

Hush - a - by, don't you cry, Go to sleep-y, lit-tle ba - by.

EXPRESSION

Listen: The children will enjoy listening to the teacher sing this beautiful song in the minor mode. Before teaching it to the children, use it often during rest periods or for a break during the day.

Discuss the kind of tone one would want to use in singing this song. **Should it be sung SOFTLY or LOUDLY?**

MELODY

Sing: The children may learn this melody by first joining in with the teacher on the repeated TONAL PATTERN for "Hushaby, don't you cry" each time it appears. Later, they may join in on the pattern for "Go to sleepy, little baby" each time it occurs. Finally, they may learn the contrasting third phrase.

Listen: **Find the place in the tune where it moves down the scale by steps.** ("Go to sleepy, little baby.") **What other song do we know that has such a scale in it?** ("Lavender's Blue.")

Play: **Can you play the descending scale pattern of this song on the bells as you did in "Lavender's Blue?"** Allow the children to arrange the bells into a MAJOR scale (E major) starting with E. Help them to decide that they need only seven bells (E to D) for this tune.

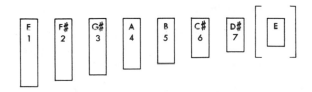

Now, play the descending scale, starting on "7." Does it sound like "Go to sleepy, little baby?" Why not?

Show the children how to exchange Steps 3, 6, and 7 for bells that are lower.

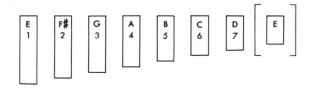

Play it again. Does it sound like our tune now? (Yes.)

This is a scale also, but we call this one a MINOR scale, while the one we played for "Lavender's Blue" was a MAJOR scale.

Let children experiment with the bells, playing major and minor scales starting from different tones.

PRINCE OF DENMARK MARCH*

Columbia Records, ML 5754   Jeremiah Clarke

This composition has long been known as the "Trumpet Voluntary in D" by Henry Purcell; however, it has now been determined that the music was written by Jeremiah Clarke, a lesser known composer who lived at the same time as Purcell.

EXPRESSION

Listen: Play the entire composition for the children, suggesting that they decide "what kind of music" they are hearing. The children may decide that it is a march. **Would you hear this kind of march at a football game or at a parade?** Help the children conclude that it is a more dignified march, one that might be used on very important occasions such as when a king is crowned, a president is installed, or for a church procession.

What helps to make this music interesting? As the children offer their answers, help them decide that changes in the music make for interest; if one hears the same thing throughout the music, it becomes monotonous. In this music there are contrasts between loud and soft; sometimes only a few instruments play and at other times many instruments are heard; different melodies are introduced; although the tempo is steady most of the time, the music slows down gradually at the end.

Help the children learn the names of some of the instruments they are hearing: such as TRUMPET, TROMBONE, TYMPANI, and ORGAN. Locate pictures of the instruments and help the class learn to associate sight with sound.

Move: To help the children become more aware of the contrasting instrumental qualities, divide the class into four groups. Assign each group a different instrument or instrumental combination: (1) trumpet, (2) organ, (3) percussion, (4) brass ensemble. If pictures are available, ask one child in each group to be the leader and hold up the picture of the instrument that is heard. The rest of the group may pretend playing the instrument. Draw attention to the fact that sometimes only two instruments are heard, and at other times many instruments are heard in combination. **Which instrument plays all the time?** (The trumpet.)

The sequence of instrumental combination is as follows:

A   Trumpet and organ
A   Trumpet, brass, and percussion
B   Trumpet and organ
B   Trumpet, organ, and percussion
A   Trumpet, brass, and percussion
C   Trumpet, brass, and percussion
C   Trumpet, brass, and percussion
A   Trumpet and organ
A   Trumpet, brass, and percussion

FORM

Move: When the children have enjoyed the music on several days, draw attention to its sectional structure. Invite some children to pretend they are marching in a dignified procession. Ask them to turn a corner each time a section of the music comes to an end (identified by the long tones). While some children march, ask others to count the number of SECTIONS. (Nine.)

Read: When the children can hear and identify the beginning and ending of each of the nine sections, ask them to listen for repetition of melodies and introduction of new ones. Discover that there are three DIFFERENT melodies:

The melodies are heard in this sequence: AABBACCAA.

To help the children understand the design of this composition, cut out three geometric shapes of different color paper or felt. Assign a different shape and color to each of the melodies:

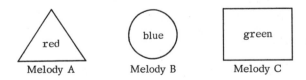

Ask three children to hold up the appropriate shape each time a melody is heard.

Later, cut out nine shapes: five for melody A, two for melody B, and two for melody C. Give them to nine children and ask them to put the shapes in correct sequence as they listen to the music:

Guiding Musical Growth
in the Third Grade

	Listening	Singing	Playing
SKILL	Constantly stress improvement in ability to listen with discrimination.	Strive for improvement of tone quality and diction.	Provide situations in which the children may develop skill with the autoharp. Stress improvement in playing common percussion instruments.
CONCEPTS *Melody*	Help the children to identify scale-line (1-2-3 or do-re-mi, and so forth) and chord-line (1-3-5 or do-mi-so) tonal patterns with increasing specificity.	Practice singing tonal patterns with numbers and/or syllables to improve tonal accuracy.	Help the children to play familiar tunes on bells and piano with the aid of numbers and/or syllables.
Rhythm	Identify music as moving in twos and threes. Help the children to sense note relationships within rhythm patterns in terms of "same" as the beat, "longer," or "shorter" than the beat.	Emphasize importance of singing rhythmic patterns precisely, paying close attention to note relationships.	Encourage independent reproduction of rhythmic patterns in accompaniments to songs. Call the children's attention to note relationships within rhythmic patterns when using these patterns as percussion accompaniments.
Harmony	Encourage the children to help determine appropriate chord accompaniments.	Increase the children's perceptivity of multiple sounds by singing rounds and chants.	Arouse an interest in chord qualities through the use of autoharp accompaniments. Increase the perceptivity of multiple sounds by playing countermelodies on bells and piano.
Form	Draw attention to repetition and contrast of sections within short compositions. Guide the children to recognize the design of simple two- and three-part song forms.	Constantly stress phrase-singing.	Draw attention to repetition and contrast by varying or repeating accompaniment patterns in accordance with song structure. Provide opportunities for playing introductions and codas for songs.
Expression	Help the children to determine ways in which contrasts are achieved melodically, rhythmically, and instrumentally. Call attention to variations in tempo, dynamics, tone color, and so forth, as expressive devices.	Motivate children to consider expressive contributions of dynamic and tempo variations in singing.	Prompt the children to consider tone color, dynamics, and tempo in playing melodies and accompaniments.

Moving	Creating	Reading
Offer the children a variety of experiences through which they may expand their ability to move expressively to music.	Foster creative participation by individuals through the composition of songs and the addition of accompaniments.	Guide the children to associate symbols of music with musical concepts.
	Motivate the children to create more expressive and extensive dance movements.	Provide opportunities to use musical notation as an aid to listening and performing.
Guide the children to consider melodic contour in planning dance movements.	Encourage the children to use their understanding of melodic movement in creating their own songs.	Employ numbers, syllables, and letter names associated with the staff in singing and playing.
		Show the children how to notate their own melodies in numbers and/or syllables.
Improve the children's awareness of beat, accent, and rhythmic relationships by clapping, stepping, and so on.	Involve individuals in creating original rhythmic patterns for accompaniments.	Provide opportunities for children to interpret rhythmic notation in terms of relative durational values ($\downharpoonleft = \downharpoonright \downharpoonright = \text{♫♫}$).
Guide the children to consider accent grouping and rhythmic relationships in planning dance movements.	Guide the children to consider meter and rhythmic relationships in creating their own songs.	Extend the children's awareness of accent groupings to include an understanding of meter signatures.
	Encourage improvisation of melodic ostinati as accompaniments for pentatonic songs.	Draw the children's attention to the notation of multiple sounds, observing the relationship of chant to melodic line.
Suggest that the children plan dance movements to coincide with the repeated or contrasting sections of the music.	Help the children become sensitive to the importance of using repetition and contrast in their own compositions and dances.	In learning new songs, help the children to use their knowledge of repetition and contrast of melodic and rhythmic patterns and of phrases as they scan the notation.
Encourage children to give thought to dynamics, tempo, and instrumentation when planning dance movements.	Suggest that children consider the expressive properties of instruments when creating accompaniments.	
	Help the children to consider the expressive possibilities of tempo and dynamic variations in their own compositions.	

VESPER HYMN

Music Attributed to Dmitri Bortniansky
Words by Thomas Moore

Allegretto

Hark, the ves - per hymn is steal - ing,
Near - er yet and near - er peal - ing,

O'er the wa - ters soft and clear.
Soft it breaks up - on the ear.

Refrain

Ju - bi - la - te!

Ju - bi - la - te! Ju - bi - la - te! A - men.

RHYTHM

Read: **Notice how the rhythm of the melody moves steadily and evenly through each phrase until the last note is reached. How much longer will you hold this last note than any of the others?** (TWICE AS LONG.)

Play: As the children plan an introduction for this song, as suggested under "expression," they will need to decide what kind of rhythmic relationships to use. The concepts of TWICE AS LONG and HALF AS LONG may be reinforced by planning the introduction to move in these relationships:

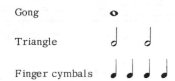

FORM

Read: Draw the children's attention to the repeat signs at the end of each phrase. **This REPEAT sign (‖:   :‖) tells us that each phrase must be repeated.**

Sing: Take the form into consideration as children plan variations in dynamics in singing. **Will you want to sing the repeated phrases exactly the same as you did the first time?** Guide the children to experiment; they might sing the repetition of the refrain softly as an echo, or loudly as the final climax.

EXPRESSION

Sing: **Do the words help you decide when to sing SOFTLY, and when to sing LOUDER? Can you sing with a clear bell-like tone?** Experiment with different TONE QUALITIES and different DYNAMIC LEVELS. Have the children decide which they like best.

Play: Resonator bells and piano may also be used to accompany this song. The following patterns may be used:

First phrase   Second phrase   Throughout

Create: The children may plan a bell-like introduction and an accompaniment using percussion instruments. **Which instruments have bell-like qualities?** (Finger cymbals, triangle, and gong.)

Discuss the manner in which these instruments might be used to create the most expressive accompaniment. **Should they be played loudly or softly? Should they be played the same way throughout?**

CHEBOGAH (Beetle)*

Hungarian Folk Dance
Words adapted

With spirit

In a cir - cle slide to left and don't be slow.
For - ward with a walk - ing step, then back in place.

To the right we slide a - gain as back we go.
Skip with el - bows joined and then your part - ner face.

Side - ward glide, side - ward glide, to the cen - ter glide;
Fast - er now, fast - er now, fast - er in and out;

Back a - gain, back a - gain, part - ners side by side.
Part - ners swing, part - ners swing, end - ing with a shout. *Hey!*

RHYTHM

Move: Sing the song for the children with accompaniment, or listen to the recording. Invite the children to tap the beat lightly, or step quietly in place. **How does the music move, in twos or in threes?** (In twos.)

Read: **There is a way to tell how music will move before you hear it. Look at the song in your book and try to find something that could have told you how this music was going to move.** Give the children time to make suggestions until someone locates the "2" at the beginning of the song. **This is the METER SIGNATURE. The top number tells you how the music will move. Look at the rest of the song; is there anything else that helps you know that this song will move in twos?** Guide the children to notice that vertical lines across the staff (BAR LINES) group the notes and rests into "sets of twos." **Each of these sets is called a MEASURE. How many different sets can you find?** As the children locate different measures, put them on the board:

Read: As you sing the song again, invite the class to tap the beat. **Can you hear words that sound with the beat?** ("don't be slow.") **What kind of note is found above these words?** (Quarter note.) **The lower number "4" in the meter signature stands for the quarter note. That number tells us that the quarter note will be the BEAT NOTE in this song.**

Can you find places in the music where the rhythm moves with two tones to the beat? ("In a circle.") **What kind of notes are used here?** (Eighth notes.)

Listen as I sing again and see if you can decide what the symbol (⸓) at the end of each phrase tells me to do. (Be silent.) **It is called a QUARTER REST.**

FORM

Read: Draw attention to the repeat signs at the end of the second phrase, at the beginning of the third phrase, and at the end of the song. **Listen as I sing and tell me what these signs tell me to do.** (Repeat sections.)

The design of a song may be described with capital letters. Help the children determine that the design of this song is AABB. (Each section is made up of two phrases.)

Move: Plan a dance as suggested by the words of the song. Discuss how the dance and the design of the song must match. When the children have worked out their plan, dance to the music of the recording.

The children should be in a single circle, with girls on their partner's right:

A   Measures   1–4   Move with a "step-together" pattern, to the left. Take one step-together during each measure.

5–9   Repeat actions of first phrase, now moving to the right.

A   (repeat)   1–4   Take four steps toward center of circle (two measures), then four steps back to place.

5–8   Hook right elbows with partner; take six steps in a small circle. Drop hands and face partner during last measure.

B   9–12   Facing partner, hold hands and take four sliding steps (step-together) toward center of circle, one pattern per measure.

13–16   Move back to place with four sliding steps.

B (repeat)   9–12   Still holding hands, partners now take two sliding steps to center and two back to place.

13–16   Hook right elbows with partner; take six steps in a small circle. During last measure raise left arms high as everyone shouts, "Hey!"

MELODY

Listen: Listen to the melody of section A and draw attention to the similarity between the two phrases. Guide the children to discover that the second phrase is the same as the first phrase, sounded one step lower. Another SEQUENCE occurs in section B.

AWAKE AND SING

Old German Hymn
Words translated by
Catherine Winkworth

Joyously

Heav-en and__ earth and sea and air, All__ their Mak-er's praise de - clare;

Wake, my__ soul, a - wake and sing: Now thy grate - ful prais - es bring.

MELODY

Read: Scan the notation of the song and discover that the first phrase moves UP by STEPS. **If the first step of the song is 1 (do), can you sing the entire phrase with number (syllables)?** (Notice that the fifth step is repeated.) Identify this passage as a SCALE.

Give eight children the bells for the D-major scale, D-E-F♯-G-A-B-C♯-D. Place the scale on the staff on the chalkboard; ask the children to give you the letter name of their bell for each step. Draw attention to the F♯ and C♯. To help the children understand the need for these bells, replace them with F and C natural. Ask the children to play the scale again; notice that it sounds "wrong" or "different." Discover that the bells with the SHARP (♯) after their name sound a little HIGHER than those without sharps. Conclude that "sharps tell us to sing or play a tone a little higher." Look in the book and notice the sharps at the beginning of the song. **This is the KEY SIGNATURE for the D scale.**

Can you decide what bells we would need for the C scale? Allow the children to experiment until they find the correct bells: C-D-E-F-G-A-B-C. Put this scale on the chalkboard next to the D scale:

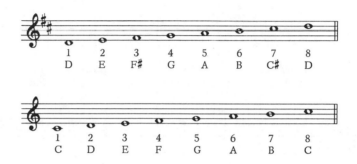

Notice that the same letter name always appears on the same line or space of the staff. Give the children the names for all the lines and spaces of the staff; include middle C.

Return to the song and ask the class to sing the first phrase with numbers (syllables), then with words. **Can you find a phrase that moves DOWN the scale?** (Third phrase.) Determine the numbers (syllables) noticing that, after the first skip from 5 (*so*) to high 1 (*do*), the melody moves stepwise down the scale to 2 (*re*).

Sing: Sing the third phrase with numbers (syllables). Next, ask the class to sing the first and third phrase with words. Teacher should sing the second and fourth phrases. Then ask the class to sing the entire song.

Play: Place the bells for the D scale in order. One child may play the first and third phrases while the class sings the song.

Find the bells for the C scale and ask a child to play the same phrases. Discover that it sounds like the same melody, except that it sounds LOWER.

EXPRESSION

Discuss: Talk about the meaning of the words. **In what ways did the composer support the meaning of the words by the music he composed? Why, do you suppose, did he create a melody that moves upwards for the first phrase?**

Sing: **What kind of voice should you use to help express the meaning of this song?** Decide that it should be sung with a strong, full voice to communicate the mood of praise. Each phrase should be sung on a single breath. Remind the children to sustain the long tone at the end of each phrase.

COME TEND THE GEESE

RHYTHM

Read: Review the discussion of meter signature held when learning "Chebogah." **Look at this song. Can you decide how it will move?** Help the children notice the "3" in the meter signature. **What kind of note will move with the beat?** (Quarter note.) Sing the song as the children tap the beat; help them decide whether or not their answers are correct.

Did you find measures which include sets of three notes? What kind of notes are used? (Quarter notes.) Find measures which do not include sets of three notes, such as the third measure. Sing the song as the class taps the beat. **What did you do while I sang the word "tend"?** (Tapped two beats.) **What kind of note is above that word?** (Half note.) Conclude that the half note is TWICE AS LONG as the quarter note. Therefore, a half note plus a quarter note constitutes a "set of three."

Notice the measures which include only one note, a DOTTED HALF NOTE. Sing the song again as the children tap the beat; discover that they clapped three beats while you sang the words "-way," "-day," "break," "morn," "been," "corn," and "late." Conclude that the dotted half note is THREE TIMES AS LONG as the quarter note. It can be a "set of three" all by itself.

Play: Ask one child to tap the BEAT softly on the wood block while another plays the finger cymbals on the ACCENTS. The class may chant the words. **Be sure to hold the dotted half note for three full beats.**

FORM

Move: The phrase structure of this song is somewhat unusual in that all the phrases are not of equal length. As the class sings, ask a few children to walk in a circle, one step to the measure. Change directions at the beginning of each new phrase. Notice that all phrases end with a sustained tone. **Did you walk the same number of steps for each phrase?** Help the children realize that their pattern should be: six steps- six steps- four steps- four steps- six steps.

Read: Look at the notation and determine the design of the song by phrases. It is A (two six-measure phrases) B (two four-measure phrases) A (one six-measure phrase).

MELODY

Listen: As the children listen for the sustained tone at the end of each phrase, ask them to decide if they give one a feeling of "rest" or "unrest." Compare the feeling of these phrases with the feeling of those in "Vesper Hymn." Notice that all of the phrases in "Vesper Hymn" end on 1 (*do*) or home tone, and that they give a feeling of "rest." **On what step of the scale do the phrases in "Come Tend the Geese" end?** (On 3 [*mi*].) Help the children realize that this creates a feeling of "unrest." Discuss the fact that most songs they know end on 1 (*do*) and that the change from such a usual ending adds to the interest of this song.

ARE YOU SLEEPING (Frère Jacques)

Moderato   Traditional

Are   you   sleep - ing,   are   you   sleep - ing,   Broth - er   John,
Frè - re   Jac - ques,   Frè - re   Jac - ques,   Dor - mez   vous,

Broth - er   John?   Morn - ing   bells   are   ring - ing,
dor - mez   vous?   Son - nez   les   ma - ti - nes,

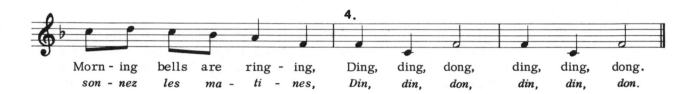

Morn - ing   bells   are   ring - ing,   Ding,   ding,   dong,   ding,   ding,   dong.
son - nez   les   ma - ti - nes,   Din,   din,   don,   din,   din,   don.

MELODY

Listen: This melody will undoubtedly be familiar to most children. As they sing, ask them to listen carefully. **When does the music move by STEPS? When does it move by SKIPS?**

Read: **Can you write this melody in numbers (or syllables)?**

     1   2   3   1   1   2   3   1

Are you sleep-ing, Are you sleep-ing? . . .

After the children have completed this task, help them to translate the numbers (syllables) into staff notation. **Let us notate this song in the key of F. F will be 1 (do); can you find this on the staff?** (First space.) **Can you write the entire F scale in notes on the staff?** Put the letter names underneath the notes.

With the aid of the bells, guide the children to discover that they need bells F-G-A-B♭-C-D-E-F to make up the scale. As they look for the fourth step, B♭, help them realize that they must now use a bell with a slightly LOWER sound than B. **This bell has a FLAT (♭) after its name and a flat tells us to sing or play a tone a little lower.**

Show the class how to put the flat at the beginning of the song to make a KEY SIGNATURE for the scale of F. Then help them notate the melody in whole notes, adding the rhythm later.

Play: When the melody has been notated, the children may play the melody on the bells, using both ears and eyes to help them.

RHYTHM

Read: After the children have determined the melodic notation, notate the rhythm of the melody. Help the class decide how the music moves by clapping or stepping as they chant the words. They will probably respond with "twos."

Ask the class to look at the METER SIGNATURE in the book. Discover that the top number is "4." Discuss the fact that sometimes the small "sets of twos" are combined into larger "sets of fours." Sing the song for them, accenting every other beat as though it were in "twos." Then sing it again, accenting every fourth beat. Discover that the second way helps to make the song move more smoothly.

Look at the lower number of the meter signature and review its function with the children. Determine that the quarter note is the BEAT NOTE. Close the books and help the class notate the rhythm of the melody.

Write the words on the chalkboard and chant them as the class taps the beats in "fours." Decide which words should be grouped into "sets of four" to make the measure. Draw a vertical line between each group:

Are you sleep-ing, | Are you sleep-ing, | . . . etc.

Will we use notes that are alike for "Are you sleeping," or will some be different? (All alike, because the rhythm is even and moves with the beat.) **What kind of note will we use?** (Quarter note, because it is the beat note.) **In what way will the notes for "Brother John" be different?** (The last note is TWICE AS LONG and will be a half note.) **What kind of notes are needed for "morning bells are"?** (Short notes that are half as long as the beat, eighth notes.)

When the children have finished notating the rhythm of the melody, ask them to compare their notation with that in their books. Make any corrections that are necessary.

HARMONY

Sing: After the song is learned, it may be sung as a round by dividing the class into two groups. Later, classes made up of good independent singers may sing this as a four-part round by dividing the class into four groups.

This song may also be used for a harmonic experience by having one group of children sing the last phrase "Ding, ding, dong" as a chant throughout.

Play: The "Ding, ding, dong" fragment may also be played on the piano as an accompaniment. Play it in the octave below middle C:

This song may be accompanied on the autoharp with a single chord. It may be used for an introductory experience in teaching the children to play the autoharp.

GET ON BOARD

Rhythmically

Spiritual

Refrain Autoharp in F:

Get on board, lit-tle chil-dren, Get on board, lit-tle

chil-dren, Get on board, lit-tle chil-dren, There's room for man-y a more. *Fine*

Verse

The gos-pel train's a - com-ing, I hear it just at hand,＿＿ I

hear the car-wheels rum-bling and roll-ing through the land, So

D.C. al Fine

RHYTHM

Listen: **Where is the rhythm of this song different from that of many of the songs we have sung before?** (On "Get on.") **What makes this rhythm different?** (The short-long pattern ♪ ♩.) **Ordinarily we would say "Get on" evenly.** (Long-long or short-short ♪ ♪ or ♫.) **When a pattern moves short-long as this one does we call it** SYNCOPATION.

Create: Plan an introduction that will describe the mood of this song. **What kind of introduction might we use for this song? If a train is coming what will you**

hear? Children may suggest such things as the sound of the whistle at the crossing, the sound of the engine as it comes closer, the train slowing down, and so forth. As the train leaves the station, these sounds might be heard in reverse order, preceded by the conductor calling out "All aboard!"

Play: Select appropriate instruments and rhythm patterns for sound effects:

Emphasize the expressive quality of the TEMPO changes: Start fast and slow down as the train nears the station; reverse as it departs from the station. Continue the stick and sand-block patterns as an accompaniment throughout the song.

MELODY

Read: Ask the children to scan the notation to discover how many tones are used in this song. As they find these tones, place them on the staff in the key of G flat.

How many tones do we have? (Five.) **This is also a scale, but it has only five tones instead of eight. We call this a PENTATONIC scale.**

Compare the sound of the pentatonic scale with that of the major scale; help the children to discover that scale tones 4 and 7 are "missing" in the pentatonic scale.

Play: Find the five bells and have the children play the tune by ear. Show them that the song can be played in its entirety on the black keys on the piano.

HARMONY

Play: The children may experiment with any of the five tones to make up an accompaniment on the piano; the following patterns might be used:

Sing: After the song is learned, some strong independent singers might accompany the song with the following chant:

Ooh _____
or
Toot _____

IN THE HALL OF THE MOUNTAIN KING

Bowmar Orchestral Library, BOL #59   From the "Peer Gynt Suite" No. 1 by Edvard Grieg

MELODY

Listen: **Listen carefully to the opening section. Is this melody in MAJOR or in MINOR?** (Minor.)

Sing: Learn the main theme by humming along as the recording is played.

RHYTHM

Read: Help the children to picture the RHYTHM OF THE MELODY in line notation and in musical notation:

Play: The children may accompany the opening section with rhythm sticks or tone blocks. It will move too quickly toward the end to be able to keep up with the pattern.

EXPRESSION

Listen: **What is the MOOD of this music?** ("Spooky," "scary," or "exciting.") **What prompts these feelings?** Conclude that it is the following: The minor quality of the melody and the PIANISSIMO beginning add to the "spookiness"; the melody is repeated eighteen times, each time a little louder; upon each repetition the melody becomes higher in pitch and the tempo increases; and tension is created by adding more instruments each time the melody is repeated, until the whole orchestra is playing FORTISSIMO.

Move: Tap the beat lightly as the music begins. Compare the TEMPO of this beat with that of the beat at the end, which moves almost twice as fast.

The children may wish to dramatize this exciting music. Help them to plan dance movements that reflect their recognition of the expressive qualities of the music. For example, eighteen children might be selected to dance, a new one joining in each time the theme is repeated.

STYLE

Discuss: The Norwegian composer Edvard Grieg wrote this music to accompany a play, "Peer Gynt." This music did not tell the story of the play, but was supposed to set the mood for various parts of it.

"In the Hall of the Mountain King" describes an imaginary place where "trolls" lived. These creatures were supernatural beings, sometimes conceived as giants and sometimes as dwarfs, who inhabited caves and subterranean dwellings. They play an important role in Norwegian folklore.

Peer had discovered the home of the Troll King accidentally. At first he thought he wanted to become a troll himself and marry the King's daughter, but later he changed his mind. This music describes what happened when the trolls decided to chase Peer out of their mountain home after he had decided he did not want to become one of them.

Listen: **Listen again to the music. Can you picture the trolls giving Peer a wild chase?**

CANOE SONG

Andante

Arranged by Margaret B. McGee

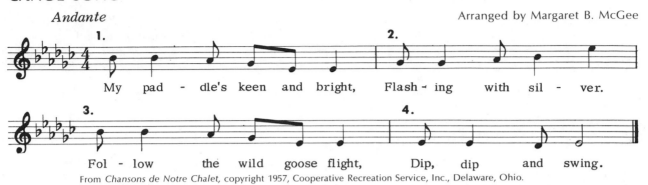

My pad - dle's keen and bright, Flash - ing with sil - ver.

Fol - low the wild goose flight, Dip, dip and swing.

From *Chansons de Notre Chalet*, copyright 1957, Cooperative Recreation Service, Inc., Delaware, Ohio.

STYLE

Listen: **What kind of song do you think this is? Who sang it? What in the music makes you think so?** The children should conclude that the "strange" melodic line and the steady beat make them think of Indians. Suggest that the songs of the Indians are often repetitious, using the same tonal patterns over and over.

Play: This song can be played on the black keys of the piano. Encourage the children to find out for themselves by starting them on B flat.

How many different tones do we need to play this song? (Five.) **Do you remember what we call a scale that is made up of five tones?** (Pentatonic scale.) **Most Indian melodies are based on the five-tone scale.**

Create: **Could you plan an accompaniment that would be appropriate for an Indian song? What instruments would you use?** (Drums, rain rattles, and so forth.) **What kinds of rhythmic patterns would you use?** (Drums might play steady ♩ ♩ ♩ ♩ with a strong accent while the rattles might play a rhythmic pattern that moves twice as fast: ♫ ♫ ♫ ♫.)

RHYTHM

Listen: **What is different about the rhythm of the melody in this song? Are there places where the rhythmic pattern is** UNEVEN? Help the children discover that these places move in a SHORT-LONG sequence (♪ ♩). **What other song used this kind of pattern?** ("Get on Board.")

Play: The activities suggested under *Style* will also help children become increasingly aware of the relationship of BEAT to RHYTHMIC PATTERN.

HARMONY

Sing: After the song is very familiar it may be sung as a two- or four-part round. Another experience with multiple sounds might be to have a small group of children sing the last measure as a chant throughout:

Play: Use the above chant as an accompaniment on the piano, bells, or xylophone. One child could play the following pattern on the piano as an accompaniment for the song:

TURN THE GLASSES OVER

Moderato   American Singing Game

> I've been to Har - lem, I've been to Do - ver, I've trav - eled this wide

> world all o - ver, O - ver, o - ver, three times o - ver, Drink what you have to drink and

> turn the glas - ses o - ver. Sail - ing east, sail - ing west,

> Sail - ing o - ver the o - cean, Bet - ter watch out when the

> boat be - gins to rock, Or you'll lose your girl in the o - cean.

RHYTHM

Read: **Look at the METER SIGNATURE; how will this song move?** (In fours.) **Can you find a measure where the rhythm of the melody moves with the beat? What kind of notes will you look for?** (Quarter notes.) **Can you find measures that include notes that are shorter than the beat? Longer than the beat? How many different "sets of four" can you find?** (Eight.) As the children locate the different patterns, put them on the chalkboard:

Clap the patterns, then chant the words of the song while observing the notation.

To help the children review the relationship of various note values to the BEAT NOTE, place these rhythmic patterns on the chalkboard:

Divide the class into three groups, each clapping a different pattern.

Move: The children may wish to play the following traditional game, or create their own.

> *Formation:* A double circle, facing counterclockwise, girls inside, holding partners' hands.
>
> Measures 1–6 Walk slowly around the circle, two steps to the measure.
>
> Measures 7–8 Face partner; take both hands, turn under partner's arms away from partner.
>
> Measures 9–14 Girls reverse and circles move in opposite directions.
>
> Measures 15–16 Link elbows with new partner and swing.

MELODY

Read: The children should be able to read this song with numbers or syllables with very little assistance from the teacher. Scan the song. Discover the repeated melodic patterns. For example, these four tones are used repeatedly with different rhythmic patterns:

Find the two-measure pattern that is made up of 1-3-5 (do-mi-so).

Find measures that are made up of 3-2-1 (mi-re-do).

HARMONY

Play: This song can be accompanied in two ways: with the F and Dm chords as indicated in the score, or with the F and C₇ chords. Experiment with both chord patterns as accompaniment. Have the children decide which they prefer and why.

The children may also enjoy playing the following OSTINATO on the bells, xylophone, or piano as an accompaniment for all or part of the song:

SANDY LAND

Lively   American Singing Game

1. Make my liv-ing in sand-y land, Make my liv-ing in sand-y land,
2. Raise my 'ta-ters in sand-y land, Raise my 'ta-ters in sand-y land,
3. Keep on dig-ging in sand-y land, Keep on dig-ging in sand-y land,

Make my liv-ing in sand - y land, La-dies fare you well.
Raise my 'ta-ters in sand - y land, La-dies fare you well.
Keep on dig-ging in sand - y land, La-dies fare you well.

MELODY

Read: The children should be able to sing this song from notation with very little help. Scan the song carefully. Discover the melodic patterns for measures 1–2 and 5–6 are the SAME.

What about the pattern in measures 3–4? Help the children realize that this pattern is almost the same as that in measures 1–2, only that it begins one step lower.

Look at measures 7–8. How does this pattern move? (Mostly by steps.)

In this song 1 (do) is G, which is on the second line. Can you decide the number (syllable) for the third note, D? Help the children realize that when notes are lower than 1 (*do*), one must count down backwards. Recall that high 1 (*do*) is also called 8 (*do*), therefore the step just below 1 (*do*) will be 7 (*ti*). Count down lines and spaces to find that D is low 5 (*so*).

Sing: **Do you think you could sing the pattern of the first two measures with words by yourself?** If the tonality has been well established by singing 1-3-5-3-1-5̲-1 (*do-mi-so-mi-do-so-do*), the children should sing it correctly the first time.

Good! This time go right on and sing the pattern for the third and fourth measures also. What will you remember about this pattern?

Encourage the children to determine the melody for the seventh and eighth measures by singing these measures with numbers or syllables.

RHYTHM

Read: **Will this music move in "twos" or "threes"?**

How will the rhythm for "Sandy Land" move? (Unevenly.) **Who can say "Sandy Land" correctly?**

Play: Select one child to establish the two-beat meter on the drum. Discuss whether or not the beat he establishes is too fast or too slow. **Did he make his first beat HEAVY and the second beat LIGHT?**

HARMONY

Play: The children can easily add an autoharp accompaniment to this song, because it requires only two chords (G, D₇). **Guess where you will need to change chords.** Use one stroke on the autoharp for each measure.

BANSHEE*

Sounds of New Music, Folkways Records, FX 6160

Henry Cowell

EXPRESSION

Listen: Ask the children to listen to the music and be ready to suggest a title for it. As they offer their ideas, guide them to support their choices with musical reasons. When all have had an opportunity to express their reactions to the music, explain the meaning of Cowell's title. **A banshee was a ghost that people once imagined lived in Ireland and Scotland. It was invisible but one could hear its wail as it wandered over the countryside.** Listen again and discuss the eerie sounds; decide which sections describe the wail of the banshee. **Can you tell when the banshee is coming closer?**

What instruments do you think are used in this music? The children will probably be surprised to learn that only a piano is being used. **This piano doesn't sound like the ones we usually hear, does it? That is because the music is being played on the strings by plucking, striking, and scratching, instead of by pressing down the keys.**

If a grand piano is available in the school, take the children to see it and explain how the performer of "Banshee" would have to stand in the curve of the piano to play, instead of sitting at the keyboard. Show them the mechanism that attaches the keys to the hammers that strike the strings. Compare the sound produced by the hammer striking the string with the sound resulting from the string being plucked.

Discuss the difference between the music of "Banshee" and other music the children have heard. **What things do we expect to hear in music?** Guide the children to decide that they usually expect to hear a MELODY which moves in RHYTHM, and that often more than one sound is heard at the time, creating HARMONY. **Is there a melody in this music?** Agree that one could not sing the "melody" they hear, but it does seem to move up and down as there are differences in high and low; however, the tones slide from one to another so quickly that one cannot describe the "tune" in precise terms. **Is there rhythm?** There is no steady beat which one can tap, but the longer and shorter sounds do create a kind of pattern. **Is there harmony?** At times, more than one pattern of tones is heard together and this creates a sort of harmony.

Create: Suggest that the children experiment with new ways to play their own instruments. Explore the possibilities of using some of the same techniques Cowell used on the piano with the autoharp, such as:

   a. Pluck separate strings, using different types of picks.
   b. Tap the strings with the hand, a piece of paper, a soft felt mallet.

c. Rub the thumb up and down the length of the low (wrapped) strings.
d. Press down all the chord bars and tap or sweep the strings with a pencil.
e. Loosen one string with the autoharp tuner key; pluck the string and then tighten it while the string is still vibrating.
f. Pluck single strings in a melodic pattern while someone else uses one of the above-mentioned ways to add an accompaniment.
g. Explore the body of the autoharp for sound-producing possibilities. Scrape across the chord bars with a stick, tap the body and sides with a mallet.

When the children have experimented with different ways of producing sound, help them organize the separate sounds into a composition. Tape the final product, play it for another class and ask the children to identify the instrument used.

THE FROG AND THE MOUSE

2. He rode till he came to Mouse's Hall,
     Whipsee . . .
   Where he most tenderly did call. Whipsee . . .
   "O, Mistress Mouse, are you at home?
   And if you are, oh, please come down."
     With a harum . . .

3. "My Uncle Rat is not at home,
     Whipsee . . .
   I dare not for my life come down." Whipsee . . .
   Then Uncle Rat he soon comes home,
   "And who's been here since I've been gone?"
     With a harum . . .

4. "Here's been a fine young gentleman,
    Whipsee . . .
   Who swears he'll have me if he can." Whipsee . . .
   Then Uncle Rat gave his consent
   And made a handsome settlement.
    With a harum . . .

5. Four partridge pies with season made,
    Whipsee . . .
   Two potted larks and marmalade. Whipsee . . .
   Four woodcocks and a venison pie.
   I would that at that feast were I.
    With a harum . . .

MELODY

Listen: **Can you decide what is different about this melody?** To help the children discover the MINOR quality, play the first phrase on the bells as follows:

Discuss the difference in sound and which version might be more appropriate.

Read: As the children look at the notation, help them to recall the letter names of the staff and to find all the different notes that are used. As they name the notes, ask one child to locate the bells that are needed to play the melody.

Play: Place the bells in order from low to high: D-E-F-G-A-Bb-C-D. Play them up and down and discover that this is a kind of "scale" also. **We call this a MINOR SCALE. This song is in a MINOR KEY; most of the songs we have learned have been in a MAJOR KEY.**

To help the children sense the difference between major and minor, replace bells F, Bb, and C with bells F#, B, and C#. Compare the sound of the two scales.

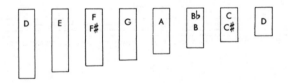

FORM

Listen: The phrase structure of this song is somewhat more complex than many. Help the children find the four phrases (counting the repeat), each four measures long. Find the REPEATED and the CONTRASTING phrases; then picture them on the chalkboard, using colored chalk.

The fourth phrase ends like the first phrase, but begins differently. How can we show this in color? (Use two colors.)

EXPRESSION

Move: This is a wonderful ballad to dramatize with children taking turns at being Frog, Mouse, and Rat. Encourage them to match their movements to the phrase structure and to the rhythmic flow of the melody.

Sing: Dramatization will afford opportunities for individual singing. **Should the frog sing with the same TONE QUALITY that the mouse uses?**

Listen: This song is a good one to help children realize that minor music is not always sad or scary.

CLOUDS

Music by Arthur Frackenpohl
Words by Christina Rossetti

EXPRESSION

Create: Read the poem in its original form aloud to the children without mentioning
its title.

White sheep, white sheep,
on a blue hill.
When the wind stops
you all stand still.
But when the wind blows
you walk away slow.
White sheep, white sheep,
where do you go?

Discuss the meaning of the poem. **Is the poet really talking about sheep? What suggests that he isn't? Would sheep be on a blue hill? Would they move with the wind? Can you think of something white that would be on a blue hill and move with the wind?**

Invite the children to create a melody for this poem. **What kind of music does the poem suggest? Will the rhythm move in twos or threes? Will it be even or uneven? Will the melody move with many skips or mostly stepwise? Will it cover a wide range from high to low or a narrow range? Are there words that suggest that the melody should go in a certain direction?**

When the children have given their ideas, guide them to chant the words until they have developed a rhythm they like. Help them to notate this rhythm over the words for reference. Next, ask them to pick bells to make a scale for their melody. Play the scale several times, then invite the children to take turns making up a melody on the bells for the first phrase. Ask the class to choose the melody that seems most appropriate for the words. Sing the melody together, then ask the children to experiment with the second phrase. Follow this procedure until the song is completed. When the melody is complete, you may notate it for the children, or help them write it on a staff on the chalkboard as a class project.

Listen: **You are not the only composers who have written a melody for this poem. Listen to this melody written by a composer by the name of Frackenpohl.** (Play or sing the melody.) **Did this composer have some of the same ideas that you had? What is different about the two songs? Which do you like the better?**

(Other settings of this poem may be found in *Growing with Music,* Book 2, *Making Music Your Own,* Book 3, and *Magic of Music,* Book 3. See Appendix D,I for names of publishers of these. Children may enjoy comparing the various versions.)

MELODY

Listen: During the children's discussion of the Frackenpohl setting they may have discovered that his melody is in a MINOR KEY. Recall the discussion they held while studying "The Frog and the Mouse." Sing or play the first phrase of "Clouds" in major, substituting C♯ and G♯ for C and G. Discuss how the minor key adds to the quiet, wistful mood of the song.

Notice that this melody moves primarily by steps or small skips. Most of the time it remains within a four-note range (G-C) which also helps create the peaceful mood.

FORM

Read: As the children study the notation, help them to discover that this song has five PHRASES. **Are any of these phrases alike?** Determine that none are exactly alike, but the first, second, and fifth are similar, as are the third and fourth phrases.

Discuss possible reasons for repeating the words of the first phrase. Perhaps the composer felt that these words were so important that they needed to be repeated.

TINGA LAYO*

Calypso Song from
the West Indies

EXPRESSION

Listen: Listen to the recording of this song. Discuss the different instruments that are heard in the introduction. The children should be able to identify the guitar playing the melody, the xylophone on the countermelody, the maracas making a swishing sound, and the bongo drums playing the rhythmic ostinato. Notice the two different pitch levels of the drums.

The distinctive rhythms, the repetitious melody, and the interesting sounds of the instruments help to give this music a unique flavor. **This music is from the West Indies. It is called Calypso music.** Help the children locate the West Indies on a map.

Play: When the children know the song well, they may wish to add their own calypso accompaniment.

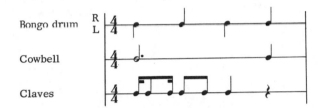

Practice each of the rhythms separately, then add them to the song one at a time. (Note that these are not the accompaniment patterns heard on the recording.)

RHYTHM

Listen: Place this rhythm pattern on the chalkboard: ♫ ♩ ♫ ♩. **How many times do you hear this pattern in the song?** (Five times.) **What makes this rhythm so interesting?** Help the children decide that the UNEVEN rhythm with the SHORT tone preceding the LONG tone is what makes this rhythm unusual. **This SYNCOPATED pattern is typical of music from the West Indies.**

Move: Invite the children to clap the rhythm pattern lightly each time it is heard.

FORM

Listen: Listen to the song again and ask the children to discover the number of phrases it contains. (Five two-measure phrases.) Notice that the first and second phrases are similar and that the fourth and fifth phrases are repetitions of these two phrases. The third phrase is different and offers contrast (variety). **Why would this be an ABA form?** (Because the first and last sections are the same.)

Read: Notice the SEQUENCE in the third phrase:

Compare the rhythmic pattern with the rhythm of the fourth phrase. **How are they different?**

MELODY

Sing: After the children have listened to the song several times and have discussed the items mentioned in the preceding paragraphs, invite them to sing the first two phrases without assistance. Listen again to the recording to be sure they have sung it correctly; then challenge the class to sing the entire song. Again, use the recording to check for accuracy.

HARMONY

Sing: Some third graders who are strong singers may be able to sing a harmonizing part during the refrain.

THEME FROM THIRD MOVEMENT, SYMPHONY NO. 1

Bowmar Orchestral Library, BOL #62   Gustav Mahler

MELODY

Discuss: Before playing this composition, talk about ways that a composer creates music. Sometimes he will write a short melody with words and then it is called a SONG. He can also take this short melody and "stretch it out" by playing it in many different ways in order to create a longer composition. The melody then is called a THEME. It is the composer's main idea, which he tells us over and over; however, he keeps us interested by changing it in different ways each time it is repeated.

Listen: Play the composition and ask the children to see if they can find a theme in this music. **Raise your hand when you think you have found a theme and know the name of the song the composer has used for this.** ("Are You Sleeping.")

Does this theme sound the same as the song does when you sing it? (No.) Guide the children to verbalize the differences: the melody is slightly altered; it is in minor; it is played by instruments much lower than when sung; the tempo is slower.

Play: Some children may not be able to sense the difference between the MAJOR and MINOR versions of the melody. To help them grasp the reasons for the difference, place bells D-E-F♯ on the table. Ask one child to play the first motive: D-E-F♯-D or D-E-F♯-E-D. Substitute F for F♯ and repeat the pattern. Talk about the differences. Some children may be able to play the complete melody, first in major and then in minor. (You will need to add the G-A-B bells for major and the G-A-B♭ bells for minor.)

Listen: **Does the composition begin with the theme?** (No, it begins with an INTRODUCTION played by the tympani.) Help the children realize that the pattern they hear in the introduction is based on the tones used for the final phrase of "Are You Sleeping" (Ding, Dong, Bell, 1–5–1) and that this pattern continues throughout the composition as an OSTINATO.

   The melody is familiar. Does the composer do anything that is similar to the way you sing this melody? (We sing it as a round, and the composer treats it in the same way using different instruments for each new entrance.)

   Can you find something the composer does which is different from the way you sing the melody? Draw attention to the added melody—DESCANT, or COUNTERMELODY—played by the oboe. It is heard twice.

Create: Suggest that the children develop their own VARIATION of "Are You Sleeping" (p. 122), using some of the ideas they have discovered by listening to Mahler's arrangement. They may want to sing the melody in F minor instead of F major in a tempo similar to that heard on the recording; they may also want to create their own countermelody. "Are You Sleeping" can be harmonized with a single chord, the I chord, and a countermelody based on the tones of this chord would be appropriate.

   When singing in major, use bells F-A-C (in all octaves); when singing in minor, use bells F-A♭-C. Allow several children to improvise a descant as the class sings. Notate the one the children like most.

   The children will enjoy adding an ostinato to the melody, also. The following may be played on the piano or bells:

EXPRESSION

Listen: Help the children identify the main instruments heard. The introduction is played by the TYMPANI. The first statement of the theme is given to the STRING BASS; other statements are played by the BASSOON, TUBA, and CLARINET. The descant is played by the OBOE.

COMING OF SPRING

Joyous

Autoharp in C:

German Folk Song

1. All the birds are here a - gain, Lis - ten to their sing - ing,
2. All the birds are here a - gain, Lis - ten to their sing - ing.

Chirp - ing, war - bling, all day_ through, Sing - ing hap - py songs to__ you,
Rob - in, star - ling, thrush, and_ lark, Twit - ter - ing from dawn to__ dark;

Spring will soon be com - ing__ too, Joy and mu - sic bring - ing.
Wish - ing you a hap - py__ year, What a mer - ry greet - ing.

FORM

Discuss: Use this song to help the children summarize the musical learnings they have absorbed during the year. Discuss the steps one needs to go through to learn a new song. Agree that the first step is to look at the entire song to discover its form.

Read: Determine the phrase structure of the song by studying the notation. Discover that there are three phrases, each four measures long. Notice that the first and third phrases are the SAME. Observe that the second phrase is made up of a two-measure pattern which is repeated. Describe the over-all design with letter names, ABA.

RHYTHM

Read: Discuss the steps one must follow to learn the rhythm of a new song. Agree that one must first determine how the song will move. Look at the meter signature; decide that it will move in fours and that the quarter note is the BEAT NOTE. Ask the children to scan the notation. **Are the measures grouped in "sets of four"? Can you find a measure where the tones move with the beat?** (Measures 5 and 7.) **Find measures that include tones that are TWICE AS LONG as the beat.** (Every second measure.)

Put each different measure on the chalkboard as the children locate them. Draw attention to the pattern with the dotted quarter note. Review the function of the dot; it makes the note a little longer. Notice that the second note is an eighth note, which is short. This pattern will sound UNEVEN: Lo-ong-short-long-long.

Practice clapping all the different rhythm patterns:

Chant the words of the song in rhythm.

MELODY

Read: **In this song, 1 (do) is in the space below the staff. Do you recall its letter name?** (D.) **Who can find the bells needed for the D scale?** (D-E-F♯-G-A-B-C♯-D.) Ask one child to play up and down the scale to establish the tonality.

Sing: **Who can find a pattern that moves 1–3–5–8 (do-mi-so-do)?** ("All the birds are") **A pattern that moves 5–5–4–4–3 (so-so-fa-fa-mi)?** ("chirping, warbling, all") Draw attention to other tonal patterns in the same manner. Practice singing each pattern with numbers (syllables); then challenge the class to follow the notation in the book and sing as much of the song as possible, first with numbers (syllables) and then with words. If problems arise, help the children solve them by practicing the difficult section on the bells; then sing the entire song again.

EXPRESSION

Listen: **What is the mood of this song?** (Bright, sprightly, gay, and so forth.) **What gives it this feeling?** (The wide sweep of the melodic line and the lilting rhythm.)

Sing: **How must this song be sung so as to convey this mood to our listeners?** Sing with a light, bright TONE QUALITY and with rhythmic accuracy.

Guiding Musical Growth
in the Fourth Grade

	Listening	Singing	Playing
SKILL	Strive for continual improvement in the ability to listen with discrimination.	Work for good tone production over a wide vocal range.	Provide increased opportunities for chording on the autoharp and piano.
		Help each child to develop skill in maintaining a harmonizing vocal line.	Foster improvement in ability to play a variety of percussion instruments accurately.
			Provide opportunities to acquire some skill in playing recorder-type instruments.
CONCEPTS *Melody*	Help the children to become conscious of differences in tonality (major, minor, pentatonic).	Increase an awareness of tonal relationships within melodic line by singing tonal patterns with numbers and/or syllables.	Extend the understanding of melodic movement through playing simple tunes on bells, piano, and recorder-type instruments from notation as well as by ear.
	Draw attention to melodic patterns based on scale-line or chord-line movement.		Reinforce the understanding of scale pattern by constructing major and pentatonic scales by ear.
	Develop sensitivity to tonal sequences within melodic line.		Develop ability to establish tonality for songs by playing appropriate patterns on bells, piano, or autoharp.
Rhythm	Stress understanding of meter, beat, accent, and rhythmic patterns.	Continually stress the need for accurate reproduction of rhythmic patterns.	Provide opportunities for the children to demonstrate their understanding of meter and rhythm patterns, including syncopation, based on 2-1 and 3-1 relationships.
	Direct attention to 2-1 (♩ ♩ ♩, ♩ ♫, ♩ ♫) or 3-1 (♩. ♩,) (♩. ♪, ♩. ♫) relationships and syncopation (♪♩ ♪) within rhythmic patterns.		Encourage independent reproduction of rhythmic patterns as accompaniments to songs.
Harmony	Emphasize differences in the quality of I, IV, V_7 chords.	Include many rounds, descants, and two-part songs as a means of increasing the understanding of multiple sounds.	Expand experiences in adding chordal accompaniments to include the voice.
	Draw attention to the feeling of finality (rest) engendered by the V_7-1 cadential progression.	Encourage the children to establish tonality of new songs by singing tonic triad (1-3-5 or do-mi-so).	Provide experiences in playing ostinati and descants.
	Develop recognition of common harmonic intervals (thirds and sixths).		
Form	Help the children recognize repetition and contrast of phrases and sections within a composition.	Stress the importance of singing long melodic lines with adequate breath support.	Draw attention to phrase repetition and contrast by varying or repeating accompaniment patterns in accordance with song structure.
	Plan experiences to familiarize children with two- and three-part forms, rondo, and theme and variation.		Encourage improvisations to demonstrate understanding of introduction and coda.
Expression	Stimulate the children's interest in the many ways in which tonality, tempo, dynamics, and tone quality can be combined to create varying musical expressions.	Encourage the use of appropriate tone quality and dynamics for expressive purposes.	Explore the expressive qualities of instrumental tone colors and of variations in tempo and dynamics in playing melodies and accompaniments.
	Point out ways in which musical climaxes can be attained.		
Style	Guide the children toward recognition of musical style by providing experiences with music from different cultures and with the music of different composers.		

Moving	Creating	Reading
Expand the children's vocabulary of movements to include formalized folk dance steps.	Foster creative participation by individuals through composition of songs and the addition of accompaniments. Motivate the children to create more extensive and expressive dance movements.	Extend the children's knowledge of musical symbols to include key signatures, expression markings, and so on, through the meaningful use of symbols.
Suggest that the children adapt body movements to the melodic contour of music.	Suggest exploration of major, minor, and pentatonic tonalities when creating original melodies. Stimulate children to use their understanding of scale and chord-line patterns, as well as melodic sequence and alteration, in their own improvisations and compositions.	Help the children interpret key signatures to determine tonality. Apply recognition of scale- and chord-line patterns in singing and playing melodies from notation. Use numbers, syllables and/or letters as aids to develop music reading skill.
Encourage the children to respond with increasing sensitivity to rhythmic nuance in planning dance movements. Emphasize differences in rhythmic structure in execution of folk dances.	Strive to include a variety of rhythmic patterns in the children's original compositions and accompaniments.	Provide opportunities for the children to interpret meter signatures to establish meter and to determine durational relationships of various notes.
Guide the children in developing dance movements that reflect their awareness of countermelodies and cadential progressions.	Encourage the children to add autoharp accompaniments to original melodies. Stimulate improvisation of ostinati to pentatonic melodies.	Stress the reading of simple two-part music at sight. Encourage the children to read chord symbols (letters and Roman numerals) when playing autoharp and piano accompaniments.
Stress the importance of adjusting dance movements to the form structure of music.	Help the children reveal their understanding of part-forms, rondo, theme and variations in developing compositions based on these designs.	Guide the children to recognize repetition and contrast in notation when learning new songs. Help the children schematize compositional designs with appropriate letters: AB, ABA, ABACA, and so forth.
Interpret with increasing sensitivity variations in tempo, dynamics, and tone color through physical movement.	Suggest that the children consider the expressive properties of instruments when creating accompaniments. Interest children in considering expressive possibilities of variations in tempo and dynamics in their compositions.	Stress the importance of observing tempo and dynamic markings in the score.
Emphasize the stylistic characteristics of folk dances.	Guide the children to consider cultural characteristics when selecting instruments for creating accompaniments.	

DONKEY RIDING

Marcato
Autoharp in C:

Canadian Folk Song

1. Were you ev - er in Que - bec, Stow - ing tim - ber on a deck,
2. Were you ev - er in Car - diff Bay, Where the folks all shout, "Hoo - ray!

Where there's a king with a gold - en crown, Rid - ing on a don - key?
Here comes___ John with his three month's pay, Rid - ing on a don - key"?

Refrain

Hey - ho! A - way we go! Don - key rid - ing, don - key rid - ing,

Hey - ho! A - way we go! Rid - ing on a don - key!

RHYTHM

Read: Before the children study this song, place the following rhythm patterns on the chalkboard:

Review the meter signature; determine that the rhythm moves in twos and that the quarter note is the beat note.

Point out that both lines of rhythms are to be sounded simultaneously. Stressing the relationships between notes by comparing the two lines, guide the children to answer the following questions. Give them the names of new notes as needed.

Find a measure where both parts sound with the BEAT. (Measure 1.) **Where does one part sound with a tone that is TWICE AS LONG as the beat?** (Measure 8, HALF NOTE.) **Find a measure where the pattern sounds with two tones to the beat.** (Measure 2, EIGHTH NOTES.) **Find a measure where the pattern moves with four tones to the beat.** (Measures 5, 6, and 7, SIXTEENTH NOTES.) **What measures include patterns that are UNEVEN?** (Measures 3, 4, 6, and 7.) **Compare the two different patterns in these measures. Can you decide how much longer the DOTTED QUARTER NOTE is than the eighth note?** (THREE TIMES AS LONG.) **How much longer is the DOTTED EIGHTH NOTE than the sixteenth note?** (THREE TIMES AS LONG.)

Play: When the class can clap these rhythms, choose two children to play the patterns on instruments of contrasting tone colors, such as wood block and drum.

Read: Look at the notation for "Donkey Riding." Draw on the discoveries made about the relationships of notes to help the children determine the rhythm of the melody. Locate distinctive rhythm patterns; practice these and then chant the words for the entire song.

MELODY

Read: Scan the melody and discover that the first and second phrases are similar, as are the third and fourth phrases. Notice that the melody moves primarily by steps. **This song begins on 1 (do); sing the first two phrases with numbers (syllables).** Discuss the difference in the two phrase endings. **Which phrase gives a feeling of "unrest"? Of coming to "rest"?** Agree that the second phrase gives a feeling of "rest" because it ends on 1 (do), the home tone; the first phrase ends on 2 (re) and gives a feeling of "unrest" or continuation.

On which tone do the third and fourth phrases begin? (On 6 [la].) Find this tone on the bells, then proceed to sing these two phrases with numbers (syllables).

EXPRESSION

Discuss: This is a work song from Canada. The donkey referred to is not an animal, but a small engine used on docks to haul cargo. These engines used less than one horse power, therefore they were called "donkeys."

Sing: **This song was sung by dockworkers as they loaded cargo onto the ships. How should it be sung?** Agree that it should be sung with a strong rhythmic feeling, with firm accents to help the workers move in rhythm as they lifted heavy loads of ore or lumber.

HOLLA-HI! HOLLA-HO!

German Folk Song
Translated by Peter Kunkel

RHYTHM

Read: Review the function of the METER SIGNATURE. Help the children recall that this meter signature tells that the rhythm will move in fours and that the quarter note will sound as the BEAT NOTE. **Can you find a measure where the rhythm of the melody sounds with the beat?** (Next to the last measure.) Locate distinctive rhythm patterns and put these on the chalkboard.

Move: Practice clapping each pattern, then clap the rhythm of the melody while one child plays a steady beat on a woodblock. Next, chant the words of the song.

MELODY

Read: **The melody of this song begins on 1 (do). Can you sing the complete song with numbers (syllables)?** Before the children sing, ask them to study the notation to find patterns that move by steps or skips.

Sing: Establish the tonality by singing 1-3-5-3-1 (*do-mi-so-mi-do*) and invite the children to sing the melody with numbers (syllables). If they encounter difficulties with the skips in the second and fourth measures, help them find the problem intervals on the bells. Return to singing the melody with numbers (syllables), and finally sing with words.

Play: **Look at the first phrase; how many different bells will you need to play it?** (Eight.) Guide the children to determine the names of the bells by studying the notation. Review the names of the lines and spaces of the staff. As the children identify the letter name of each different tone, place the notes on the staff from low to high:

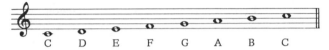

Put the chromatic bells in one long line from C to C:

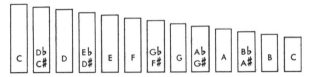

Ask one child to locate and play the bells which the class had identified. Discover that he has played a MAJOR SCALE. **We call this the C SCALE because the first tone is C.**

Scan the remainder of the song to see if other bells are needed to play the complete melody. Discover that high D is needed. **Does this new bell change our scale?** (No, because all tones of the same name belong to the same scale, regardless of whether they are high or low.)

Draw attention to the fact that the complete melody uses only tones from the C scale. **We say that this song is in the KEY OF C because it uses the tones that make up the C scale. C is the home tone of this melody, the first tone of the scale upon which it is built.**

Some children may learn to play the entire melody on the bells.

Read: On another day, draw a diagram on the chalkboard showing the letter names of the chromatic scale. Review the letter names of the C scale, and then ask the children to fill in the spaces in the second row of the diagram to show which tones were used in this scale.

	Db		Eb			Gb		Ab		Bb		
C	C♯	D	D♯	E	F	F♯	G	G♯	A	A♯	B	C
C		D		E	F		G		A		B	C

Ask the children to build scales starting on F and G. Allow them to experiment with the bells until they find the sequence of tones which "sound right." Write the letter names for these scales on the chart, leaving spaces whenever a bell in the chromatic scale is omitted.

F		G		A	B♭		C		D		E	F
G		A		B	C		D		E		F♯	G

Draw attention to the fact that the empty spaces occur in the same order in each scale. Guide the children to conclude that the MAJOR SCALE must always follow this particular pattern. Help the children to develop their own terminology to describe this pattern, or give them the terms of HALF STEPS (represented by bells next to each other) and WHOLE STEPS (occurring when one bell is omitted or skipped).

Describe the structure of the major-scale pattern as:

1	2	3	4	5	6	7	8
whole step	whole step	half step	whole step	whole step	whole step	half step	

HARMONY

Play: When the children have learned the melody, determine the autoharp accompaniment through experimentation. Ask the children to assist you as you play the chords by telling you when the chords should be changed. Put the chord names on the chalkboard as they are determined. (Use two chords per measure.)

C C G₇ C C C G₇ C

F F C C G₇ G₇ C C

F F C C G₇ G₇ C C

Draw attention to the fact that the first chord is named C. **This song is in the key of C and C is the home tone I (do). We call this chord the I chord, also, because it is the chord that is built on the first step of the scale.** Observe that the C chord is used at the end of each phrase and that it gives a feeling of rest.

Sing: Some children may be able to sing the following descant during the last two phrases. It may also be played on the bells.

Hol - la - hi,   Hol - la - ho,   Hol - la - hi,   Ho!

Hol - la - hi,   Hol - la - ho,   Hol - la - hi - a - ho!

FOLLOW ME

Gaily

Traditional

Come a - long, Sing a song,
Come a - long, Sing a

Fol - low me; It is eas - y, you can
song, Fol - low me; It is

see. Ev - 'ry day, In this way,
eas - y, you can see. Ev - 'ry day, In this

Just re - peat 'Til the tune's com - plete.
way, Just re - peat, com - plete.

FORM

Read: Ask the children to look at the notation. **Do you see anything unusual about the way this song has been notated?** (It is written on two staffs.) Point out that the two staffs are connected with a heavy black line and that this indicates that the notes on both staffs should be read and sung simultaneously.

Compare the melodies written on the two staffs. Discover that the lower part is an exact repetition of the upper part. **This design is called a CANON.** (*Canon* is a Greek word meaning "law" or "rule.") Explain that a canon is similar to a round in that all parts have the same melody throughout, although starting at different times. Rounds can be repeated immediately; this canon cannot because the ending of the lower part has been altered.

RHYTHM

Read: Study the rhythm of the upper part and notice that it includes notes and rests. **How many different kinds of rests do you see?** (Two.) Remind the children that the QUARTER REST (𝄽) receives the same time value as the quarter note (♩) or two eight notes (♪ ♪), and that the EIGHTH REST (𝄾) receives the same time value as the eighth note (♪).

Determine from the meter signature that this song moves in twos. Establish a two-beat pattern at a comfortable tempo and chant the words of the upper part while tapping the beat. When the children can do this accurately, paying special attention to observing the appropriate rests, divide the class into two groups and chant the words of both parts.

Play: Two groups of children may play the two parts on different percussion instruments as a rhythmic canon.

MELODY

Read: Sing the upper part with numbers (syllables) and then with words.

HARMONY

Sing: Divide the class into two groups and have them sing the song as a canon.

Play: The two parts can also be played on two sets of bells or on any other melody instruments available.

THE MARCH OF THE SIAMESE CHILDREN

Bowmar Orchestral Library, BOL #54   From *The King and I* by Richard Rodgers

STYLE

Listen: Play the composition for the class. **What kind of music is this? What part of the world does the music suggest?** Agree that it is a march and that it reminds one of the Orient. Give the children the title of the composition and locate Siam (Thailand) on a map. The instruments used in this composition (wood block, Temple blocks, gong, and English horn) are reminiscent of instrumental sounds used in the Far East. The use of GRACE NOTES (very short tones that precede the main melody tones) are also typical of Oriental melodies. This can be most easily noted in the statement of the B theme.

How would you know that this music was not written by an Oriental composer? (The sound of the full orchestra, the choice of melodies, and the design of the composition are more typical of Western music than music of the Orient.) Tell the children that it was composed by the American composer Richard Rodgers, who has written music for many musical plays including *The King and I.*

FORM

Listen: **Long compositions are often divided into shorter sections. How many sections did you hear in this music? Are they the same, similar, or different?** Listen again; discuss proffered answers and reasons for differences of opinions. **How can you tell when one section ends and a new one begins?** (The music may seem to pause or come to rest; or it may begin to introduce a new musical idea.)

How many sections did you hear that were the same or similar? Which sections were different? Replay the march, pausing at the end of each section to discuss its characteristics. Discuss differences in sections in terms of melodic contour, rhythmic organization, instrumentation, and so on. Determine finally that the design of this composition is ABACABA. Talk about the balanced design achieved by the single contrasting section appearing in the middle between the ABA sequences on each side.

This design is called a RONDO. Ask the children to draw geometric designs to represent the rondo form, using a different shape and color for each section.

Create: Invite the children to create their own rondo. At first, confine this to the development of rhythmic patterns that may be clapped or played on percussion instruments. Divide the class into three groups and ask each group to plan one section. Before they begin to work they may wish to agree on an over-all design for their rondo. **What meter should be used? Will each section have the same meter?** (Not necessarily.) **How long should each section be? If percussion instruments are used, should the same instruments be used in all sections? How may the A and B sections be varied during the repetitions?**

EXPRESSION

Listen: Discuss the fact that although the three sections are quite contrasting, they are combined to make an interesting, unified composition. **What helps to give UNITY to this composition?** (The rhythmic pattern ♪♪♩ ♪♪♩, which is constant throughout, and the many repetitions of theme A.)

Listen to the repetitions of sections A and B. Are they always the same? (No; instrumentation and dynamics are changed.) **Why, do you suppose, did the composer make these changes?** (To provide VARIETY in the expressive design.)

As the children listen to this composition, draw attention to the following details:

A. The opening melody, which begins with an outline of the I chord, is played by the flute. **What instrument plays this pattern: ♩♩♩ ♩♩♩ ?** (Woodblock.)

B. Listen for the nasal quality of the English horn. Notice the reverberating sound of the gong. **When the melody is repeated, what instruments play?** (Strings.) **How can you tell that theme A is about to return?** (The flute begins playing a melody reminiscent of the A theme.)

A. **Is this statement the same as the beginning statement?** (Yes, but it is much louder and many instruments have been added.) **What instrument now plays the repeated pattern?** (Low drum.)

C. **How does this section contrast with the other two sections?** (The melody is strongly accented and accompanied with more full chords than previously. The full orchestra is playing, creating a loud climax.)

A. The full orchestra now joins in on the A theme, and a countermelody played by the French horn has been added.

B. The strings state the B theme, giving a richer and fuller sound to this repetition.

A. The piccolo returns with the A theme and is joined by the full orchestra in a final, climactic statement to end the composition.

Move: Invite the class to divide into three groups to develop a dance reflecting the design and expressive nature of the composition.

LOVELY EVENING

Moderato   Three-Part Round

Oh, how love-ly is the eve-ning, is the eve-ning,

'When the bells are sweet-ly ring-ing, sweet-ly ring-ing!

Ding,   dong,   ding,   dong,   ding,   dong.

MELODY

Read: **Before we sing this song, look at the first phrase. What do you see that will help you sing it from notation more easily?** (Discover that the tonal pattern for "is the evening" is repeated.)

This song begins on 1 (do). Can you sing the first phrase with numbers (syllables)? The teacher listens.

Look at the notation as I sing the second phrase and see what you can tell me about this phrase. The children should conclude that it is the same melody as the first phrase, only a little higher.

Can you identify the letter names of the melody for the first phrase? Ask one child to find the proper bells as the children give the letter names. They will probably name B instead of B♭. Ask the child to play the bells he has located: F-G-A-B. **Does this sound right?** (No.) **What do we need to do to make it sound right?** (Lower the fourth step to B♭.)

Remind the class of the discoveries made about major scales when studying "Holla-Hi! Holla-Ho!" **This song is in the key of F because it uses the tones that make up the F scale. F is the home tone of this melody and it is the 1 (do) of the scale upon which the melody is built.**

Use this as an opportunity to discuss the purpose of the KEY SIGNATURE. **There is a way to tell what tones need to be lowered (flatted) or raised (sharped) before we play or sing a melody from the notation. Look at the notation for "Lovely Evening" again. At the very beginning there is a FLAT (♭) on the B line. This is called the KEY SIGNATURE. It tells us which key the song is in. Which step of the scale of F is B?** (Fourth.) **If you know the fourth step of a scale, could you find the first step?** (Count down to 1 [*do*].) **This is how I knew that 1 (do) was in the first space of the staff, before we started to sing the song.**

Experiment with other scales, using flats represented by key signatures. Start on B♭ and build the scale, using the chart on page 147 as a guide. Discover that the fourth step, E, must be flatted. Repeat the process starting on E♭ and A♭.

filling in the chart each time with correct letter names. Help the children conclude that, in scales using flats, the fourth step is always lowered.

B♭		C		D	E♭	F		G		A	B♭
E♭		F		G	A♭	B♭		C		D	E♭
A♭		B♭		C	D♭	E♭		F		G	A♭

Turn the process around; write key signatures using flats on the chalkboard. Ask the children to locate the home tone, 1 (*do*), reminding them that the flatted fourth step will be represented by the last flat to the right in the key signature.

Sing: After the children have discussed the key signatures, return to the key of F and establish the tonality for "Lovely Evening." Challenge the class to sing the entire song with numbers (syllables) and then with words.

HARMONY

Sing: This is a particularly lovely round and one that children will enjoy singing often after it is learned. Be sure to use an appropriate TONE QUALITY and to sing with accurate pitch and rhythm.

Listen: Draw the children's attention to the pleasing sounds created when the parts are sung simultaneously. **Why do you suppose the first and second phrases sound so well when sung together?**

Read: To help the children decide the answer to the above-mentioned question, write the two phrases on the same staff.

If we call the bottom note of each pair "1" and count up, the top note will be "3." When two tones are this far apart they are a THIRD apart. Conclude that THIRDS are "pleasing" sounds.

EXPRESSION

Listen: **What makes this music appropriate for a song about bells?** (The rhythmic movement suggests the swaying of a bell back and forth.)

The HARMONY created by the combination of the three phrases gives the impression of many bells ringing at the same time.

Sing: **How can we create a bell-like effect with our voices?** (By singing with a sustained tone in a clear voice and by maintaining a steady rhythmic flow.)

A bell-like effect can also be achieved by accenting the "ding, dong" in the last phrase.

An added effect can be created by having each group of singers continue to sing "ding, dong" until all have finished the song.

VRENELI

In march time

Swiss Folk Song

1. "O Vren - e - li, my pret - ty one, Pray tell me where's your home?"
2. "O Vren - e - li, my pret - ty one, Pray tell me where's your heart?"
3. "O Vren - e - li, my pret - ty one, Pray tell me where's your head?"

"My home it is in Swit - zer - land, It's made of wood and stone." stone."
"O, that," she said, "I gave a - way, Its pain will not de - part." part."
"O, that, I al - so gave a - way, 'Tis with my heart," she said. said.

Refrain

Yo, ho, ho, tra - la - la - la; Yo, ho, ho, tra - la - la - la; Yo - ho

ho, tra - la - la - la; Yo, ho, ho, tra - la - la - la; ho, tra - la - la - la, Yo, ho, ho.

RHYTHM

Read: Observe that this song is made up largely of alternating EVEN and UNEVEN rhythmic

patterns, ♪♪ and ♪.♪ Have the children chant the words together as the teacher, or one child, maintains a steady beat by clapping.

To help the children read the rhythm of this song accurately, review the relationships between the various note values. Have the children clap these rhythm patterns from notation on the chalkboard:

There is one pattern in this song that moves with the BEAT. Can you find it? (Next to the last measure.) **When you come to this place, be sure you do not make that pattern sound like the previous one.**

Sing: Sing this song crisply, with marked rhythm and good enunciation, so that the contrasting rhythmic patterns can be heard distinctly.

FORM

Discuss: This is a dialogue song. The verse is made up of two PHRASES. Have the children decide which phrase should be sung by the boys and which by the girls.

The refrain is made up of two MOTIVES. A motive is a short melodic or rhythmic pattern. Decide which motives should be sung by the boys and which ones by the girls.

Sing: **Who can sing the boys' motive? Who can sing the girls' motive?** After the song is learned, give the children an opportunity to sing individually; some may be able to sing the entire song as a duet.

Read: Review *1.* and *2.* ENDINGS, noting the melodic differences.

HARMONY

Sing: A harmonizing part can be added to the refrain very simply by having the boys sustain the last tone of each "Yo, ho, ho" motive while the girls sing "tra-la-la-la."

Listen: **How much lower are the girls' voices than the boys' on the first two motives?** (A third.)

EXPRESSION

Read: Identify the FERMATAS (⌒) at the beginning of the refrain. **These symbols tell us to emphasize these tones by holding them longer than the value of the note would require.**

Listen: Sing the first measure of the refrain with and without the fermatas, and ask the children to decide which version they like best.

What is the musical purpose of the fermata in this song? Help the children realize that it provides a CLIMAX. **All good songs have climaxes, that is, one or more places that are most "important." One way to provide a climax is to emphasize that place by interrupting the rhythmic flow of the melody, as the fermata suggests be done here. Notice that the climax occurs in the highest place of the melodic line.**

Have the children look at other songs to see where the climaxes occur and decide how they are created.

Sing: **Show your recognition of the climaxes in this song with your voices by sustaining the tones marked with a fermata and by singing these tones a little louder.**

STODOLA PUMPA

Slowly

Czechoslovakian Folk Song
Words by A. D. Zanzig

1. Walk - ing at night a - long the mead - ow way,
2. Near - ing the wood, we heard the night - in - gale,
3. Man - y the stars that bright - ly shone a - bove,

Home from the dance be - side my maid - en gay.   Walk - ing at night a -
Sweet - ly it helped me tell my beg - ging tale.   Near - ing the wood, we
But none so bright as her one word of love.   Man - y the stars that

long the mead - ow way,   Home from the dance be - side my maid - en gay. *Hey!*
heard the night - in - gale,   Sweet - ly it helped me tell my beg - ging tale. *Hey!*
bright - ly shone a - bove,   But none so bright as her one word of love. *Hey!*

Quickly
Refrain

Sto - do - la,   Sto - do - la,   sto - do - la   pum - pa,

sto - do - la,   pum - pa,   sto - do - la,   pum - pa,   pum, pum, pum.

Words from *Singing America,* copyright 1941, Summy-Birchard Company, Evanston, Ill. Used by permission.

EXPRESSION

Discuss: **This is a song describing the ways of boys and girls long ago in Czechoslovakia. Today when we go to a party and get thirsty we have a cold glass of pop. The Czech boys and girls did not have such drinks, so they would go to the village pump for cold water. The refrain of this song describes the sound of the pump as the boys competed to see who could pump the fastest.**

Listen: **What makes this song interesting?** Conclude that the contrast between verse and refrain provides interest. The verse moves slowly with a flowing melodic line, has a wide range and an even rhythmic pattern; the melody moves primarily in skips. The refrain moves at a much faster TEMPO; the melody has a narrow range and a repetitious rhythmic pattern, and progresses by steps.

Sing: **Sing in a manner that shows that you recognize the contrasting sections.** The verse should be sung smoothly (LEGATO) with as beautiful a tone as possible. The refrain should be sung quickly and exuberantly. Caution the children to be ready to change the mood with the word "Hey!" which must be short and quick so as not to interrupt the rhythmic beat. Experiment with various tempos; singing the refrain exactly twice as fast as the verse will probably prove to be most effective.

RHYTHM

Read: Observe that this song has two meter signatures, 4/4 and 2/4. Scan the rhythmic notation of the song. Notice that the rhythmic pattern of the first three phrases is the same. **How does the rhythmic pattern of the fourth phrase differ?** (♩ ♩ takes the place of ♩. ♪).

Move: Emphasize the difference in these patterns by clapping ♩. ♪ against ♩ ♩. Review the relationship of the dotted quarter note to the eighth note.

(♩. ♪ = ♪♪♪♪ , THREE TIMES AS LONG.)

STYLE

Discuss: Songs such as this, with a slow verse and a fast refrain, are very common in the eastern European countries which include Czechoslovakia. These songs were originally danced. Perhaps that is the reason for their slow-fast form, which would allow the dancers to "catch their breath" on the slow part.

Move: Learn the dance that is traditionally performed with this song. Look at pictures of European folk dancers to discover what positions and formations seem to be typical of their dances.

Formation: Partners stand side by side, girls on the right, holding crossed hands, in a double circle facing counterclockwise.

Verse: Measures 1–6   Walk with slow, sauntering steps.
Measures 7   Drop hands; turn in a circle away from partner.
Measures 8   Join inside hands with partner, "strike a pose" shouting "Hey!"

Refrain: Measures 1–4   Start with outside foot; heel goes forward, toe backward:

heel   toe   step   step   step   hop   step   step   step   hop   step   step   step   hop

Measures 5–8   Start with inside foot and repeat:

OLD TEXAS

Leisurely

Cowboy Song

2. They've plowed and fenced my cattle range,
   And the people there are all so strange.
3. I'll take my horse, I'll take my rope,
   And hit the trail upon a lope.
4. Say adios to the Alamo,
   And turn my head toward Mexico.

MELODY

Read: **Look at the KEY SIGNATURE. Can you tell me where the HOME TONE is? In what key is this song? Upon what scale is this melody based?** Remind the children of the discussion of key signatures in connection with "Lovely Evening." Help them realize that "F" is the answer to all three questions.

Play: Invite one child to locate the bells needed for the first motive: C-F-A-C. Ask him to play this pattern to establish a feeling for the tonality.

Sing: Challenge the class to sing the entire melody with numbers (syllables) or on "loo." Call attention to the sequential nature of the last two measures of each phrase.

RHYTHM

Read: Draw attention to the curved lines above the notes for "leave" and "old."

What is different about these two curved lines? (The first line connects two notes on the same space; the second connects notes on different lines and spaces.)

We call the first curved line a TIE. It tells us to hold the word "leave" through both notes. The second one is a SLUR. It tells us to sing the word "old" on two notes.

Observe the meter signature which tells that this song moves in twos and that the quarter note is the beat note. Emphasize the importance of feeling the ACCENTED BEAT and draw attention to the fact that each new motive starts on the last part of the first beat:

Play: Children may add a "clip-clop" pattern (♩ ♩ | ♩ ♩) on wood blocks or coconut shells to help underline the beat against the sustained tones (♩ | ♪) and the "off-beat" entrances (𝄾 ♪ ♪ ♩) of each new pattern.

HARMONY

Sing: When the children know the melody, they may divide into two groups, one group echoing the other.

I'm goin' to leave ———— old Tex-as now, ————   etc.

I'm goin' to leave ———————— old Tex-as now,

Draw attention to the effect created when the long tone in each motive is sustained against the moving pattern of the echo.

Another day, add the following chant as another experience in singing an independent melodic line:

Leave old Tex - as,   leav-ing old Tex - as

This sounds best if it is used only with the melody and the accompaniment.

EXPRESSION

Create: Plan an introduction and a coda for this song. The chant pattern may be used for this in different ways: sung, or played on wood blocks, coconut shells, and so forth.

Play: Start the introduction very softly, getting gradually louder (CRESCENDO) as the cowboy rides nearer. The coda should get gradually softer (DIMINUENDO) as he rides off into the distance.

BUFFALO GALS

Jauntily

American Folk Song

1. As I was walk-ing down the street, Down the street, down the street, A
2. I stopped her and we had some talk, Had some talk, had some talk, Her
3. I asked her if she'd be my wife, Be my wife, be my wife, Then

pret - ty gal I chanced to meet, And she was fair to view.
feet took up the whole side-walk, And left no room for me.
I'd be hap - py all my life, If she would mar - ry me.

Refrain

Oh, Buf - fa - lo gals, will you come out to - night, Will you

come out to - night, will you come out to - night, Oh, Buf - fa - lo gals, will you

come out to - night, And dance by the light of the moon?

MELODY

Play: **In what key is this song?** The children will know from looking at the key signature that it is in the key of F. They may learn to establish the TONALITY of the song by finding the home tone 1 (*do*) on the bells or piano and playing or singing 1–3–5 (*do-mi-so*) from that pitch.

Sing: Help the children establish the beginning interval of a sixth, 5–3 (*so-mi*), then encourage them to read the verse at sight with numbers and/or syllables.

FORM

Listen: The teacher sings the refrain. **Are there any similarities between the melody of the refrain and the melody of the verse?** The children may need some guidance to realize that the two melodies are similar: The melody of the refrain is a VARIATION of the verse.

RHYTHM

Read: **What is unusual about the rhythmic pattern for "come out tonight"?** (It moves in a short-long relationship—SYNCOPATION.) Practice clapping and chanting the words of this pattern.

HARMONY

Sing: The following chant may be used throughout the song:

Buf-fa-lo gals,   Buf-fa-lo gals,

Play: Add an autoharp accompaniment. **This song can be harmonized with just two chords. The key signature can help us to decide what chords to use.**

What key are we in? (F.) **We will need the F chord, then. Find this on the autoharp. We call this the I chord, also, because it is the chord that starts on the first step of the scale.**

The other chord we need for the accompaniment is named for a step in the scale that we use a great deal in our melodies, 5 or so. A chord that starts on this fifth step of the scale we call the V chord. By adding one more note to this chord, a V$_7$ may be formed. On the autoharp this will be the C$_7$ chord.

With which chord do you suppose we shall start? With which shall we end? Help the children to draw the conclusion that, just as most songs start and end on the home tone, so will the accompaniment start and end with the I chord.

As one child plays the accompaniment, the class may suggest when to change the chords.

WINDY NIGHTS

Mysteriously

Music by William S. Haynie
Words by Robert Louis Stevenson

1. When-ev-er the moon and stars are set, When-ev-er the wind is high,___
2. When-ev-er the trees are cry-ing-a-loud, And ships are tossed at sea,___

All night long in the dark and wet, A man goes rid-ing by.___
By on the high-way low and loud, By at the gal-lop goes he:___

Late in the night when the fires are out, Why does he gal-lop and
By at the gal-lop he goes, and then,

gal-lop a-bout? By he comes back at the gal-lop a-gain.

EXPRESSION

Create: Before studying this song, read this famous poem to the children. Discuss the the pictures suggested by the words. Invite the class to recite the poem as a "choral reading." Divide the children into three groups of high, medium, and low voices. Experiment with different sequences of voices to help convey the changing mood. The following might be appropriate:

Whenever the moon and stars are set,	*(medium voices)*
Whenever the wind is high,	*(low voices)*
All night long in the dark and wet,	*(medium voices)*
A man goes riding by.	*(low voices)*
Late in the night when the fires are out,	*(high voices)*
Why does he gallop and gallop about?	*(high voices)*
Whenever the trees are crying aloud,	*(medium voices)*
And ships are tossed at sea,	*(low voices)*
By on the highway, low and loud,	*(medium voices)*
By at the gallop goes he:	*(low voices)*
By at the gallop he goes, and then,	*(high voices)*
By he comes back at the gallop again.	*(high voices)*

At another time, ask the children to develop an expressive accompaniment for the poem, using classroom percussion instruments. It might be similar to the following:

Lines 1 and 2	sand blocks in a sustained rhythm, or lightly stroked autoharp strings
Lines 3 and 4	galloping rhythm on wood blocks or sticks
Lines 5 and 6	pattern on drum to suggest falling rain
Lines 7 and 8	same as lines 1 and 2, but louder; perhaps additional instruments
Lines 9 and 10	same as lines 3 and 4 with different instruments (coconut shells)
Lines 11 and 12	galloping rhythm continued with varying dynamics to match word meaning

RHYTHM

Read: Ask the children to read the poem aloud again and to tap the beat as they read. Try to determine a meter signature. **Does the rhythm of the poem seem to move in twos, threes, or some combination?** The children may offer a variety of answers. As these are accepted, experiment with notating the first phrase in different meters:

When the children have completed experimentation, ask them to look at the song in their books. Locate the meter signature and discuss its meaning. (The rhythm moves in sixes with the eighth note as the beat note.) Examine the notation, notice the groupings of even and uneven patterns: ♪♪♪ , ♩ ♪.

Read the poem aloud in the rhythm of the song for the children and ask them to tap the accented pulse as they listen. **How does the rhythm seem to move?** (In twos.) **Why did the composer use a meter signature suggesting six beats?** Help the children to feel the division of each strong beat into three weaker pulsations: ♩♩♩ ♩♩♩. **The meter is written in ⅝, but we only feel two strong beats. The real beat note of this song is therefore the dotted quarter note (♩.), but there is no way to write this in numbers in the signature. The composer uses the ⅝ meter signature, but organizes his rhythm patterns in two groups, or sets, within each measure to let us know that the strong first and fourth beats are the most important ones.**

Practice chanting the words in the rhythm of the melody as notated.

MELODY

Read: Examine the notation and discover that the melody for each four-measure phrase moves down by steps, except for the one skip at the beginning:

Play: Ask the children to use their knowledge of the letter names of the lines and spaces to locate the bells that are needed to play the melody. Remind the class to look at the key signature to discover what notes are flatted (B♭ and E♭). Ask one child to play the stepwise patterns resulting from playing the first note in each measure (ignore the repeated notes).

As the children listen carefully, help them realize that this melody is in MINOR. Play the complete G-minor scale for them and compare it with the sound of the G-major scale.

Sing: Sing the descending patterns on "loo" first, ignoring the repeated tones; then the entire melody in rhythm. Finally, sing the song with words.

THE TWITTERING MACHINE

Mercury Olympian Series, MG 50282A; RCA Victor, LSC 2879

From "Seven Studies on Themes of Paul Klee"
by Gunther Schuller

EXPRESSION

Listen: **Composers sometimes find ideas for their music in the works of other artists. This composition is based on a painting. Listen to the music and see if you can decide what the title of this painting might have been.**

Play the composition and invite the children to make suggestions; urge them to give musical reasons for their choices. After all have had an opportunity to propose possible titles for the composition, give the correct title, "The Twittering Machine." **Listen again to the music. What has the composer done to reflect the title of his music?**

Guide the children's attention to the "buzzing" pattern at the beginning of the composition which is suggestive of the reverberation of the machinery. Listen for the twittering sounds that are tossed around among the woodwinds; the piccolo has a major role in this section. The twittering remains at a high-pitch level most of the time. Near the middle of the composition, however, the machine seems to begin to "run down" as the twittering becomes lower and slower. Then there is another buzzing pattern which might suggest the "rewinding" of the machine, and the twittering takes up again. Not for long, however, because it stops rather abruptly with a final "buzz" and two rapid pulsations as if its gears got jammed.

Create: Postcard reproductions of the original painting may be obtained from the Museum of Modern Art, New York City. Before showing the children the Klee painting, invite them to draw or paint their own version of a twittering machine. Compare their efforts with that of Paul Klee.

If possible, obtain reproductions of some of the other paintings depicted by Schuller in his suite. These include *Antique Harmonies, Abstract Trio, Little Blue Devil, Arab Village, An Eerie Moment,* and *Pastorale* (subtitled *Rhythms*). Invite the children to select one of the paintings and create their own composition. Secure the complete recording of "Seven Studies on Themes of Paul Klee" and compare their compositions with those of Schuller.

Not only do musicians receive inspiration from painters; sometimes painters might get the idea for a painting from a favorite composition. Invite the children to choose a favorite piece of music and to draw or paint their reactions to it.

STYLE

Discuss: **This music was written by a contemporary American composer, Gunther Schuller. What in this music would help you to know that this music was written by a composer of today instead of a composer of long ago?** To help the children answer this question, compare the sounds of "The Twittering Machine" with the Second Movement from the "Surprise Symphony." Help them conclude that some clues might be:

1. There is no easily discernible melody that can be sung. One reason why there seems to be no melody is because the tones cover such a wide range.
2. The "melody" does not stay with one instrument, as it does in the Haydn composition, but is tossed about from one instrument to another.
3. Although there is a steady underlying pulse, the accents do not recur regularly as they do in traditional music.
4. There are many complex rhythms sounding simultaneously.
5. There is no feeling of "home tone" because all of the tones of the chromatic scale are used; each tone is as important as the other.

Paul Klee, the artist, lived in the early 1900s. Not only was he a fine artist who produced hundreds of paintings during his lifetime, he was also a fine musician. This may be the reason that many of his pictures were based on musical terms and forms, as reflected in the titles which use words such as *harmony, rhythm, trio,* and so on.

THE CUCKOO

Austrian Folk Song

Lively

1. Oh I went to Pe-ter's flow-ing spring Where the wa-ter's so
2. Aft-er East-er come sun-ny days That will melt all the
3. When I've mar-ried my maid-en fair, What then can I de-

good, And I heard there the cuck-oo As she sang from the wood.
snow; Then I'll mar-ry my maid-en fair, We'll be hap-py, I know.
sire? Oh, a home for her tend-ing And some wood for the fire.

Refrain

Ho-li-ah, ho-le-rah-hi-hi-ah, Ho-le-rah cuck-oo! Ho-le-rah-hi-hi-ah,

Ho-le-rah cuck-oo! Ho-le-rah-hi-hi-ah, Ho-le-rah cuck-oo! Ho-le-rah-hi-hi-ah-ho!

From *Songs of Many Nations,* Cooperative Recreation Service, Inc., Delaware, Ohio.

MELODY

Listen: **Can you decide where the HOME TONE in this song is? If you are not sure by looking at the key signature, perhaps you can tell by listening to the melody. What kind of feeling will you have when the melody arrives at the home tone?** (A feeling of rest, of completion.) Sing the song for the children and help them conclude that the melody comes to rest at the end of the verse and again at the end of the refrain, on G.

Read: Recall the discussion regarding scales and key signatures carried on during previous lessons. Ask the children to build the scale of G again, referring to the chart on page 147 as needed. **Which step of the scale had to be altered? (7.) Did it need to be raised or lowered?** (Raised.) **Recall the symbol ♯ (sharp) which indicates a raised tone.**

Ask the children to experiment with the bells and build scales on D and A. Fill in the chart.

D		E		F♯	G		A		B		C♯	D
A		B		C♯	D		E		F♯		G♯	A

Which step of the scale was always altered? (7.) **Keeping this in mind, could you find the home tone 1** (do) **if I gave you a key signature with sharps in it?**

Write several key signatures with sharps on the chalkboard. Help the children conclude that the last sharp to the right will always be the seventh step and that one must count down seven or up one to find the letter name of the home tone.

Sing: Return to "The Cuckoo" and scan the notation. Notice the similarity of the two phrases of the verse. Both begin with a pattern that centers around 1 3 5 (*do-mi-so*), but starting on 3 (*mi*). Establish the tonality by singing 1–3–5–3–1–5–1 (*do-mi-so-mi-do-so-do*) and ask the children to sing as much of the verse as possible on a neutral syllable. When problems arise, return to numbers (syllables) or play the bells to help solve them.

RHYTHM

Read: Look at the meter signature and observe that this song moves in threes and that the quarter note is the beat note. Notice that the song begins on the third beat, the UP beat. Also notice the "surprise" rhythm at the beginning of the second phrase (measure 4) where the accent is shifted because the longest note is now in the middle of the measure. Compare this with the beginning pattern of the first phrase.

Notice the FERMATAS and the alternating even and uneven rhythm patterns in the refrain which add interest to this song.

Move: The children may do these actions as they sing the refrain:

First measure: Tap knees rapidly.
Remaining measures: Beat 1 Slap knees.
                                 Beat 2 Clap hands.
                                 Beat 3 Snap fingers.

HARMONY

Play: Determine the name of the I and V_7 chords in the key of G (G and D_7); develop an autoharp accompaniment. Experiment with various rhythmic patterns for the chords; for example, on the verse one might stroke once to each measure (♩.), and on the refrain add interest by stroking twice (♩ ♩.).

SAN SERENI

Gaily   Spanish Singing Game

From *Music Across Our Country*, copyright 1959, Follett Publishing Company, Chicago, Ill. Used by permission.

2. We wash the clothes clean.   4. We build our new house.
3. We iron the clean clothes.   5. We weave serapes.

HARMONY

Read: Discover that this two-part song moves consistently in THIRDS, just as the children have added a second part in thirds to other songs. Observe also that the second phrase is a SEQUENCE to the first phrase, one step lower.

Sing: Sing the scale up and down in thirds to help the children become accustomed to the sound of the harmony:

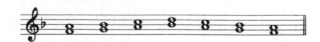

Divide the class into two groups and have them sing the first motive, "working like this," with words, both groups singing simultaneously. Discuss the problems encountered, then resing. Proceed to learn the entire song by this same process.

Play: Add an autoharp accompaniment. Help the children to recall that the I and V_7 chords are the most common chords. Determine from the key signature that in this song the I chord will be F and the V_7 chord will be C_7. Determine the chord sequence needed for the accompaniment by ear.

A simple piano accompaniment could be played by one child:

STYLE

Listen: **What people do you think first sang this song?** (Mexican or Spanish.) **What in the music makes you think so?** The children will, no doubt, say that it is the Spanish words that indicate the national origin. Explain that harmonizing a melody in thirds and using only the I and V_7 chords are very characteristic of music from countries with a Spanish heritage.

Move: Ask the children to clap the rhythm patterns that they associate with Latin-American music. Perhaps the most common patterns are ♩. ♪ ♫ ♩ and

♩ ♩ | ⅞ ♪♩

Play: Plan a percussion accompaniment for this song using rhythmic patterns such as those suggested, or other patterns taken from the song. Select instruments typical of Latin America such as maracas, claves, tambourines, and conga and bongo drums. (Any drum may be used to imitate the latter.) The autoharp may represent the guitar, which is another typical Latin-American instrument.

The following patterns may be used:

Sing: Learn the Spanish words to the song.

MARCHING TO PRETORIA

In march time

South African Folk Song

"Marching to Pretoria" from *Songs from the Veld* by Josef Marais, copyright 1942, by G. Schirmer, Inc., New York, N.Y. Used by permission.

RHYTHM

Read: Observe the METER SIGNATURE and determine that this song moves in twos. **What note will be the BEAT NOTE?** To help the children answer this question, sing the melody for them as they tap the beat lightly. **Can you find a place where the rhythm of the melody moves with the beat?** ("As we march a-.") **What kind of note is this?** (Half note.) Conclude that in this song the beat note is the half note and that the lower number "2" in the meter signature indicates this.

Scan the notation and look for difficult rhythm patterns. Review the function of the quarter rest (𝄽). Practice the uneven rhythm of the dotted quarter- and eighth-note pattern (𝅘𝅥. 𝅘𝅥𝅮) and the tied-note patterns in the refrain.

MELODY

Read: **This song will be easy to learn because the same melodic pattern is used over and over, each time sounding a step lower.**

So   we   are   all to-geth-er,   so   we   are   all to-geth-er

We call this a SEQUENCE. Can you find another melodic pattern that moves in a sequence? Help the children to find the sequence occurring on "Pretoria" in the refrain.

Sing: Encourage the children to sight-sing as much of the verse as possible with words. They should be able to do this with very little help.

HARMONY

Sing: Remind the children of the discovery they made about the pleasing sound of THIRDS when they were studying "Lovely Evening." **The refrain of this song can also be sung in thirds. Do you think you could add a second part below the melody all by yourselves?** Divide the class into two groups and give each group their starting tone, F♯ for the low part and A for the high part. Have both groups hum the starting tones together to establish the tonality; then invite them to sing as much of the refrain as they can. Point out to those singing the lower part that they will still be singing the familiar melody, but a third lower.

When the children sing the last four measures, they will sense that the thirds no longer sound "right." Help the lower part learn the following harmonization:

Pre - to - ri - a, hur - rah!_____

STYLE

Discuss: **This is a song from Southern Africa, sung by the miners as they marched to and from the diamond mines. These miners were Dutch, many of them far from home and families who had remained in Holland. So they did sing, eat, and live together.**

Some of the children may do research to discover where Pretoria is, how the Dutch came to be in South Africa, and so forth.

Sing: **What kind of song is this?** (A marching song and also a work song.)

How will you want to sing this song to reflect its style? Help the children to conclude that it should be sung vigorously with marked rhythm to help everyone stay "in step" as they march to work.

AU CLAIR DE LA LUNE

Andante   French Folk Song

1. Au clair de la lu - ne, Mon a - mi Pier - rot,
2. Au clair de la lu - ne, Pier - rot re - pon - dit;

Prê - te moi ta plu - me, Pour é - crire un mot.
Je n'ai pas de plu - me, Je suis dans mon lit.

Ma chan - delle est mor - te, Je n'ai plus de feu;
Va chez la voi - si - ne, Je crois qu'elle y est,

Ou - vre - moi ta por - te, Pour l'a - mour de Dieu.
Car dans la cui - si - ne On bat le bri - quet.

FORM

Read: Challenge the children to use all the knowledge they have gained about musical notation during the year to sing this song without assistance. Scan the notation and discover that the first, second, and fourth phrases are the same. Compare these phrases with the contrasting third phrase. Discuss the importance of contrast to create musical interest, and also the role of unity to hold the form together. Note that the melody at the beginning of the first phrase is ascending and that the melody in the third phrase is descending. Discover that the rhythm of the melody is the same in all four phrases.

Sing: Review the key signature and establish that G is 1 (*do*). Sing the first phrase with numbers (syllables), then sing the second and fourth phrases on a neutral syllable. Learn the third phrase in the same manner. When the children can sing the whole melody on a neutral syllable, sing it with words. The French words tell the following story:

> A friend asks Pierrot to lend him his pen to write a note by the moonlight, explaining that his candle has gone out and that he has no more fire. Pierrot answers that he has no pen and that he is in bed. He tells his friend to go to the neighbor, who must be in because a fire is being made in the kitchen.

HARMONY

Sing: Suggest to the children that a harmonizing part might be created for this song. Remind them of the songs they have harmonized by THIRDS. Let them try harmonizing the first phrase melody a third above. Then point out that the same tones can be sung an OCTAVE (eight steps) lower, making the two parts a SIXTH apart.

Discuss the fact that a sixth is an "upside down" third. Invite the children to sing as much as they can of the melody in sixths.

Listen: **Is there a place where the SIXTHS will not work?** (Third phrase.)

This time, as you sing the melody of the third phrase, I shall sing a harmonizing part. Listen as you sing and see if you can tell me how the part moved.

Read: Place the third phrase melody with its harmony on the board:

Discover that there are only two tones in the harmonizing part, D and C♯. Have the children practice singing D to C and D to C♯, listening carefully to the difference in the two patterns. Then sing the third phrase with both parts together on "loo" as they watch the notation.

EXPRESSION

Sing: **Because there is so much repetition in this song, we shall need to add interest by providing contrast in other ways.** Discuss ways that the DYNAMICS might be varied from phrase to phrase.

MISTER URIAN

Music by Ludwig van Beethoven
Words Translated by Ronald Duncan

ven - t'rous man, So tell us some more, Mis-ter U - ri - an.

From *Classical Songs for Children* by the Countess of Harewood
and Ronald Duncan. Copyright 1964 by Marion Harewood and
Ronald Duncan. Used by permission of Clarkson N. Potter, Inc.

STYLE

Discuss: This song was written by Ludwig van Beethoven, one of the most famous composers of all times. He lived in Germany in the late 1700s, about the time when our country was gaining its independence. Beethoven is most famous for the many symphonies that he composed, but he also wrote numerous songs.

Listen: **How might you have known by listening that this was a composed song rather than a folk song?** After the children have listened to the song, discuss the fact that this melody is more complex than are most melodies of folk songs. There are no repeated patterns in the melody, and the rhythm of the melody is made up of a variety of rhythmic patterns. The piano accompaniment is also more elaborate than one would expect to hear with an ordinary folk song.

RHYTHM

Read: Examine the rhythm of the melody and review the relationships of rhythmic patterns to the beat. **In this song the beat note is the quarter note. What rhythm pattern will move EVENLY with two notes to the beat?** (♪ ♪ .) **What rhythm pattern will move EVENLY with four notes to the beat?** (♬ ♬ .)

Divide the class into two groups. Ask one child to clap the beat while one group taps the eighth-note pattern and the second group taps the sixteenth-note pattern. Listen carefully to the 2 to 1 relationship of these patterns.

Find an UNEVEN rhythmic pattern that equals one beat. (♪. ♪ .) Review the function of the dot and note that the dotted eighth note should be three times as long as the sixteenth note. As one group taps the even sixteenth-note pattern, the second group may tap the uneven dotted eighth- and sixteenth- note pattern. They should be reminded that the dotted eighth note must be equal to three sixteenth notes.

Find an UNEVEN rhythmic pattern that equals two beats (♩. ♪). Follow the same procedure as above, listening carefully for the relationship of the dotted quarter note to the eighth note (3 to 1 relationship).

As one child taps the beat, ask the class to chant the words in rhythm, paying close attention to the alternating even and uneven rhythms.

MELODY

Listen: Ask the children to listen to the complete song. **What differences do you notice between the verse and the refrain?** Help the children decide that the verse is in MINOR, but the refrain is in MAJOR.

Play the A-minor and the A-major scales on the piano or bells. Discuss the differences in sound.

FORM

Read: Study the phrase structure of the song. Discover that no two phrases have the same melody. Examine the rhythm of each phrase and discover the similarities. Help the children to realize that similarities of rhythmic pattern help to give the melody UNITY, while the changing melodic patterns provide interesting VARIETY. Discuss the fact that a good song needs both; it must have contrast to maintain interest and it must also have repetition to give it unity (a feeling of "belonging together").

FRENCH CATHEDRALS

Traditional French Round

Or - lé - ans, Beau - gen - cy, No - tre Dame de Clé - ry, Ven - dô - me, Ven - dô - me.

MELODY

Read: Study the key signature and determine that this song is based on the E scale. Write the scale on the staff and review the pitch names.

Scan the notation and discover that only four tones are used in this melody. Notice the NATURAL symbol (♮) preceding D in the third measure. **This symbol tells us to sing D natural (D♮) instead of D sharp (D♯) as indicated by the key signature.**

Play: Locate the four bells: G♯-B-C♯-D. Give one bell to each of four children and ask them to play the melody. Establish a slow tempo so that they can play the eighth-note patterns accurately.

Sing: Ask the class to sing the melody on a neutral syllable, then with words. The words name four famous French Cathedrals.

HARMONY

Sing: Divide the class into three groups and sing the song as a three-part round. Draw attention to the bell-like sounds created by the combination of tones.

Play: An interesting study of contemporary harmony may be conducted by harmonizing the melody with parallel FOURTHS. Give one child bells D♯-F♯-G♯-A. Allow him to experiment until he can play the melody, beginning on F♯. When he can play this accurately, give a second child the bells used previously. Ask the two to play the melody simultaneously.

Notice the interesting HARMONY that is created by this arrangement. It gives an even stronger impression of the ringing of cathederal bells.

Discuss the fact that most of the harmonizing they have done was based on THIRDS. However, contemporary composers have been interested in creating harmony based on different kinds of intervals, such as FOURTHS and FIFTHS. At another time, the children might wish to experiment with playing the melody a fifth below the original; use bells C♯-E-F♯-G.

Sing: Some classes may be able to sing the song as a two-part round with the second part beginning a fourth or a fifth below the first part.

SECOND MOVEMENT, "THEME AND VARIATIONS"

Bowmar Orchestral Library, BOL #62   From Symphony in G major ("Surprise") by Joseph Haydn

FORM

Listen: Begin the study of this composition by listening to the main theme. **What tune does this melody remind you of?** ("Twinkle, Twinkle, Little Star.") **How is it different?** Guide the children to realize that the over-all contour of the two melodies are the same at the beginning, but the actual intervals are different.

How many phrases do you hear in the first part of this melody? (Two.) **If we call this two-phrase melody A, can you determine the design of the entire melody?** (AABB.)

Play: Invite some children to play the A section on the piano. It can also be played on the bells in the key of G, as follows:

Listen: When the children are familiar with the theme, play the entire composition. **Do you hear any other important melodies in this composition?** (No.)

Ask the children to listen especially to the A melody as the composition is replayed. **Is the A melody repeated exactly the same each time you hear it? Do you hear anything that is new?**

After the children have discussed the things they noticed, study each section of the composition. **This music is called a THEME AND VARIATIONS.** Help the children to develop a definition for this form: "There is one main melody which is called the *theme.* Each time the theme is repeated it is *varied* in some way."

Listen to each section and discover what variations the composer has made.

VARIATION I.   The melody is played by the lower strings. Violins, sometimes joined by flutes, play a COUNTERMELODY. This added melody might also be described as an OBLIGATO or DESCANT. **Listen carefully; can you hear the main melody as it continues beneath the added melody in the violins?**

VARIATION II.   The melody is now played in MINOR. To help the children sense the change in tonality, play and sing the first phrase in C major and then in C minor. (For minor change E to Eb.) Notice that the first phrase is played by the full orchestra and that the second phrase "answer" is played softly by the violins.

Can you hear the B melody during this section? (No.) Guide the children to realize that a new part has been added. At the end of this section the violins return to the familiar melody, leading to the next variation.

VARIATION III.   The theme returns to MAJOR, and the first statement of melody A is altered rhythmically. Notice that the melody played by the oboe now sounds with four tones to the beat instead of only two. During the repetition of A, listen for the new countermelody played by the flute and oboe. This countermelody is continued during the B phrases.

VARIATION IV.   This variation begins with a pompous statement of A for full orchestra. Listen for the new countermelody played by the violins. When A is repeated, new tones are added to the melody:

The single statement of melody B is varied in the same manner. A bridge made up of strong chords leads to a concluding statement of A for this section.

CLOSING SECTION (CODA).   After a few loud chords for the full orchestra, melody A is stated once more softly by the woodwinds and strings, bringing the movement to a quiet close.

CREATE A "THEME AND VARIATIONS"

After the children have studied Haydn's "Theme and Variations," ask them to summarize the different ways he varied the theme in this composition:

1. He added a countermelody.
2. He changed the tonality from major to minor.
3. He altered the rhythm of the melody.
4. He added tones to the melodic line.
5. He used a variety of instruments.
6. He made frequent changes in dynamics.

Ask the children to think of other ways that the theme might be altered. They might suggest such things as:

1. Change the meter from twos to threes.
2. Change the harmony.
3. Change the key (place melody higher or lower).

When children have thought of as many ways as possible to vary a theme, invite them to create their own "theme and variations." Select a familiar melody, such as "Go Tell Aunt Rhodie," (page 94) for the theme.

Divide the class into small groups and assign each group a different kind of variation to develop on the agreed-upon melody. Remind the children that they must either notate their "variation" or practice it carefully enough so that they can perform it for the class. Some possible variations might be the following:

1. Add a countermelody. To do this, first determine the harmony for each measure of the melody. The harmony for "Go Tell Aunt Rhodie" is as follows for the first phrase: C–C–G_7–C–. Choose tones from the appropriate chord in each measure to create the new melody. It should include tones that are higher than the main melody:

2. Alter the rhythm of the melody. When changing the rhythm, remind the children that the patterns for each measure must include the same number of beats:

3. Change the tonality from C major to C minor. This can be done easily by substituting E♭ for E in the melody.

4. Add new tones to the melodic line:

5. Change the meter:

6. Change the harmony. Try the following chord sequence for the entire melody: A–A–D–A–G–A–D–A.

When the different groups have planned their variations, listen to each. Decide on an appropriate sequence for the variations and perform them as a complete composition, beginning with the class singing the song as the main theme.

LULLABY

Tranquillo

Johannes Brahms

STYLE

Discuss: We have sung many lullabies. Some of these songs were made up by mothers as they sang to their babies, but we have no idea who sang them first. We think of these songs as belonging to our FOLK SONGS, songs that have been transmitted from generation to generation without having been written down by any specific person.

This song, "Lullaby," might be called a combination folk and composed song, because it was "arranged" by a composer, Johannes Brahms, who based it on an old Austrian folk melody.

Brahms was a great German composer who wrote his greatest music in the late 1800's, about the time our country was expanding westward. He wrote many beautiful songs such as this lullaby, as well as many lovely compositions for various instruments.

FORM

Listen: The children listen as the teacher sings or plays a recording of this song. **How many phrases does this song have?** (Four.)

Guide the children to observe that none of these phrases is alike, but that the first and third phrases end on the fifth tone of the scale (B♭), while the second and fourth phrases end on the first tone (E♭). **Each pair of phrases, first-second and third-fourth, seems to make a complete unit. These units we call PERIODS. A song that is made up of two periods is called a TWO-PART SONG FORM.**

RHYTHM

Read: This song may present some rhythmic problems, especially the first phrase. Chant the words of this phrase while watching the notation. In particular, draw the children's attention to the rhythmic pattern of the first full measure.

HARMONY

Play: Transpose the song to the key of C. Have the children help decide what chords to use. They will no doubt suggest the I (C) and V₇ (G₇) chords. **At the beginning of the third phrase we must use a new chord, the IV chord. What will be the letter name for the IV chord?** The children should reason, based on their experience with the I and V₇ chords, that this will be the F chord.

Sing: Add the following DESCANT after the song is thoroughly familiar:

Guiding Musical Growth
in the **Fifth Grade**

	Listening	Singing	Playing
SKILL	Stress the importance of developing habits of attentive and discriminating listening.	Strive for continual improvement in tone quality and diction.	Work for increased facility in autoharp and piano chording. Provide opportunities to gain skill in playing diverse instruments (Latin-American, Hawaiian, and so on).
CONCEPTS *Melody*	Help the children to distinguish melodic variations (sequence, and so forth). Stress the awareness of differences in major, minor, and pentatonic scale structures. Strive for recognition of common intervals.	Encourage independent reproduction of new songs with numbers and/or syllables in major and minor keys.	Encourage independent reproduction of simple melodies on bells, piano, and recorder-type instruments from notation as well as by ear. Explore major, minor, and pentatonic scale structures on bells and piano.
Rhythm	Strive for the awareness of more extended and complex rhythmic relationships.	Stress the accurate reproduction of all rhythmic patterns. Strive for rhythmic flow in singing, reflecting the ongoingness of the rhythmic movement.	Encourage the improvisation of extended rhythmic patterns on a variety of percussion instruments. Stress the independent maintenance of rhythmic patterns.
Harmony	Work for a consciousness of common harmonic intervals (thirds, sixths, and octaves). Help the children to discriminate between qualities of I, IV, and V_7 chords in major and minor tonalities.	Include a variety of two-part songs, canons, and descants to help the children become increasingly independent in reproducing multiple sounds. Help the children to develop an awareness of chord progressions through vocal chording (roots or triads).	Extend chording experiences with the autoharp to include accompaniments to songs in minor keys. Encourage the children to establish tonality on the bells, piano, and autoharp.
Form	Provide many experiences for the children to become aware of the form structures of rondo, theme and variations, and sonata-allegro in terms of repeated and contrasting sections.	Encourage the children to reflect an understanding of phrase structure in singing.	Plan accompaniments that reveal an awareness of repetition, contrast, and variation.
Expression	Help the children become aware of ways in which tempo and dynamics contribute to musical expressiveness. Draw attention to melodic, rhythmic, and harmonic organization as contributing to expressiveness. Stress the contributions that various instrumental tone colors make to expressiveness.	Help the children to achieve more expressive singing through varying tone qualities, dynamics, and tempos (crescendo and ritardando.)	Motivate the children to apply their understanding of the expressive value of rhythmic, melodic, and harmonic organization in their playing. Encourage the children to consider variations in dynamics and tempos in planning accompaniments and performing melodies.
Style	Help the children to become sensitive to elements that characterize the music of different composers and cultures.		Foster a consciousness of style by planning accompaniments based on characteristic patterns to be played on representative instruments.

Moving	Creating	Reading
Provide opportunities for attaining skill in a variety of formalized dance steps.	Help the children to develop skill in composing instrumental as well as vocal compositions.	Strive for skill in independent reproduction of songs from notation vocally and instrumentally. Provide opportunities for acquiring ability to notate original compositions.
Suggest that the children adapt interpretive movement to melodic contour.	Motivate the composition of melodies showing an awareness of melodic variation (sequence, and so forth). Provide experiences in composing melodies in various tonalities.	Encourage independent reproduction of all common tonal patterns, including chromatics, from notation. Apply an understanding of scale structure to the interpretation of the score. Guide the children to interpret key signatures to determine major and minor tonalities.
Guide the children to reveal an awareness of rhythmic nuance in interpretive dances.	Stimulate interest in the use of varied and complex rhythmic patterns in individual composition.	Help the children to use a knowledge of rhythmic relationships in reproducing complex rhythmic patterns from notation. Extend the children's experiences in the interpretation of a variety of meter signatures.
Plan dance movements to reflect an awareness of countermelodies and cadential progressions.	Help the children to experiment with multiple sounds in their compositions. Involve the children in creating accompaniments as a means of expanding sensitivity to different chord qualities.	Provide many experiences in reproducing multiple sounds from notation vocally and instrumentally. Encourage the independent reading of chord symbols in playing accompaniments.
Encourage the children to develop dances that reveal an increasing sensitivity to repetition, contrast, and variation. Draw attention to the relation between musical form and dance form in folk dances.	Foster an awareness of formal structure by composing compositions in specific forms (rondo, theme and variation).	Stress the importance of recognizing repetition, contrast, and variation in the notation as an aid in score-reading.
Stimulate the development of dances revealing increasing sensitivity to the expressive possibilities of rhythmic, melodic, and harmonic organization.	Encourage the children to consider ways of organizing rhythm, melody, and harmony to achieve expressiveness in their own compositions.	Stress the independent interpretation of expressive markings: dynamics, tempo, and so forth.
Develop a sensitivity to musical style through learning characteristic dances.	Provide opportunities for composing in various styles to increase sensitivity to authentic stylistic characteristics.	

MORNING COMES EARLY

Slovak Folk Song
Words Adapted

1. Morn - ing comes ear - ly, the dew so bright,
2. Lis - ten my com - rade: when work seems long,

Come with me, lad - die, in day's first light.
Light - en each mo - ment with mer - ry song.

Dawn o - ver - takes me, morn - ing a - wakes me,
Wel - come to - mor - row, wait not for sor - row,

To the green mead - ows the herd I lead.
Mu - sic and laugh - ter are all we need!

RHYTHM

Read: Use this song as an opportunity to review with the children some of the musical understandings they have acquired in previous grades. Help them to develop a list of steps to be followed whenever they wish to learn a new song from notation.

As you study the rhythm of a song, what information do you look for first?
Conclude that one must first decide how the rhythm will move (in twos,

threes, or a combination) by observing the meter signature and scanning the notation. **What can you learn by studying the meter signature?** (How the rhythm will move and the name of the note that will sound with the beat.) Decide that this song will move in twos with the quarter note sounding as the beat note.

Are you ready to tap the rhythm of this song? Some children may assume that they are; through trial and error, help them decide that they should first scan the notation to determine the relation of the RHYTHM OF THE MELODY to the RHYTHM OF THE BEAT. Discover measures in which the rhythm of the melody sounds with the beat. Look for rhythm patterns that are repeated and for unusual patterns that may be difficult.

As the children scan the notation, help them to observe that the rhythm of the melody is the same in the first, second, and fourth phrases, and that the third phrase is made up of two identical two-measure patterns.

If the children do not mention the recurrent syncopated pattern (♪♩ ♪), draw their attention to it. Notice that the second tone is longer than the first, and that this is somewhat unusual. Because of its extra length, this tone seems more important than the first and therefore it is ACCENTED more strongly than the first tone. **When an accented tone occurs after the beat, we say that the rhythm is SYNCOPATED. One way to create syncopation is to use patterns that sound SHORT-LONG, with the long tone occurring after the beat.**

Tap measures one and two and compare the different patterns. Discuss the added interest created by shifting the accent in the second measure.

Play: **Are we now ready to tap the rhythm of this song?** (Yes.) **Before we begin, what must we do?** (Determine the tempo of the beat.) Ask one child to establish the beat on the drum, not too fast. While he plays, ask the other children to tap the rhythm of the melody on rhythm sticks.

MELODY

Read: **Now that we have determined the rhythm of the song, let us study the melody. What do we need to discover first when learning a new melody?** Guide the children to conclude that they must first determine the TONALITY, that is, they must locate the HOME TONE (1 or *do*). **How might you do this?** Through discussion, agree that one must observe the KEY SIGNATURE and also scan the notation to discover typical patterns. Observe that in this song there is no key signature, indicating that this melody is in the KEY OF C and that the home tone is C. Recall that most melodies they have studied center around 1–3–5 (*do-mi-so*). Scan the notation and discover that this melody does indeed center around C–E–G.

Invite one child to locate the bells needed for the C scale. As he locates the bells, put the notation on the chalkboard:

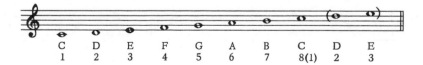

Compare the tones he has selected with the song notation. **Are all these tones used in our song?** (Yes.) **Are any additional tones used?** Some children may feel that high D (fourth line) and E (fifth space) are "additional tones." Help them realize that a scale may continue over several octaves; as long as the letter names of the tones remain the same, they still belong to the scale.

Return to the song and agree that the next step is to scan the notation to discover familiar patterns that will serve as guides when learning the song. Notice that the melody moves primarily by steps with a few skips of a third. Compare the melody of the first two phrases; help the children realize that they are identical, except that the second phrase begins five steps higher.

Sing: Challenge the children to sing the entire melody with numbers (syllables). Establish the tonality by singing 1–3–5–3–1 (*do-mi-so-mi-do*) and choose a comfortable tempo for the beat. When problems arise, ask one child to play the difficult passage on the bells; then sing the same with numbers (syllables).

DOWN IN THE VALLEY

STYLE

Read: The children will know different versions of this song. Study the notation to see if it is the same tune as the ones they already know.

Why, do you suppose, are there different tunes for the same song? Help the children to realize that since folk songs were transmitted by "ear" rather than by being written down, there will undoubtedly be many versions of the same song.

Can we say that one tune is right and another wrong? (No, because we do not know the original version.)

The children might look through various folk song collections to find different versions of this song, or of other folk songs.

Play: As nearly as we know, this song originated in the Southern mountains. Folk singers in that part of the country often accompany themselves on guitars or banjos. Plan an appropriate accompaniment on the autoharp.

RHYTHM

Read: Review the steps discussed in "Morning Comes Early." **What is the meter signature for this song?** (9/8.) **How many beats will there be in each measure?** (Nine.) **Will we actually "feel" nine beats?**

Move: To help decide the last question, suggest that the children clap lightly as they sing. Some children will clap each beat: ♪♪♪ ♪♪♪ ♪♪♪ ; others will undoubtedly clap ♩. ♩. ♩. . Have the children try clapping both patterns. They will probably conclude that clapping "threes" rather than "nines" will be easier.

The BEAT NOTE in this song will be the dotted quarter note (♩.) rather than the eighth note (♪). Remind the children that this is similar to some of the songs written in 6/8 meter, where the beat was moving in twos rather than sixes.

HARMONY

Listen: Determine the autoharp accompaniment by ear.

When we say that we are going to use the I CHORD or V₇ CHORD, what do we mean? How are these chords different?

The children are already familiar with the different QUALITIES of these two chords, but they do not know the reasons for this difference. To help them decide, strum the I chord very slowly on the autoharp, asking the children to hum any tone they hear. As they hum, place these tones on the staff. Continue until they have reproduced all the tones within the chord. Follow the same procedure with the V₇ chord.

I chord   V₇ chord

Read: **Look at the notation for the I chord. How many tones with different letter names did you find?** (Three.)

How far apart are the three tones from each other? (A third.) **Where else have we heard thirds?** (In two-part songs.)

When we combine two thirds we have a CHORD. Why, do you suppose, do we call this chord the I chord? (Because the bottom tone is the first step of the scale.)

What is different about the V$_7$ chord? Help the children to discover that it starts on the fifth tone of the scale and that it has four tones, a third apart, rather than three. **We call this a "7" chord because the fourth tone is seven steps above the first tone. If there were only three tones, we would call it a V chord.**

Can you decide what notes would be included in the IV chord? (B flat, D, F.)

As the children write the I, IV, and V$_7$ chords in other keys, guide them to discover that if one begins on a line, then the other tones will be on lines; and that if one begins on a space, the other tones will also be on spaces.

Sing: **If these chords make a pleasing accompaniment, then any single tone from them should also sound "right" when sung or played against the melody.** Using the chord progression established earlier (under *Listen*), encourage the children to experiment with various tones from the two chords. Guide them to realize that the CHORD ROOTS (F and C) will make a pleasing accompaniment when sung or played in the proper sequence.

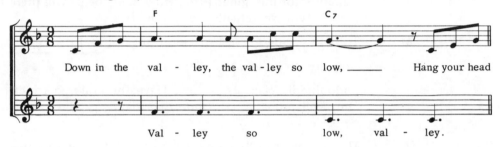

The chords can also be sung as well as played. Divide the class into three groups, each one humming a different note of the chord. Introduce the chord changes I to V$_7$ before attempting to accompany the song. Then choose a few children to sing the melody while the rest of the class provides the chordal accompaniment by humming or singing on a neutral syllable such as "ooh."

Would there be one single tone that one might sing throughout the entire song? Help the children to see that the tone C belongs to both chords and that this tone could be used to accompany the entire song. Divide the class into two groups, one singing the melody, the other humming C throughout.

Play: Extend the children's experience with chord tones by having them play the F and C$_7$ chordal accompaniment on the bells or the piano.

The tones of each chord may be played simultaneously on the bells. Distribute the bells needed between two groups of children, one for the I chord and one for the V$_7$ chord. Have them sustain each chord by playing with light, rapid taps on the bells in no regular rhythmic pattern.

The bells might also be played in an ARPEGGIO fashion, as could the piano:

IFCA'S CASTLE

Smoothly   Round

A - bove the plain of gold and green, A young boy's head is

plain - ly seen.   A hu - ya, hu - ya, hu - ya - ya, Swift - ly flow - ing

riv - er,   A hu - ya, hu - ya, hu - ya - ya, Swift - ly flow - ing riv - er.

MELODY

Read: Scan the notation, noticing the sequential movement of the melody in the first two phrases:

Notice also that the last two phrases are based on the same tonal pattern as the first phrase:

Sing: Establish the tonality by singing the major scale and then the I-chord pattern, 1-3-5-3-1-5-1 (*do-mi-so-mi-do-so-do*.) Sight-sing the song with words.

Play: Provide opportunities for individual children to play this melody on the bells and the piano, using the notation as well as playing by ear.

HARMONY

Sing: This round can be sung in as many as eight parts. Begin with two or four groups and add others as the children become increasingly independent in reproducing the melody accurately.

Play: Play the melody as a round between the bells and the piano. It might also be performed as a round between voices and instruments in a variety of combinations.

Create: Every two measures of this song can be harmonized with the following chord progression: I-V$_7$-I-I. Help the children to develop a chant, based on these chords, to sing or play with this melody. First select a word pattern that will fit the two-measure pattern, such as "huya, huya, huya ya!" or "river flowing." Then select tones from the appropriate chords for each beat. Two suitable patterns might be the following:

Huy - a, huy - a, huy - a ya!   Ri - ver flow - ing.

THIS LAND IS YOUR LAND

EXPRESSION

Listen: **Most of the songs we learn to sing in class are folk songs. This song is not a folk song, for we know the name of the man who wrote it. Yet, if one were to hear this song for the first time, he might call it a folk song. Listen and see if you can think of some reasons why it gives this impression.**

Decide that the song has a folklike character: The melody is simple and repetitious, as is the rhythmic pattern, and it can be harmonized with the I, IV, and V$_7$ chords, which is true of most American folk songs.

Sing: **As you sing, try to express the pride and wonder you might feel if you were standing beneath a giant California redwood or if you were gazing up at a mighty skyscraper in New York City. Sing with assurance, in a good brisk rhythm, carrying each phrase through without a break.**

MELODY

Read: Review the steps discussed when learning the melody of "Morning Comes Early." As the children determine the key (F) from the key signature and scan the notation, draw attention to the melody of the first phrase. Discover that it is made up of four MOTIVES that are of a sequential nature, making the melody easy to learn:

Notice that each phrase is made up of four of these MOTIVES.

Sing: Sing the refrain with numbers (syllables) if needed, then with words. Sight-sing the verse with words, since the melody is the same as the refrain.

FORM

Read: **How many phrases are there in the verse?** (Two.) **How do they compare?** (They are similar: A, A'.)

What is the relationship of the verse to the refrain? (Identical.)

As there is only one basic musical idea stated in this song, we call this a ONE-PART SONG FORM.

Discuss: **Why is it important to recognize the form of a song? How can it help us to know that the verse of this song is made up of motives that are sequential, that the two phrases are similar, and that the refrain is an exact repetition of the verse?**

Help the children to conclude that if we recognize the sequential nature of the melody, we can use the knowledge of the sound of the first motive in learning the others; that knowing that the two phrases are similar will make the learning of the second phrase easier; and that if we are aware that the verse and refrain are the same, we can use the same chord progressions to accompany both.

RHYTHM

Read: **Do you see anything unusual about the rhythmic notation?** (The meter signature.) **This sign ₵ is called** ALLA BREVE **and indicates that there should be two beats to each measure and that the** BEAT NOTE **is a half note. Another way of writing this signature would be 2/2.**

Call attention to the TIES at the end of each motive and to the syncopated pattern on "This land was."

Move: Stepping about the room as though "Walking the ribbon highway" while singing will help the children become sensitive to the relationship of beat to rhythmic pattern and to the necessity of holding the tied tones *through* the accented beat of the next measure.

HARMONY

Play: In playing the autoharp accompaniment from the notation, try strumming once or twice to each measure; decide which pattern is most suitable to the rhythmic movement of this song.

Some children may be able to play an accompaniment on the piano. Determine which tones are needed for the I, IV, and V_7 chords, and write them on the chalkboard.

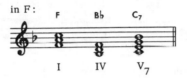

Show the children how these tones can be arranged so that it will be easy to move from one chord to the next with very little shifting of the hand position.

Sing: Learn the harmonizing part as written in the score. Later, add a third part by having one group sing the chord roots.

SIMPLE GIFTS

Moderato

Shaker Song

'Tis the gift to be sim - ple, 'tis the gift to be free, 'Tis the gift to come down where you ought to be, And when we find our- selves in the place just right, 'Twill be in the val - ley of love and de - light. When true sim - pli - ci - ty is gained, To bow and to bend we shan't be a - shamed, To turn, turn will be our de - light, Till by turn - ing, turn - ing we come round right.

STYLE

Discuss: This is a song of the American Shakers, a religious group that lived in New England about the time of the American Revolution. Music, both song and dance, was an important part of the Shaker religious service. The words "bow," "bend," and "turn" may possibly refer to the dancing that often took place during these services.

"Simple Gifts" is one of the most famous of the Shaker hymns. The "simplicity" it describes was one of the most important Shaker virtues.

Shaker songs were often created spontaneously by an individual, sometimes during a service. Others would then learn the song and teach it to friends and neighbors, thus making it part of the community repertoire.

Shaker hymns are somewhat different from other hymns in that:

1. The texts do not usually follow a stanza form.

2. Their tempos are generally quite spirited.

3. Harmony is never used, nor are instruments used for accompaniments.

4. The rhythms are very free, with little repetition of pattern.

5. The melodies do not follow the typical repetitious pattern found in most folk hymns.

Listen: Listen to this Shaker hymn and decide which of the above characteristics can be found. (All of them.)

RHYTHM

Read: Observe the notation carefully and notice the rhythmic changes from one pattern to another. None of the rhythmic patterns is difficult, but the sequence is unpredictable. Chanting the words will help to establish the rhythm, because it follows the natural word rhythm in most instances.

MELODY

Read: Ask the children to scan the score. Guide them to observe the absence of exact repetition or sequence in the melody. Establish tonality and sing with numbers (syllables).

Sing: This melody is appealing and haunting. Sing it simply as the Shakers might have done. Notice that each phrase seems to grow from the preceding one, although there is no repetition in this melody.

THEME AND VARIATIONS ON "SIMPLE GIFTS"

Bowmar Orchestral Library, BOL #65   From "Appalachian Spring" by Aaron Copland

FORM

Listen: When the children are familiar with the song "Simple Gifts," play these variations written by the American composer Aaron Copland. The music is an excerpt from a ballet titled *Appalachian Spring*.

Review what the children know about the form of theme and variations. Guide them to discuss the differences they hear in each variation of "Simple Gifts."

INTRODUCTION: Only the first section of the melody is heard. It is played by the strings as a canon.

THEME: The theme is stated by the clarinets. Suggest that the children follow the melodic notation in their books and discuss any differences they notice in the melody. Listen for the bridge passage that announces the beginning of the first variation.

VARIATION I. This variation is played by the OBOE with other woodwinds echoing the melody at a lower pitch. Notice the quick tempo and the addition of tones to the melodic line.

VARIATION II. The cellos announce the theme in a more dignified mood. Violins enter, repeating the melody to create a canon (round) with the cellos. Once more a bridge passage made up of melodic fragments prepares for the next variation.

VARIATION III. The trumpets and trombones play a duet in martial style with separated tones and strongly accented rhythm.

VARIATION IV. The woodwinds take up the theme for the final statement. Notice that only the first section of the melody is played this time.

THE PEDDLER

Reprinted from *Time for Music*, by Ehret, Barr, and Blair. Copyright 1959, Prentice-Hall, Inc., Englewood Cliffs, N.J.

MELODY

Listen: **Is this song in MAJOR or MINOR?** (Minor.) **What do we mean when we say that a song is in minor rather than major?**

Discuss: **Look at the key signature; it has one sharp (F sharp), which would indicate that this song is in G major.**

What tones would we use if this song were in G major? As the children construct the scale on the bells, the teacher places the G-major scale on the chalkboard. (Take this opportunity to review the major scale pattern.)

Look at the notation for the verse. Are there any tones we need that we do not have in the scale on the board? (The first line E and first space F sharp.) The teacher adds these tones, omitting the high F sharp and G.

The name of this scale is E minor because it begins on E.

Where does the E-minor scale sound different from G major?

Play 1–2–3 of both scales, discovering the difference between steps 2 and 3.

What kind of step do you hear between 2 and 3 in the minor scale? (A half step.) **In the major scale?** (A whole step.)

Find other places where the two scales differ. The children discover that the natural minor scale has a half step between 5 and 6, and a whole step between 7 and 8.

The pattern for this minor scale, then, is:

1	–	2	⌣	3	–	4	–	5	⌣	6	–	7	–	8
whole step		half step		whole step		whole step		half step		whole step		whole step		

Read: Look at the notation of the song and discover that the melody constantly returns to E rather than G. This is another indication that the song is in E minor and not in G major.

A key signature of one sharp (F sharp), therefore, may indicate that the song can be either in G major or in E minor.

Play: Build other minor scales with the bells. Use the ear and knowledge of the minor scale pattern to check the accuracy. Compare with major scales starting on the same tone.

Sing: Sing the major and minor scales starting from the same tone. (The teacher must decide whether to use numbers 1–8 for the minor scale or the syllables *la-la.*)

Sing 1–3–5 in major (*do-mi-so*) and in minor (*la-do-mi*).

Sing the song with words, using an awareness of the sound of the minor scale to help in reading the melody at sight.

HARMONY

Listen: The teacher plays the I, IV, and V₇ chords in E minor, while the children listen.

Which of these chords are minor, and which are major, in quality? (I and IV are minor; V₇ is major.)

To help the children understand the differences between MAJOR and MINOR chords, place the chromatic bells in order in a single line:

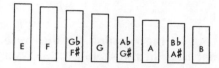

Help a child to locate the tones needed for the E-MAJOR chord, E–G♯–B. Count the bells from E to G♯ (5), then count those from G♯ to B (4).

Although we say that both skips, E to G♯ and G♯ to B, are a THIRD, we can see that one third is "bigger" than the other. Can you hear the difference? Experiment with playing "big" and "little" thirds, asking the children to decide what they hear.

Next, locate the bells needed for the E-MINOR chord, E–G–B, and count the bells between E and G (4) and between G and B (5). Notice that the intervals are now reversed with the "little" interval on the bottom.

When the "big" third is lowest, we say that the chord is MAJOR; when the "little" third is lowest, we say that the chord is MINOR.

Read: **In order to play the accompaniment for this song on the autoharp, we must change the key to D minor. We say that the song is TRANSPOSED from E minor to D minor.**

Help the children to interpret the Roman numerals used as chord designations in the score. **What will be the letter names for the I, IV, and V₇ chords in D minor?** Guide the children to conclude that the I will be Dm (the name of the key), the IV will be Gm (four steps above I), and the V₇ will be A₇ (five steps above I).

Play: As the children experiment with the accompaniment to this song, note that it is unusual in that it begins with the V₇ chord rather than I.

The following pattern may be played on the autoharp imitating a Russian *balalaika*. Children who may be learning to play a string instrument might play this pattern on their instrument to accompany the singing. Try both bowing and plucking, deciding which is most pleasing.

STYLE

Discuss: This is a Russian folk song. After studying this song and listening to others, try to list some characteristics of Russian music.

1. Many of the songs seem to be in the minor.
2. The melodies move in descending patterns.
3. Intervals of fourths and fifths are common in the melodies.
4. A characteristic rhythmic pattern is "short-short-long."
5. The songs are strongly rhythmic, moving in a variety of accent groupings, some of which may be unusual, such as 2–3 or 3–2.
6. Harmonizing voices move as countermelody rather than simultaneously.
7. Typical instruments are the balalaika, the bagpipe, the hunting horn, the flute, the tambourine (*buben*), drums, and bells.

SHALOM CHAVERIM[1]

Israeli Round

MELODY

Read: Ask the children to determine the TONALITY of this song, reminding them that one must look at both the key signature and the melodic line to decide whether it is major or minor. Decide that it is D minor rather than F major because the melody centers around D and the other tones of the D-minor I chord, F and A.

Sing: Establish a feeling for tonality by singing 1–3–5–3–1 (*la-do-mi-do-la*). Then sing the song at sight, keeping these tones in mind as "anchors" to which the melody is hitched.

HARMONY

Sing: This is a beautiful round when sung in two or three parts. For added effectiveness the following ending might be used:

EXPRESSION

Sing: This song is a "benediction," a well-wishing song that one might use in taking leave of one's friends. "Shalom" (*shah-lōm'*) means peace; "chaverim" (*khah-vay-reem'*) means friends; and "lehitraot" (*lay-heet'-rah-ot*) means "till we meet again." **Sing this song in a manner that communicates this mood: "Peace to you, friend, until we meet again."**

Listen: **Every song, to be truly satisfying, must have a CLIMAX, a point of interest toward which the melody seems to move.**

Listen and see if you can find the climax in this song. (In the third measure.) **Can you decide how the music builds up this climax?** (The first melodic motive is repeated at a higher pitch in the second measure, building up a feeling of excitement as it reaches the third measure, where the melodic rhythm takes on a different character with the long tones on "Shalom.")

Sing: In singing this song, add to the climactic effect by making a CRESCENDO on the first phrase and a DIMINUENDO on the last phrase.

---

[1] Pronounced shah-lōm' kha-vay-reem'

THE LITTLE BLACK TRAIN

Collected, adapted, and arranged by John A. and Alan Lomax. Copyright 1941 by John A. Lomax in *Our Singing Country*. Copyright assigned 1957, Ludlow Music, Inc., New York, N.Y. Used by permission.

MELODY

Read: Ask the children to determine the key of this song. They will probably say F major, because the key signature has one flat. Scan the notation and locate the different pitches that are used. Place the notes on a staff, beginning with F, which seems to act as the "home tone."

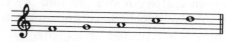

Discuss the fact that only five different pitch names are used. Determine the relationship between these tones:

1 whole step	2 whole step	3 whole-half steps	4	5 whole step

Do you remember what we call a scale with only five tones? (PENTATONIC scale.) Compare the pattern of this scale with that of the MAJOR scale. Notice that there are no half steps between any of the tones in the pentatonic scale.

Pentatonic scales differ from major and minor scales in that they seem to lack a definite "home tone." Many different pentatonic scales can be developed, each with its own pattern of half, whole, and whole-half step intervals between tones.

Create: Encourage the children to invent their own pentatonic scales, starting on any tone and using any sequence of intervals they wish. Then invite them to improvise melodies based on their new scales.

STYLE

Discuss: **What kind of song do you think this is?** Some children may suggest that it is a Negro spiritual. **What makes you think so?** (The words, the syncopated rhythms, the simple diatonic melody.)

Explain that this is a type of song that in folk song collections is described as a "white" spiritual. It is an example of how the customs of people living together over a long period of time become so nearly alike that it is hard to decide to whom they belong.

We discovered that this song is based on the pentatonic scale. Many American Indian and Oriental songs are also based on pentatonic scales. Why didn't you think that this was a song sung by one of those groups? Help the children realize that the arrangement of tones in this melody is different from the way Indian or Oriental melodies would be organized. The rhythm patterns and harmony are also different.

Conclude that musical STYLE is caused by a particular *combination* of several elements of music, and that no *single* element can determine style.

Listen: To help clarify the discussion given above, play the following melodic patterns, which are based on the same tones used in "The Little Black Train." **Can you tell where these tunes might come from?**

("Chinese")

("Indian")

EXPRESSION

Create: Plan an introduction, a coda, and an accompaniment to suggest the idea of a train coming or going; consider changes of tempo and dynamics as means of making the "sound effects" more realistic.

FAREWELL, MY OWN TRUE LOVE*

American Folk Song
Collected by William S. Haynie

Pensively

Fare - well, my own true love, Fare - well a lit - tle while, I'm goin' a - way but I'll come a - gain, If I go ten thou - sand mile.

2. Ten thousand mile, my love,
Through England, France and Spain;
My roving mind shall never rest
Till I see your face again.

3. Oh, don't you see that dove
That flies from vine to vine,
A-mourning for his own true love,
Just as I will mourn for mine.

MELODY

Listen: Sing the complete song with accompaniment for the children, or play the recording. After discussing the mood of the song, ask the children to determine its tonality.

Read: To help them in their decision, remind the class that one determines tonality by studying the key signature *and* by looking for tonal patterns that center around the I chord of the key. The children may suggest that the key signature indicates that this song is either in F major or D minor. **What tones are included in the I chord in F major?** (F-A-C.) **What tones are included in the I chord in D minor?** (D-F-A.) Ask the children to scan the melody and look for patterns which include these tones. As they study the notation, they will discover that this melody seems to keep "changing its mind." The first phrase begins with the skip C-F, which would suggest that the song is in F major. However, the phrase ends by outlining the D minor chord, A-F-D. This shifting from major to minor continues throughout the song; neither tonality seems to gain control.

Discuss: **This is a very old song which comes from the Appalachian Mountains. It probably originated in England.** Discuss the fact that many of the first settlers in this area of America came from England, bringing their songs with them. **Many ancient folk songs are based on scales that are unfamiliar to us. These scales we call** MODES. **Modes have patterns of whole and half steps that are similar to, but not the same as, our major and minor scales.**

Play: Show the children that various modes can be created by starting on any white key of the piano and playing up eight white keys. **Each of the different modes has a different name. This song is based on the** AEOLIAN MODE, **which is the sequence of whole and half steps you hear when you start on A.** Discover that this is the same as the A-minor scale.

However, the Aeolian mode which "Farewell, My Own True Love" is based on is not built on A, but on D; that is, it has been TRANSPOSED.

One of the clues to help one determine if a song is modal is the lack of a consistent feeling of either major or minor tonality.

EXPRESSION

Listen: Listen to the recording again and discuss the way the melody supports the mood of the words. Read the poem aloud. Notice that each stanza of the poem presents a single thought, with each new phrase simply adding something to this main idea. The music is organized in the same way. Each new melodic phrase seems to grow out of the previous one. The words in lines one and two are very similar in their idea; this is also true of the first two musical phrases. Phrase 3 contains the most important section of the poem's idea: I may have to leave, but I *will* return! The music helps give the words emphasis; the highest point of the melody occurs in this phrase and the rhythm adds intensity by using more short tones.

Notice how the lack of a strong tonal ending adds to the "lonesome" mood. To help the children sense this more vividly, change the ending as follows:

FENGYANG DRUM

Moderato

Chinese Folk Song

Man: 1. I hold a drum; she holds a gong; With drum and gong we
Wife: 2. Sad is my life, sad my fate, I must live with
Man: 3. Sad is my fate, sad my life, I have mar-ried

sing a song. No oth-er tune do we know;
such a mate! He is so poor, begs door to door,
such a wife! She is so dumb; she is so dumb;

We sing this Feng-yang song as we go.
Sing-ing his Feng-yang song all day long.
She on-ly beats this Feng-yang drum.

Refrain

Feng-yang, Feng-yang song,

Ai ya ai hee ya, Terl pang tang piao yi piao, Terl lang tang piao yi piao,

Terl, piao, terl, piao, Terl lang tang piao yi piao.

MELODY

Read: Scan the notation and discover all the different pitches that are used in this song. As the children name the pitches by letter name, place them on the staff:

How many tones does this melody use? (Five.) **What do we call a scale that has only five tones?** (PENTATONIC.)

STYLE

Listen: Listen to a recording of the "Fengyang Drum" and other Chinse songs. **What makes Chinese music sound strange to our ears?** Help the children to decide that the strangeness is caused by the different way in which the Chinese organize melody, rhythm, and harmony in their music. Conclude that Chinese music has the following characteristics:

1. The melodies make use of the pentatonic scale.
2. The melodies are long and seem to wander without repetition of tonal patterns. Melodic intervals of thirds and fourths are common.
3. The rhythm of the melody is monotonous, with little change of pattern.
4. Traditionally, the only multiple sounds used are countermelodies. The melodic instruments usually play in unison.
5. The rhythmic accompaniment played by percussion instruments is made up of "linear" patterns, meaning that each note in the pattern may often be played by a different instrument.

(Chinese instruments are classified into eight families according to the materials used, rather than our four families which are grouped by the way they are played. The families of Chinese instruments are skin, stone, metal, silk, wood, bamboo, clay, and gourd.)

Play: Add a "linear" accompaniment to this song. Use a word pattern from the song and assign a different instrument to each word syllable in the pattern. Use instruments from different families. Play the pattern throughout the song.

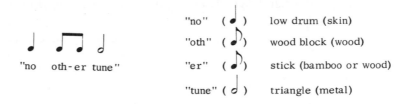

"no" (♩)	low drum (skin)
"oth" (♪)	wood block (wood)
"er" (♪)	stick (bamboo or wood)
"tune" (♩)	triangle (metal)

Use this pattern for an introduction and a coda, also, adding a gong for an extra effect:

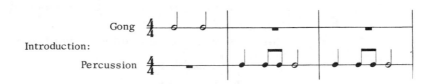

Coda: reverse above pattern

SURREY APPLE-HOWLER'S SONG*

A Round by Virgil Thomson
Traditional Words

Here stands— a good ap - ple tree.— Stand fast at root,

Bear well at top;   Ev - ery lit - tle twig   Bear an ap - ple big;

Ev - ery lit - tle bough   Bear an ap - ple now;   Hats full! Caps full!

Three score sacks full!   Hul - lo, boys! Hul - lo!   Hul - lo, boys! Hul - lo!

Copyright 1966 by Virgil Thomson. Reprinted by permission of the copyright owner.

RHYTHM

Create: Before the children learn this round, discuss the effect of accent on word meaning. **It is possible to completely change the meaning of a sentence by accenting different words. How can we create accent?** Invite the children to experiment and help them to discover that one can say a word louder or that one can stress it by saying it "longer."

What happens to the meaning of this sentence, "Here stands a good apple tree," if we accent different words? Ask the children to chant the sentence over and over, stressing the first word; for example:

Chant again, stressing the second word:

Repeat this process, stressing a different word each time:

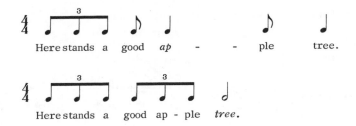

As each pattern is developed, discuss the changes in meaning that have occurred. When all the patterns have been chanted, help the class notate them as suggested in the examples given above. Then clap each pattern in succession to create a rhythmic composition. At another time, divide the class into two groups and clap as a rhythmic canon.

Read: After the children have developed their own canon, open the book and look at the song. **What did the composer do with this sentence?** Observe that he has expanded the sentence to cover two measures and that the words "stands" and "apple" are stressed. Notice that he has created emphasis for "apple" by *anticipating* the accent on the first beat of the second measure, in contrast to the stress on "stands" where the accent has been *delayed*, occurring after the beat where it normally would fall.

Practice clapping each phrase separately, beginning with the fifth phrase, where the melody moves with the beat.

HARMONY

Sing: Learn the melody in unison, paying particular attention to rhythmic accuracy in singing. After the children have worked on the melody, play the recording. Ask the children to follow the notation and evaluate their performance in comparison to what they have just heard. **Did you sing all the intervals correctly? Was your rhythm accurate?** Listen again, then sing without the recording. Repeat this procedure until the children have mastered the complex melodic and rhythmic patterns.

When the children are secure in their singing, divide them into two groups and have them sing it as a round. Gradually divide into more groups until the class can sing it as a six-part round.

Read: Write the I (D-F♯-A) and V_7 (A-C♯-E-G) chords on the chalkboard. Examine the notation and help the children discover that the tones of the first and third beats of each measure are included in the I chord and that the tones of the second and fourth beats belong to the V_7 chord.

Play: Transpose the melody to the key of C. One child may accompany the singing on the autoharp, playing the I-V_7 (C-G_7) pattern over and over, one chord on every beat.

SKYE BOAT SONG

Con moto

Refrain

Autoharp in F and Dm:

Scottish Folk Song

Speed, bon-nie boat, like a bird on the wing, On-ward, the sail-ors cry.

Car-ry the lad that's born to be king, O-ver the sea to Skye.

Verse

1. Loud the winds howl, loud the waves roar, Thun-der-clouds rend the air;
2. Tho' the waves leap, soft shall ye sleep, O-cean's a roy-al bed.
3. Man-y's the lad fought on that day, Well the clay-more could wield.
4. Burn'd are our homes; ex-ile and death Scat-ter the loy-al men;

Baf-fled, our foes stand by the shore; Fol-low they will not dare.
Rock'd in the deep, Flor-a will keep Watch by your wea-ry head.
When the night came, si-lent-ly lay Dead on Cul-lo-den's Field.
Yet ere the sword cool in the sheath, Char-lie will come a-gain.

From *Voices of the World,* copyright 1960, Follet Publishing Company, Chicago, Ill. Used by permission.

EXPRESSION

Discuss: Folk songs are used for many purposes: People sing at work, at play, and at worship. Another way that people use music is to express pride in their country and its history. This song is an example of such a song—it tells of an important event in Scottish history.

Skye is one of the islands of the Hebrides off the coast of Scotland. This song describes the escape to Skye of a Scottish leader, Bonnie Prince Charlie. He had been a leader in a revolt against the English, which ended disastrously at the Battle of Culloden Field. Flora MacDonald was a loyal patriot who helped the Prince escape in a small fishing boat during a severe storm. Claymore is a large two-edged sword used by the Scottish Highlanders.

Sing: Discuss the mood of this song. It should be sung with vigor, reflecting the energy of the men as they bend over their oars. Help communicate this mood by using appropriate TONE QUALITY and DYNAMICS.

Create: Add an accompaniment for the verse that might describe the fury of the storm. A "rolling" octave accompaniment in the low register of the piano, reinforced by a muffled roll on a deep-toned drum (using a soft mallet) might prove effective:

STYLE

Listen: Of all the folk music of the European countries, Scottish folk songs seem to be the most unique in sound. Listen to, or sing, some of the familiar songs such as "Auld Lang Syne" and "Comin' through the Rye." **What makes this music so Scottish?**

1. Many melodies are based on the pentatonic scale; others move back and forth from major to minor.
2. Many melodies make use of a "turn"—up and then back down ("Speed, bonnie.")
3. The Scotch "snap" is the most distinctive rhythmic characteristic. It is made up of a short-long pattern (♪ ♩.) with the "short" occurring *on* the beat. (This is found in "Comin' through the Rye," but not in this song.)
4. The bagpipe gives Scottish music a unique flavor. The wailing drone of an open fifth is the most characteristic harmonic interval. The harp is another common Scottish instrument.

Play: Let the children play the drone accompaniment appearing in the score on the piano.

An autoharp may be used for the drone on the refrain. Press down both the G-major and G-minor buttons at the same time and stroke on the lower strings only.

MELODY

Listen: Help the children to hear the change from major (refrain) to minor (verse.)

Do you notice anything unusual about the way the melody of the refrain ends? It ends on the fifth tone of the scale rather than on the first, as most songs do. This gives the melody a somewhat "plaintive" or "wistful" air.

FORM

Read: **What is the form of this song?** (ABA.) It is somewhat unusual in that it begins with the refrain, moves on to the verse, and then returns to the refrain.

PRETTY PEÑA

Leisurely

Mexican Folk Melody
Words by Eunice Boardman

1. Soft -ly, a voice is sing -ing;
2. Come now, O pret -ty Pe - ña;

Gent -ly, its mes-sage bring -ing. Pe -ña, come to your win - dow! The sounds of
Hur -ry, it is Fi - es - ta! Lis -ten, the hap -py tam-bour-ines Are call -ing

ser - e -nad -ing fill the sum-mer air! _____ Gui-tars are play -ing, their mu-sic
us to join the danc -ers in the square! _____ Whirl -ing, the danc-ers

say -ing; Come pret-ty Pe - ña! No more de - lay -ing! Hur - ry! Come to your
Whirl -ing, the danc-ers

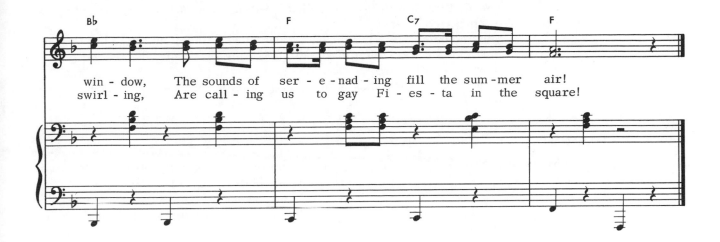

win - dow, The sounds of ser - e - nad - ing fill the sum -mer air!
swirl - ing, Are call - ing us to gay Fi - es - ta in the square!

RHYTHM

Read: **What is unusual about the meter of this song?** Draw attention to the changing accent resulting from the alternating 2/4 and 4/4 meter signatures.

Move: Locate a rhythmic pattern that includes both meter signatures, and practice tapping this pattern, making sure that the accent always occurs on the first beat of the measure.

Play: Choose one percussion instrument to play the beat and another to play the accents. A third instrument may be selected to play the rhythm of the melody.

STYLE

Discuss: **From what country do you think this song might be?** The children may suggest Mexico or Latin America.

Could it be from any other part of the world? (Spain.) **Why do you suppose that Mexican and Spanish music sound so much alike?**

Help the children to recall what they know regarding the colonization of Mexico by Spain. When one country is occupied by another nation for a long time, many things may be changed, including personal expressions such as speech and music. The Mexican language, today, is much nearer to Spanish than it is to the language of the Indians who first lived there. Mexican music is also more like Spanish music than Indian music.

Listen: After listening to this song and to other songs or music typical of Mexico, the children should be made aware of some of the characteristics of Mexican music:

1. Melodies are primarily based on the major scale (few chromatics) and move in scale or chord-line patterns.
2. The melodies are often repetitious, making use of sequential patterns.
3. The song forms most often used are AB or ABA.

4. Song melodies usually move in accent groupings of threes, like the waltz, with strong accents.
5. The rhythms are distinctive and interesting; several rhythmic patterns are often played at once.
6. The melodies are harmonized primarily with the I and V_7 chords. The melodies are most often harmonized vocally by singing the second part a third or a sixth lower.
7. Typical instruments include the guitar, tambourine, castanets, maracas, and drums.

HARMONY

Read: Scan the notation of the second section of the song and notice that the two harmonizing parts move consistently in thirds. Draw attention to the end of the unison section and observe that the lower part continues down the scale while the upper part skips up a third. The two parts then continue in thirds to the end of the song.

Sing: Divide the class into two sections and challenge the children to read the two parts simultaneously, singing on "loo." If problems occur, return to the use of numbers (syllables) to help solve them. Finally, sing the song with words.

Play: One child may provide an accompaniment on the autoharp. Remind him that he should always strum on the ACCENTED beat and that he must therefore observe the meter signature carefully.

ROUMANIAN FOLK DANCES*

Vanguard, VRS 1023; Mercury, 90367; Vox, VBX 426

Bela Bartok

STYLE

Discuss: This set of dances was written by Bela Bartok, a contemporary composer who was born in Hungary and later moved to the United States. These dances were written while Bartok still lived in Hungary. Like much of his music they reflect the folk music of his country. Many of the compositional devices used— intricate rhythms and shifting meters, unusual scales and harmonies—are typical of many twentieth-century composers.

Listen: Play the complete set of dances, then listen to each separately, noticing specific details.

DANCE WITH STICKS.   The gaily syncopated melody is a two-part form: A (repeated one octave higher), B (repeated). Guide the children's attention to the piano accompaniment; the harmonization is different during the repeated sections. This changing harmonization, in addition to the constant shifting of the melody between major and minor, contributes to the mercurial mood of the dance.

WAISTBAND DANCE.   This brief dance is made up of short, four-measure melodies. Each draws from the previous melody, but none is exactly alike.

The complete dance is repeated. The melody is in the Dorian mode, as are many Hungarian melodies. To play the Dorian mode for the class, play all white keys on the piano from D to D. Compare it to the minor scale.

STAMPING DANCE. The high-pitched melody is suggestive of the bagpipe, a Hungarian folk instrument. This melody is based on what is sometimes described as the Gypsy "gapped" scale. This melody is based on the following scale:

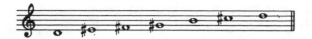

HORNPIPE DANCE. The alternating even and uneven rhythmic patterns within the measure add to the interest of this dance. Most of this melody is based on the following scale:

Help the children to compare the sequences of whole and half steps of the two scales.

ROUMANIAN POLKA. This lively broken-chord melody is particularly intriguing because of the frequent changes in metric groupings. To help the children sense the meters diagram them as follows:

Introduction

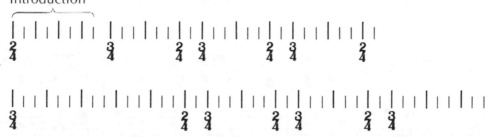

QUICK DANCE. The dance suite ends with a vigorous dance in quick tempo; listen for the increasing tempo of the middle section. Help the children determine the form: A (eight measures), A (repeated with different harmonization), B (sixteen measures), B (repeated with different harmonization), Coda (thirteen measures based on the last four measures of B).

GOOD NIGHT

Andante

German Folk Song (Translated)

EXPRESSION

Listen: **We have talked about the importance of discovering the main climax in a song. However, most good songs will also have smaller "climaxes" within each phrase or section.**

Listen to this song and see if you can locate a climax within each phrase.

Notice that these climaxes may come at different points in the phrase:

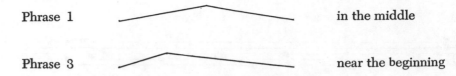

Phrase 1   in the middle

Phrase 3   near the beginning

The major climax of this song is in the third phrase.

Sing: **In singing or playing we indicate these climaxes by increasing the dynamic level at these points. As you sing this song, show your awareness of these different kinds of climaxes by making a CRESCENDO and DIMINUENDO at the proper places.**

Read: **When we want to indicate slight changes in the dynamics of a song, such as these small climaxes, we use the following symbols in the notation:**

meaning: crescendo

meaning: diminuendo

HARMONY

Read: This song provides an opportunity for two different types of part singing. In the first two and the last phrases the voices move together at the interval of a third. In the third phrase the two parts move in the manner of a round, both parts singing the same melody at different times.

Guide the children to observe these features as they scan the notation. The reading of two staves at the same time will be a new experience for most of them.

Sing: Review the sound of harmonizing in thirds, then sing the two parts in phrases one, two, and four, simultaneously.

Learn the third phrase in unison first, then sing the two parts as written in the score.

FORM

Discuss: **When we say that a song is in a TWO- or THREE-PART SONG FORM, what do we mean?** (It has two or three sections.) **How can we recognize these different sections?** (The melody is different.)

Help the children to conclude that FORM in music depends on the way repeated and contrasting sections are arranged in relation to each other.

Listen: **Is there REPETITION and CONTRAST of sections in this song?** (Yes, the first phrase is repeated twice; the third phrase provides contrast.)

In what ways do these two different phrases contrast? Guide the children to observe that the melody of the first phrase moves primarily by steps, whereas the third phrase contains wide skips; that the rhythm of the first phrase is mostly even, whereas the third phrase has mostly uneven rhythmic patterns; and that harmonizing thirds in the first phrase are in contrast to the independent parts in the third phrase.

MARY ANN

Not too fast, but rhythmically

Calypso Song
Words by Kathy Alexander

1. All day___ all night,___ Miss Mar-y Ann,___
2. If you___ come to___ this is-land fine,___

Down by___ the sea - side___ sift-ing sand,___
You'll love___ the sea and___ bright sun-shine,___

All the lit - tle chil - dren___ love Mar-y Ann,___
You will be___ en - chant - ed___ with this fair land,___

You, too,___ will love her,___ Miss Mar-y Ann.___
You'll be___ be - witched by___ Miss Mar-y Ann.___

Reprinted from *Music for Everyone* by Ehret, Barr and Blair, copyright 1959 by Prentice-Hall, Inc., Englewood Cliffs, N. J.

STYLE

Discuss: Fifth-grade children will perhaps be familiar with calypso music, for it has become quite popular in recent years. Draw as much of the following information from them as possible.

Calypso music comes from the West Indies. These islands were owned in turn
by the Spaniards, the French, and the English, each of whom imported Negro

slaves from Africa to work their sugar plantations. The language of the Negro gradually became a mixture of Spanish, French, and English; their music and songs reflected the same influences.

Music was very important in the life of the slaves, and as they worked they sang. The owners of the plantations often hired a leader ("chantwelle") whose only job was to sing while the slaves labored in the fields. To keep the workers interested, the leader would sing of current events, poking fun at the "bosses," and passing on local gossip. He was a sort of "singing newspaper," making up his verses as he sang. Modern calypso songs use similar topics; the best calypso singers improvise the words as they sing, commenting on things or people about them.

Listen: **What is distinctive about calypso music?** From listening to records in class, and drawing on out-of-school experiences, summarize the unique features of this music:

1. Interesting rhythmic patterns played simultaneously
2. The shifting of word accents to accommodate the rhythm of the melody
3. Chord-line melodies based on the I and V_7 chords in major keys
4. Accompaniments using primarily the I and V_7 chords, with the sixth step of the scale being added to the I chord for added flavor
5. The use of a variety of instruments for accompaniments: conga and bongo drums, guiro, claves, maracas, cowbell, and guitar

Play: The following are some typical calypso rhythmic patterns which can be used to accompany a variety of such songs. Some of these patterns are quite intricate; learn them one at a time and then combine them, gradually, as the children become adept in maintaining them independently.

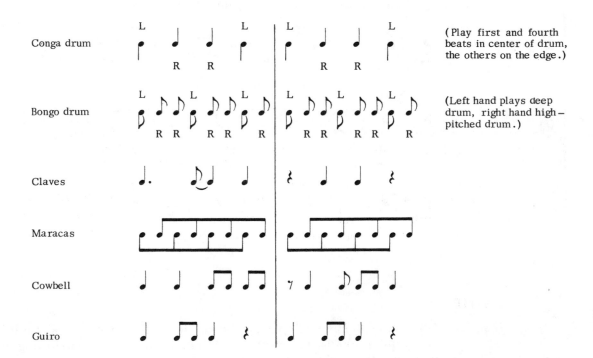

Create: Make up some calypso words about current events to fit this melody, or write a new calypso tune.

MELODY

Read:

One of the characteristics of calypso songs is that the melody usually moves along tones from I and V$_7$ chords. Look at the notation to see if this song has this characteristic.

What tones are in the I chord? (F-A-C.) **What tones are in the V$_7$ chord?** (C-E-G-B♭). Help the children to see that the melody of the first two measures (plus one beat) is made up of tones from the I chord and that the next four measures use tones from the V$_7$ chord. Notice that this pattern continues throughout the song. This can therefore be classified as a typical calypso tune.

Sing:

Sing patterns based on the I and V$_7$ chords, moving rapidly from one to another:

Sight-sing the song with words. If intervallic problems occur, review the chord tone patterns.

Move:

Observe that almost every measure is SYNCOPATED. An accurate reproduction of syncopated patterns depends on *feeling* rather than counting. Establish a steady two-beat pattern by clapping and chant the words, giving a slight accent to the eighth note that precedes and is tied to the second beat. It may take quite a bit of practice to do this correctly.

DEVELOPING CONTEMPORARY IMPROVISATIONS AND COMPOSITIONS

MELODY

Discuss with the children the fact that melodies may be based on a variety of scales. Ask them to look through their song book and discover songs based on different scales. As each song is located, sing it, then determine what scale the melody is based upon and write this on the chalkboard.

MAJOR SCALE
"Morning Comes Early"

MINOR SCALE
"The Peddler"

AEOLIAN MODE (Transposed)
"Farewell, My Own True Love"

PENTATONIC SCALE
"The Little Black Train"

As each scale is notated, review its structure in terms of whole, half, or whole-half steps.

These are not the only kinds of scales that can be used to create a musical composition. Some composers have used a scale called the WHOLE TONE SCALE. How do you think this scale would be made up? Help the children decide that it would consist entirely of whole steps:

WHOLE TONE SCALE

To help the children grasp the relationship between scale structure and melodic organization, write the numbers of a familiar song such as "Are You Sleeping?" on the chalkboard.

Without telling the children the name of the melody, ask them to play it on the bells, using the WHOLE TONE SCALE. Ask them to identify the melody and discuss the effect that the new scale had on the familiar tune.

Composers have sometimes made up their own, individual scales on which to base a melody. These are called SYNTHETIC SCALES. Invite the class to make up a synthetic scale using any sequence of intervals. (Note that a scale always ascends and encompasses no more or less than an octave.) Guide the class to avoid patterns that are similar to those found in the familiar major and minor scales. For example, the new scale might be as follows:

Play "Are You Sleeping?" in the new scale and discuss the differences in sound. Other familiar tunes may be played in the new scale, with the class trying to identify the melody.

Give the children time to work alone or in small groups to improvise their own melodies based on their synthetic scales. As they play them for the class, discuss ways of making melodies interesting. Return to favorite songs and talk about how they move. **Do the melodies move primarily by steps, by skips, or is there a balance between these? Does the melody move consistently in one direction? How is the climax attained? Do successive phrases have melodies that are similar or contrasting?** Discuss the fact that a melody with too much repetition becomes boring and that contrast is needed. On the other hand, without repetition of musical ideas a melody seems to sound confusing because the patterns do not seem to "hang together."

RHYTHM

Help the children to develop interesting rhythmic patterns for their compositions, also. Suggestions for developing rhythmic patterns from word patterns were made in connection with the "Surrey Apple-Howler's Song." Such experiences might be expanded by inviting the children to experiment with chanting word patterns in different meters.

Begin with a familiar proverb and then add new lines to it. At first, keep each syllable in the phrase the same length and provide accent only through emphasis (stress) rather than lengthening of the note value. For example:

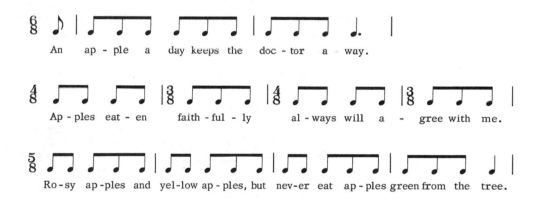

Another way to develop an interesting rhythm is to create a five-beat pattern using a quarter note as the beat note, such as $\frac{5}{4}$ ♩ ♫ ♩ ♩, and then write this pattern in different meters so that the accent falls in a different place in the pattern each time.

Combine the new rhythms with the melodies the children have developed. Some classes may wish to notate their compositions; others may work until they have memorized them. Taping the best compositions for others to hear may be a good culminating activity.

TILL EULENSPIEGEL'S MERRY PRANKS

Many LP recordings available; consult record catalogues   Richard Strauss

EXPRESSION

Discuss: Every country has its folk heroes, individuals who have once lived or personages who may be only imaginary. We have our Paul Bunyan and our Davy Crockett; in Germany they have a legendary person by the name of Till Eulenspiegel.

Till was a scamp who supposedly lived in the thirteenth century. He wandered about the country getting into all kinds of foolish scrapes. He was a mischief-maker, although he never did anything really bad, and no one disliked him, perhaps because there is a little mischief-maker in all of us.

The composer, Richard Strauss, who lived in the nineteenth century, tried to describe some of Till's escapades in this music. This type of music is called PROGRAM MUSIC because the composer had a story in mind which he was trying to describe musically. Program music is the opposite of ABSOLUTE music, which has no connection with a story.

Listen: The following description is not intended to be given to the children as written. The children may listen to a section of the piece and decide what they believe the composer might have had in mind to describe, or the title of a section might be given in advance and the children may decide whether or not the composer has succeeded in describing that event. In either case the teacher should constantly emphasize the manner in which the MELODY, HARMONY, RHYTHM, TONE QUALITY, TEMPO, and DYNAMICS are organized to contribute to the expressiveness of the music.

The various themes or motives should be notated on the chalkboard for reference.

I. "Once upon a time" the story begins with a quiet theme:

"there was a wag by the name Till Eulenspiegel" who is introduced in this manner by the FRENCH HORN:

Notice the way the composer builds up to a CLIMAX to this section. The theme is repeated several times by the horns, the oboes, the clarinets, the strings, and the other wind instruments.

Obviously Till is off to perpetrate one of his pranks as we hear the CLARINET play the first theme, which is then transformed into a flippant "rascal" theme by a change in RHYTHM:

II. "Till in the market place." A rising glissando and a trotting rhythm announce that Till is off on his horse. He is trying to make up his mind what to do, not sure where to go:

Notice that this is the first theme with altered MELODY, RHYTHM, and DYNAMICS. A sudden cymbal crash suggests that Till has ridden his horse into the market place, upsetting pots and pans, waking up the old ladies, and creating general confusion. The composer communicates this with rising DYNAMICS, higher PITCH, increased TEMPO, and harsh HARMONIES.

III. "Hidden in a mouse-hole." Lucky Till has got away from the old angry ladies. Why is this a good title for this section?

IV. "Disguised as a monk." A new melody introduces the next prank. Till dons a robe and pretends to be the very opposite of a scamp—a monk. The music helps us know this because it plays a simple hymnlike tune with a harmonization of I and V$_7$ chords.

The real Till, however, cannot stay hidden for long. Soon we hear the first theme, in altered fashion, which seems to say, "Look at me, am I not being a good boy?"

V. "Till courting pretty girls." A long glissando introduces the next section. Till is in love, but the sadness of the music tells us that the lady does not feel the same way. Till becomes angry and storms away. Evidently he is not too broken-hearted, because the clarinets are still singing his jovial theme.

VI. "The Philistines." Philistines are professors, very dull and dry ones. They are described by the composer by a persistent, plodding RHYTHM played by the wind instruments with dark TONE QUALITY. Till and the professors argue as we hear the sparkling Till theme scampering about among the dull grumbling chords of the professors.

VII. "Till's street tune." A jaunty tune tells us that Till is on his way again:

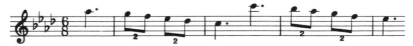

He seems a little doubtful, however. Perhaps the monks and the professors are right and he should mend his ways. The first theme is heard, rather quiet and sad, but soon the second theme is heard again in the horns; we know that Till has decided to remain his mischievous self.

VIII. "March." Till's theme is turned into a march. Suddenly the low brasses and strings begin a passage that sounds as though it were pursuing something. Could someone be after Till? A threatening roll on the drums indicates that Till has been caught.

IX. "The court of justice." We hear a conversation between the judges and Till. He is accused (drums and low brasses); he answers with his old bravado. Again he is accused; this time his answer suggests that he is not quite as sure of himself. The sentence is given: Till is to hang! Up the ladder he goes, and that is the end of Till.

X. "Finale." After a quiet, sad section, the composition ends with a final furious outburst based on the Till theme. Might this suggest that Till did not die after all? Or perhaps it is suggesting that even though the real Till is dead, the spirit of Till lives on as long as there are any scamps about who have a bit of mischief in their hearts.

Guiding Musical Growth
in the Sixth Grade

	Listening	Singing	Playing
SKILL	Continue work toward developing habits of discriminative listening.	Give help to individuals whose voices may be changing. Continue to strive for expressive singing.	Encourage the children to work independently to attain skill on a variety of classroom instruments.
CONCEPTS *Melody*	Draw the children's attention to alterations in melodic line (sequence, augmentation, diminution). Compare major and minor scales to other tonal organizations such as modes and tone row. Extend recognition of all common intervals.	Encourage individual singing of tonal patterns, as well as songs, with numbers and/or syllables.	Make frequent use of melody instruments to play familiar songs from notation, as well as by ear. Use bells and piano to experiment with tonal organizations such as tone row and modes.
Rhythm	Introduce the children to music that moves in unusual meters ("5's," "7's," and so on.) Extend awareness of complex rhythmic patterns.	Provide experiences in singing songs that move in unusual metric groupings. Stress the importance of rhythmic flow in singing.	Help the children to gain independence in maintaining a rhythmic pattern against other patterns.
Harmony	Draw attention to all common harmonic intervals. Help the children to recognize differences in qualities of primary (I, IV, V) and secondary (II, VI) chords. Introduce the children to chords based on seconds, fourths, and so on.	Include a variety of two- and three-part songs and polyphonic compositions to help the children become increasingly aware of multiple sounds. Expand vocal chording experiences to include the use of secondary chords.	Extend chording activities to include accompaniments to songs in minor keys. Experiment with the addition of secondary chords when accompanying songs with autoharp.
Form	Provide experiences involving recognition of repetition and contrast in rondo, theme and variation, and sónata-allegro forms. Foster an awareness of contrapuntal structure, including the fugue.	Stress an awareness of phrase structure in extended vocal compositions. Help the children become sensitive to melodic line and to balance in singing polyphonic music.	Help the children to use their knowledge of contrapuntal structure in adding countermelodies. Perform rounds and canons on rhythm and melody instruments to extend the understanding of polyphonic structure.
Expression	Help the children to sense the expressive values of unity and variety. Draw the children's attention to the expressive role of rhythmic, melodic, and harmonic organization.	Guide the children to consider the importance of variations in dynamics, tempo, and tone quality in the interpretation of songs.	Encourage the children to consider ways of providing unity and variety in their own performances. Stress importance of appropriate tempo, dynamics, and tone color to musical expressiveness.
Style	Help the children to become sensitive to elements that characterize the music of different composers and periods.		Foster a consciousness of style by planning accompaniments based on characteristic rhythmic and melodic patterns, using instruments representative of different cultures.

Moving	Creating	Reading
Provide opportunities to learn a variety of period dances.	Help the children to develop skill in composing for instruments as well as voices.	Stress independent interpretation of the score, vocally and instrumentally. Help the children to gain skill in notating their own compositions. Extend the children's knowledge of notation to include the bass staff and all common expressive markings.
Encourage the children to exhibit an awareness of melodic contour in executing interpretative dances.	Experiment with melodic alterations (sequence, augmentation, diminution) in original compositions. Explore possibilities of tone-row composition.	Encourage independent singing and playing of melodies from notation. Provide opportunities to interpret the key signature and establish tonality.
Help the children to increase their understanding of meter by introducing basic conducting beat patterns. Draw attention to the relationship of dance patterns to rhythmic movement.	Encourage experimentation with unusual metric groupings and complex rhythmic patterns in composing. Encourage improvisation of extended rhythmic patterns for accompaniments.	Guide the children to use their knowledge of rhythmic relationships in reproducing complex rhythmic patterns from notation.
Plan interpretive dances based on movement of independent melodic lines on polyphonic music.	Help the children to use multiple sounds, including secondary chords, in their own compositions. Experiment with chords based on seconds, fourths, and so forth, in composing.	Provide experiences in sight-reading two- and three-part songs and simple contrapuntal songs. Encourage the independent reading of chord symbols when adding harmonic accompaniments, vocally as well as instrumentally.
Focus attention on the relationship of musical form to dance form in period dances.	Foster an awareness of formal structure through composing in specific forms.	Emphasize the value of recognizing repetition and variation in notation as an aid in score-reading. Focus attention on notation as an aid to studying musical form.
Encourage the children to reveal their awareness of unity and variety through physical movement.	Encourage the children to consider possible expressive contributions of unity and variety in their own compositions. Guide the children to explore expressive possibilities of tempo, dynamics, and tone color when creating compositions and accompaniments.	Stress the importance of interpreting expressive markings accurately.
Foster a sensitivity to the styles of different periods by learning characteristic dances.	Give the children opportunities to compose in various styles as a means of increasing cognizance of stylistic characteristics.	Help the children to study the musical score for clues to musical style.

HE'S GOT THE WHOLE WORLD IN HIS HANDS

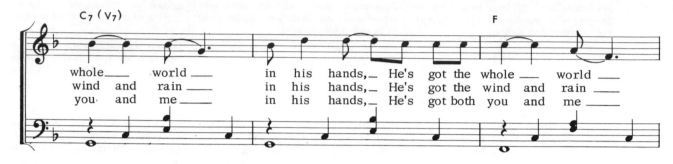

MELODY

Sing: Many children may be familiar with some version of this song. Sing it with words and discuss any discrepancy between this notated version of the melody and any that the children may have learned previously by ear. (It is often wiser to allow children to continue to sing their version of a familiar song than to attempt to change a well-established habit. After all, this *is* a folk song and no single version is necessarily the "right" one.)

Read: If there are disagreements between various versions, have the children notate theirs and compare the results with this version.

Another interesting activity, one that points up the constantly changing character of folk tunes, is to find and compare several versions of the same melody. Children might do this as individual projects, bringing to class samples of songs they have found.

HARMONY

Sing: Encourage the children to add a harmonizing part by ear. The following chant might be added:

Some of the boys whose voices are beginning to change might enjoy singing this chant, especially if the song were transposed to the key of C, thus making the chant lie in the range that is most comfortable for boys' changing voices.

Read: Determine the autoharp accompaniment from the melodic notation.

What chords should we use for each measure? We can decide what chords to use by ear, but we can also do so by studying the melodic notation.

Write the I, IV, and V₇ chords in the key of F on the chalkboard.

Look at the first full measure of the song. What tones make up the melody? (C-A-F.) To what chord do these tones belong? (I chord.) We know, then, that we will need to use the I chord for our accompaniment in this measure.

Continue this process, analyzing the melody measure by measure. Some measures may be harmonized with more than one chord (measure 3 for example). In that case, make the final choice by listening. Play the alternative chords as the class sings the melody and decide which seems most pleasing and appropriate. As chords are determined, place them on the chalkboard for future reference.

EXPRESSION

Sing: This song may be sung in two ways: as a quiet, meditative song, or as a "rocking," rhythmic song. Marian Anderson, a famous contralto, sings it in the first way. Other professional singers have preferred the more rhythmic version. Have the children sing the song both ways and decide which they prefer.

ERIE CANAL

With spirit

American Work Song

2. Git up there, Sal, we passed that lock,
   Fifteen miles on the Erie Canal!
   And we'll make Rome before six o'clock,
   Fifteen miles on the Erie Canal.
   Just one more trip and back we'll go
   Through the rain and sleet and snow,
   'Cause we know ev'ry inch of the way
   From Albany to Buffalo.

MELODY

Listen: **In what key is this song? Listen carefully before you decide. Does the first phrase sound as if it were written in MAJOR?** (It sounds MINOR.)

Listen carefully to the entire song. Does the melody sound minor all the way through? Help the children to realize that the third phrase of the verse is in major, as is the entire refrain.

When a melody shifts from one tonality to another we say that it is MODULATING.

Sing: Sing the F-major scale and the I chord and the D-minor scale and I chord. Then sing the verse with words. **Be sure to think of the different scales and remember where you need to change your "thinking" from minor to major and back.**

Before singing the refrain, practice singing half and whole steps from various tones:

RHYTHM

Read: **In what ways is the rhythm of this song interesting?** Scan the notation and discover a variety of rhythmic patterns: the syncopated pattern (♪ ♩.), the dotted eighth and sixteenth pattern (♩. ♪), and the even patterns (♩ ♩ ♩ ♩).

Move: Help the children to become more adept at reproducing a complex rhythmic pattern: Clap the beat and chant the words, "I've got a mule, her name is Sal," and "Fifteen miles on the Erie Canal." Compare the rhythm of the two patterns, noting especially the shift of the syncopation to the second beat in the latter phrase.

To emphasize the 3–1 relationship of the 𝅘𝅥. 𝅘𝅥 pattern, practice clapping this pattern while mentally subdividing the beat into four: 𝅘𝅥𝅮𝅘𝅥𝅮𝅘𝅥𝅮𝅘𝅥𝅮 .

Sing: Sing the words with crisp enunciation to make the rhythmic patterns accurate. Stress the importance of feeling the underlying beat while singing the syncopated and dotted patterns.

Play: Add the autoharp accompaniment by reading the chord symbols. This is more difficult than some accompaniments, so children may wish to practice individually before attempting to accompany the class.

Listen: Identify major and minor chords by listening. Make a game out of it, one child playing the chords and the class trying to identify them as major or minor.

STYLE

Discuss: Talk about the origin of the song. The 425-mile Erie Canal was a significant factor in the opening of the West. When it was completed in 1825 it provided for the first time an inexpensive way to transport settlers and merchandise to the new frontiers. The canal barges were towed by mules that trudged along the pathway on each side of the canal. The monotony of the trip, at fifteen miles a day, was broken by the singing of the mule driver, who probably made up verses as he sang: about the scenery he was passing, the town he expected to reach that night, the good times he had had on recent trips.

The free rhythm which reflects the natural rhythm of the words, the somewhat repetitious melody, and the repeated refrain are typical of many American folk songs.

JACOB'S LADDER

Broadly (unaccompanied)   Spiritual

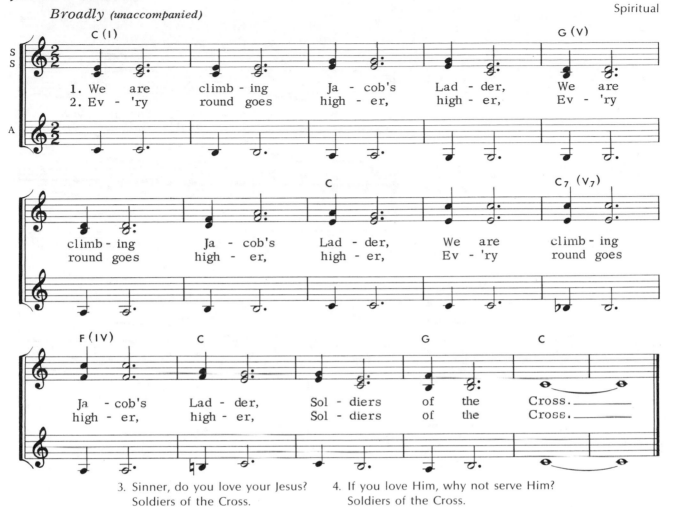

1. We are climb - ing Ja - cob's Lad - der, We are
2. Ev - 'ry round goes high - er, high - er, Ev - 'ry

climb - ing Ja - cob's Lad - der, We are climb - ing
round goes high - er, high - er, Ev - 'ry round goes

Ja - cob's Lad - der, Sol - diers of the Cross._____
high - er, high - er, Sol - diers of the Cross._____

3. Sinner, do you love your Jesus?   4. If you love Him, why not serve Him?
   Soldiers of the Cross.   Soldiers of the Cross.

HARMONY

Read: Study the notation of this three-part song; compare the chord structure of the voice parts with the chords indicated by the chord symbols. Place the suggested chords on the chalkboard:

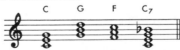

Are there some tones in the voice parts that do not belong to these chords? (Measures 2, 3, 6, 8, 11, 12, 13, and 14.)

These "foreign" tones are called PASSING TONES.

Sing: Some sixth-grade boys' voices are beginning to change. The lower voice part uses tones that are in the range of early changing voices. If children cannot sing it in this low range, transpose the song to the key of E flat.

Learn the three parts simultaneously, listening carefully to the chord progressions.

Play: The three-part arrangement should be sung A CAPPELLA (unaccompanied). It may also be sung in unison, however, or in two parts, accompanied by the autoharp or piano with the chords indicated.

FOLA, FOLA BLAKKEN[1]

In a playful mood

Edvard Grieg

1. Fo - la, fo - la blak - ken! You are ver - y tired I know, You shall have some oats and bran now, Fo - la, fo - la blak - ken. Oh, that steep and

2. Fo - la, fo - la blak - ken! Go in - to your lit - tle stall. Ver - y soon this boy will come And pat you, fo - la blak - ken. Can't you see me

From *Singing Together* of "Our Singing World" Series. Used by permission of Ginn and Company, owner of the copyright, Boston, Mass.

[1] "Blakken" is a name given to little black ponies in Norway. Prounced: fo-la block-en.

STYLE

Listen: Edvard Grieg, the composer of this song, belongs to a group of composers who often are referred to as "nationalists." His music seems to reflect the mood and character of his people and their country. Many of his songs are similar in style to Norwegian folk songs, and he uses many devices that are associated with them. One of these devices he uses in this song for the accompaniment (see piano score). One of the primitive Norwegian instruments was the "Hardanger Fele," a stringed instrument similar to the fiddle. This fele would sound not only the melody, but would also furnish a "drone bass" played on two strings a fifth apart. Notice how Grieg imitates this drone bass in the piano accompaniment to the song.

FORM

Listen: **This is an art song. What is different about the form of this song?**
Help the children to recognize that the accompaniment plays an important part in the form of the song. Listen to the INTRODUCTION and to the INTERLUDES between the various sections of the song.

Notice, also, that Grieg provides a new melody for the final verse. He uses the same melodic motives, however, which help to give UNITY to the whole song, while at the same time this melody creates VARIETY, in addition to an effective closing section.

MELODY

Read: Determine the tonality of this song by looking at the key signature. Place the tones that belong to the scale of F on the chalkboard. Review the major-scale pattern.

Look at the third phrase where there is a B natural in all places where the key signature calls for a B flat. This ♮ sign is more than an ACCIDENTAL, in this instance. It indicates a MODULATION from F major to C major. If syllables or numbers are used, this change of key must be taken into consideration.

Sing: The three sections of this song should probably be learned one at a time. Be sure to establish the TONALITY for each section firmly before trying to sight-sing with words.

EXPRESSION

Sing: **How can you best communicate the mood Grieg has suggested in this song?**
The children will probably suggest that they must sing with a light, cheerful tone. Encourage them to experiment with changes in dynamics and tempo in order to make the song more expressive.

THE SWAN

Sweet - ly the swan sings Do - de - ah - do, do - de - ah - do, do - de - ah - do.

MELODY

Read: Discover the sequential nature of the melodic line:

Sing: Sing with words, using an awareness of SEQUENCE to learn the song quickly.

HARMONY

Sing: Sing as a four-part round. After the children have mastered the problems of rhythmic accuracy and tonal blending, ask them to sing slowly and listen carefully to the interesting chord progression created by the combination of parts.

Divide the class into three groups and sing the "do-de-ah-doh" motives simultaneously. Call attention to the descending chord progression resulting from the combination of the three parts.

Read: Place the chords created by the combining of motives on the chalkboard:

IV   III   II   I

Discuss the fact that these chords move downward stepwise and that chords may be built on any step of the scale. Recall that chords are named for their bottom note and determine that the chords created are IV, III, II and I.

Listen: Play the four chords and help the children decide that they are hearing two different QUALITIES of chords. The I and IV chords are MAJOR, and the II and III chords are MINOR in quality.

To help the class become more aware of the differences, ask one child to play the chords on the bells. (Recall the discussion of major and minor chords held in connection with "The Peddler.") Discover that MAJOR CHORDS include two thirds; the lower third is made up of two tones which are four half steps apart, a MAJOR THIRD, while the upper third is made up of two tones which are three half steps apart, a MINOR THIRD. Discover that MINOR CHORDS have these intervals reversed, the smallest third being on the bottom.

Play different chords for the children and ask them to decide whether they are major or minor.

GREENSLEEVES*

2. Ah, Greensleeves, now farewell, adieu,
   To God I pray to prosper thee,
   For I am still thy sweetheart true;
   Come once again to meet me.
   Refrain

MELODY

Read: Study the key signature and scan the notation. Determine that the melody is
built around E-G-B, the I chord of the E-minor scale. Call attention to the

ACCIDENTALS preceding D and C. **These tones are often raised in the minor scale; it is then described as a MELODIC MINOR SCALE.** Play the natural minor and the melodic minor scales and compare the sounds of the two.

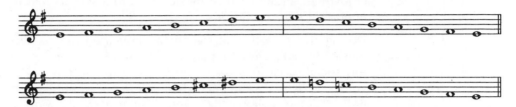

Notice that the descending melodic minor is the same as the natural minor.

Sing: Establish the tonality and encourage the children to sing as much of the song as possible on "loo." Play the recording and discuss possible errors made.

RHYTHM

Read: Discuss the 6/8 meter signature, emphasizing the fact that most music notated in this meter actually moves in twos with each beat being subdivided into three weaker pulsations. Ask one child to lightly tap the six beats on sticks while another stresses the heavy first and fourth beats on finger cymbals.

Chant the words. If necessary, practice the recurring ♩. ♫ ♩. ♫ pattern until the children sense its uneven quality and can tap and chant it correctly.

HARMONY

Listen: Draw attention to the accompaniment played by ancient instruments on the recording. Listen for the descant played by the RECORDER during the last verse.

Play: The descant may be played by a student studying the flute or violin; it might also be sung by a few voices on "loo."

STYLE

Discuss: This song is a very old English folk melody, dating back at least to the fifteenth century. It is mentioned in Shakespeare's plays and was supposedly a favorite of Queen Elizabeth I. The title, "Greensleeves," refers to the custom of the time when each family had its own colors, just as our schools today have their own colors. In contests, the knights could be identified by the colors they wore on their sleeves.

The late sixteenth-century period, known in European history as the Renaissance, is often described as England's Golden Age. By this time the English had developed a flourishing cultural life and music-making played an important role in court life as well as in the homes of the commoners. Composers wrote music to be sung and played in small groups for personal enjoyment, in addition to music of a more serious nature for the church and important court occasions.

During this period, one sign of an educated person was his ability to read music, to sing, and to play at least one instrument. People would gather for social occasions and perform music written for any combination of voices and/or instruments, depending on what happened to be available. Both "Come Follow Me" and "Greensleeves" were popular during this period.

Listen: Help the children to identify the instruments heard on the recording. These ancient instruments were popular during the Renaissance period. The melody is played on the RECORDER; its mellow sound is similar to a flute. The plucked sound in the accompaniment is made by the LUTE, an instrument similar to our modern guitar, except that it has a pear-shaped body. The VIOLA DA GAMBA supplies the sustained sound in the accompaniment. This instrument has a flat back and sloped shoulders and is held between the legs when played (*gamba* means "leg"). It usually has six strings tuned in fourths and is bowed rather than plucked like the lute.

COME, FOLLOW ME

Gaily   John Hilton

1. Come, fol - low, fol - low, fol - low, Fol - low, fol - low, fol - low me!

2. Whith-er shall I fol - low, fol - low, fol - low, Whith-er shall I fol - low, fol-low thee?

3. To the green-wood, to the green-wood, To the green-wood, green-wood tree.

RHYTHM

Read: This is a good song to review the relationship of different note values to the meter:

HARMONY

Sing: After the children know the three phrases well, sing as a three-part round. Draw attention to the interesting rhythmic and melodic contrasts created when the three phrases are combined.

Play: Suggest that the children perform this round as it might have been performed during England's Golden Age, with one or more parts played on instruments. Flute and/or violin would be suitable.

STYLE

Discuss: John Hilton was a MADRIGAL composer during the latter part of the Golden Age. Madrigals were secular songs written for from four to six independent voices, and were very popular during this time, as were rounds and canons. All were written for the enjoyment of singing in the home. The interweaving of the three melodies of the three phrases of "Come, Follow Me" is typical of the POLYPHONIC music of this period. The term POLYPHONY describes music where more than one melody is performed simultaneously.

THE NIGHT PIECE*

Music by Arthur Frackenpohl
Words by Robert Herrick

STYLE

Discuss: Robert Herrick, the poet who wrote the lyrics for this song, lived in England during the Golden Age. Recall the discussion about this period conducted when the children were studying "Greensleeves." However, the music for this poem was written by a composer of today, Arthur Frackenpohl.

Listen: After the children have learned the song, listen to the recording. Discuss reasons one might have for knowing that this song had not been written at the same time as "Greensleeves." Some children may recognize that this music has only one melody with an accompaniment instead of several independent melodies sounding polyphonically as was true of much Renaissance music.

MELODY

Read: Examine the key signature and scan the notation. Determine that this song is based on the NATURAL MINOR scale. Draw attention to the melodic sequence in phrases 1 and 2.

Sing: Establish the tonality and invite the class to sing the melody, first on "loo" and then with words.

HARMONY

Listen: Before the children begin to learn the accompanying parts, study these in relation to the melody. Discover the chords that are created by the combination of the three voices. Here is the chord sequence for the first phrase:

Notice that this chord sequence is different from the more familiar I–IV–V$_7$ sequence. This stepwise progression helps give the music a contemporary flavor.

Play the chords on the bells or piano and listen to the different chord qualities. Identify the first and the last chords as MINOR and the second and third chords as MAJOR.

Listen to the recording, drawing the children's attention to the harmony sequence. Discuss the interesting color that this adds to the composition.

Sing: Divide the class into three sections and sing the chords on "loo." Listen carefully to make sure that the chords have the appropriate major and minor qualities.

When the chords have been sung accurately, ask Group I to sing the melody while Groups II and III sing the lower tones of the chords. Notice tones in the melody that do not belong to the chords, such as D on the fourth beat of the first measure. Such tones are called PASSING TONES.

Learn the remainder of the song in the same manner: identify the chord sequence for each phrase, sing the chords listening for chord quality, and finally sing the melody with the accompanying parts.

FOURTH STRING QUARTET, OPUS 37 (Third movement, excerpt)*

Arnold Schoenberg

Columbia Records CML 4737

STYLE

Discuss: Review with the children what they have learned about various kinds of tonal organizations that composers have used for creating melodies: major, minor, modal, pentatonic, whole tone, and synthetic scales. (See "Developing Contemporary Improvisations and Compositions," page 219.) Stress the fact that all melodies are based upon tones that belong to some kind of predetermined group from which the composer selects the specific tones he wants to use.

Read: **One of the most inventive composers of the twentieth century was Arnold Schoenberg, who created a new kind of tonal organization. Here is the opening melody of his Fourth String Quartet; can you study this melody and discover the tonal organization that Schoenberg used?** Place the melody on the chalkboard, omitting the numbers below the notes:

Copyright 1939 by G. Schirmer Inc., New York, N.Y. Used by permission.

Guide the children to name the notes that have been used and put them on the staff as they are named from low to high:

How many different tones did the composer use for this melody? (Twelve.) **Can you play these on the bells?** (No.) **What could you do to make this possible?** (Transpose the tones up one octave higher.) Help the children to notate the tones in this range. Give the necessary bells to twelve children and ask them to arrange themselves in a line so that the bells would be in order from low to high. As the children play, notice that the tones move by half steps and that the composer has used every tone between low G natural and high G flat for his melody.

Number the tones of the melody as illustrated above and help the children play the different tones in the order in which they occur. **As you play these tones in succession, do you have a feeling that any one tone seems more important than another?** (No.) **Is this typical of our familiar melodies?** (No, usually one tone is more important, the home tone.)

One of Schoenberg's purposes in creating a new kind of tonal organization was to eliminate any feeling of a tonal center (home tone). (You may wish to tell the children that the word ATONAL is used to describe music that avoids a tonal center.) **This kind of tonal organization is called a TWELVE-TONE SET because it uses all twelve tones of the chromatic scale; sometimes it is called a ROW or a SERIES.**

Listen: Play the opening section of the third movement of Schoenberg's quartet. The twelve-tone set which the children have played on the bells is first played as a melody in unison by all four instruments.

After the children have listened to this, discuss ways the composer may use his row (series) to create a complete composition. **Once the composer has created his row, he may manipulate it in various ways. He continues to use the same series, but it may be played backwards (RETROGRADE), upside down (INVERSION), or backwards and upside down (RETROGRADE INVERSION).** (See "Creating Serial Music," (page 244) for a more detailed explanation of these transformations.)

The listener is not expected to be able to hear all of the different organizations of a row as he listens to SERIAL MUSIC, but it should help him to understand this new musical language a little better if through repeated listening he becomes aware of some of the devices the composer has used. As the children listen again to this excerpt, call attention to the fact that the melody is played backward and upside down (retrograde inversion) immediately after the first unison statement. They should be able to hear the interval of a fifth (the interval that ends the first statement of the row) now played by the cellos alone. The next three tones are played by the viola and second violin, and then the first violin plays the remaining seven tones. Other transformations that follow are too complex for the listener to discern.

CREATING SERIAL MUSIC

When the children have listened to the Schoenberg quartet and have had opportunities to discuss the ways some composers of the twentieth century have created new music, suggest that they apply some of these ideas in creating their own music.

Review the serial devices explained in the study of the "Fourth String Quartet." Invite the children to make up their own serial melody. You may wish to mention that some composers may at times follow a special rule when making up their melodies. This rule states that "no tone can be repeated until all tones of the chromatic scale are used."

Place the chromatic scale on the chalkboard. As the children choose the tones for their melody, cross out each note until all have been used. Remind the children that they should avoid patterns that remind them of melodies based on the major or minor scales.

When the melody has been made up, you may wish to select only a portion of it to manipulate to assist the children in becoming familiar with the procedures. For example: select a four-tone cell as the original row; describe its structure in terms of half steps between each tone and the direction of movement.

Write this melody in *retrograde;* begin with the final tone and use the same pitches. Then write it in *inversion;* remember that it is the size of the interval that is inverted, not the actual pitches. (You may need to begin an octave higher so that the melody will stay in a range that can be played on the bells.) Finally, write it in *retrograde inversion.*

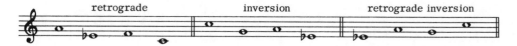

Select a poem such as "Jack Be Nimble" for your song. Choose the order in which the four possible organizations of the row should appear. Set the tones in rhythm. Sing and play the composition.

To add harmony, play the same series in a different sequence at a lower-pitch level on the piano:

COMPOSITION FOR SYNTHESIZER (Excerpt)*

Milton Babbitt

Columbia Records, MS 6566

STYLE

Listen: **We have learned earlier that some composers of the twentieth century organize the pitches of their melodies in new ways. Listen to this music; what seems to be new about it? Could it have been composed a long time ago?** The children will probably react first to the unusual tone quality.

Discuss: This music would have to be composed recently because the instrument which produces the sound was invented less than twenty years ago. It is the RCA Electronic Sound Synthesizer, the only instrument of its kind. This elaborate instrument can create whatever kinds of sound patterns the composer chooses. The possibilities of different sound qualities, of pitches ranging from high to low, of rhythms made up of any conceivable duration, are infinite. The only limitations are the composer's imagination and the ears of the audience. It is possible to create music on this instrument which moves so quickly, with tones so high or low, that no one can perceive it.

Composition on the synthesizer is difficult and time consuming. For every sound that is to be included in the music, the composer has to make five different decisions: the pitch, the duration, the tone color, the envelope (how the sound begins and ends), and how the sound should proceed to the next sound. As these decisions are made they are punched on paper tape that is fed into the synthesizer that produces the sound. The sound is recorded on a tape recorder. The composer can then decide if he wishes to alter it in any way. This procedure is followed until the entire composition is completed.

FORM

Listen: Listen again to the excerpt and discuss its form. **We often think of musical form as consisting of repetition and contrast of melodic and rhythmic patterns. Can you find such in this composition? Is there any element in this music which provides repetion and contrast?** As the children listen and make comments, guide them to discover that various tone colors help to provide the important attributes of repetition and contrast. Encourage the children to describe the different tone colors they hear. They may chart the sequence of sounds for the first segment of the composition, using a different shape for each tone color. Notice that a pattern does emerge.

Although melodic and rhythmic patterns as we are accustomed to thinking of them cannot be heard in this music, similar colors and sequences of tones do recur. Frequent listening will help the children become sensitive to these and to the unity and variety that they contribute to the musical totality.

O COME, O COME, EMMANUEL

Music adapted from plainsong
Words translated by John M. Neale

Freely

O come, O come, Em - man - u - el,
Ve - ni, Ve - ni, Em - man - u - el,

And ran - som cap - tive Is - ra - el,
Cap - ti - vum sol - ve Is - ra - el,

That mourns in lone - ly ex - ile here
Qui ge - mit in ex - i - li - o,

Un - til the Son of God ———— ap - pear.
Pri - va - tus De - i Fi - li - o.

Re - joice! Re - joice! Em - man - u - el
Gau - de! Gau - de! Em - man - u - el

Shall come to thee, O Is - ra - el.
Nas - ce - tur pro te, Is - ra - el.

STYLE

Read: **What do you notice about the notation of this song that makes it appear to be different from other songs?** Children will undoubtedly point out that there are no measure bars and no meter signature. Some children may mention the use of several notes to one syllable as on "-man-," "God," and "Is-."

Listen: **Does this song sound different from other songs we have sung?** The children may suggest that it sounds somewhat strange, seems unfinished, and seems to "wander about" without any definite pattern to it.

Discuss: **The reason this music sounds and looks different is because it is written in the style of an ancient PLAINSONG, a type of music that was sung in the earliest Christian churches.**

Plainsongs belong to a style of music called MONOPHONIC music. Mono means "one," and in plainsongs there is only one unaccompanied melody.

After listening to this and other examples of plainsong, help the children to conclude that the characteristics of this type of music are:

1. There is only a single melodic line, no harmony of any kind.
2. There are no regularly recurring accents to divide the melody into metric groupings.
3. The rhythmic pattern is determined by the rhythm of the words.
4. The melody is based on MODES rather than on the familiar major-minor tonalities. (A mode is a scale based on a whole step–half step pattern different from the usual scales. The mode of this song is very similar to the natural minor scale.)
5. The melody moves mostly by steps; skips are usually no more than a third.
6. No instrumental accompaniment is used.
7. The text is always religious, often taken from the Bible.
8. The important words are emphasized by singing several tones on the same word or a single syllable, thus giving an "ornamental" effect to the melodic line.

Play: Modes can be easily constructed by starting on any white key on the piano and playing up eight tones, always playing the white keys. In this way seven *different* modes may be created by starting on each white key: A, B, C, D, E, F, and G. Notice that each mode has a different pattern of whole and half steps. (There is a B flat in this song because it has been transposed from A, which is the beginning tone of the mode in which it is written.)

Create: Choose one of the seven modes and create a "plainsong" based on words from the Bible or other suitable words.

EXPRESSION

Listen: **We have said that "good" music has both UNITY and VARIETY and that it also must have a CLIMAX. Does this music have these qualities?** The children may feel that this song lacks all three qualities.

Help the children to realize that, while this music may seem monotonous, it *does* have both unity and variety and also what one might call a climax. Unity is provided by the consistent rhythmic pattern and the repetitious melodic ornamentation. Variety is obtained by always varying the melodic pattern and the direction. A kind of climax is reached on the word "Rejoice," which appears on the highest pitch of the melodic line and obtains importance from a contrasting rhythmic pattern.

Point out that the way unity, variety, and climax are attained is one reason why music of different historical periods sounds different. The music of this particular period places more emphasis on unity than variety. Climaxes are less important, therefore, because they require considerable contrast or variety.

Sing: If this song is to be sung with appropriate expressiveness, the tone quality must be pure and clear, the tempo must be fairly slow with steady rhythm, and the dynamics must be consistent throughout. Phrasing is determined by the word meaning, and each phrase should be sung as one thought.

CHILDREN'S PRAYER

Andante

Engelbert Humperdinck

When at night I go to sleep, Four-teen an-gels watch do keep,

Two my head are guard-ing, Two my feet are guid-ing,

Two are on my right hand, Two are on my left hand,

Two are on my right hand, Two are on my

HARMONY

Read: Have the children study the score carefully before attempting to sing this song. **This song has two kinds of harmony and is a good example of two types of music.**

At the beginning, how do the two parts move in relation to each other? (Together, mostly.) **Yes, the first voice has the melody and the second voice provides the harmony. This type of music we call HOMOPHONIC. HOMO means "one and the same" or "joint." PHONIC means "sound." So this is music where the sounds are "joined together."**

Can you find a place where the two voices do not move together? (Beginning with the ninth measure.) **Here we shall hear, not two sounds moving together, but two independent sounds, because each voice sings a separate melody.**

Do you recall what we call music where each voice has a separate melody? Remind the children of the discussion about POLYPHONIC music held when learning "Come, Follow Me."

Analyze the homophonic sections to determine the intervallic relationship between the two parts. Note that much of it moves in thirds.

In the polyphonic section observe the relationship between the independent melodic lines. Discover that the second voice often imitates the first voice, at a lower pitch. Also, compare the two voices and discover the melodic and rhythmic alterations in the imitative sections. Each melodic line might be studied separately with emphasis on the use of chromatic tones and sequential patterns.

Sing: Learn the two parts of the homophonic section simultaneously, stressing the need for listening to both parts.

In the polyphonic section each part will probably have to be learned separately; however, continually emphasize the relationship of each part to the other in so doing.

RHYTHM

Read: Good polyphonic singing requires accurate reproduction of rhythmic patterns. As the children study the score, emphasize the rhythmic relationship between the two voices. Observe how Humperdinck maintains interest by having one voice move while the other voice is stationary. By chanting the words of this section before attempting to sing them many rhythmic problems may be avoided.

Move: Show the children the basic conducting pattern for songs that move in "fours."

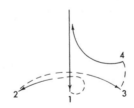

Encourage the children to conduct as they sing because it will help them to maintain a steady beat.

EXPRESSION

Discuss: Most children will be familiar with the story of "Hansel and Gretel" and some may possibly have heard the opera. Draw from them as much as possible about the story.

This song occurs at the point in the opera when the children, realizing that they are lost, decide to sleep in the forest till morning when they hope to find their way home. They then proceed to say their prayers.

Read: Discover the tempo marking (ANDANTE) and the dynamic markings (*p, f, cresc.,* and so forth). Explain these terms and discuss their appropriateness to the mood that Humperdinck is trying to create.

In what TEMPO would one probably sing a prayer? (Not too slow or too fast, but moderately.)

Would one sing loudly or softly? (Primarily softly.)

Why, do you suppose, does the composer suggest that the last phrase be sung loudly? (It is the CLIMAX of the song.) **Yes, and increasing the DYNAMIC LEVEL helps to create this feeling of climax.**

Listen: **What other things, besides the dynamics, contribute to this feeling of climax at the end?**

Guide the children to discover that both the melodic and rhythmic movements contribute to the climax. The melodic line of the polyphonic section rises constantly, each fragment ending on a higher pitch until the climax is reached on high G. Observe that prior to the last phrase, the rhythmic movement has been in short two-measure patterns. In the last phrase, however, the rhythm keeps moving steadily forward for three measures without a break, until the climactic point is reached on a long sustained note (𝅗𝅥).

Sing: Discuss the importance of singing this song with appropriate TONE QUALITY and of paying close attention to all the dynamic markings.

GHOST OF TOM

Traditional Round
Arranged by Kurt Miller

RHYTHM

Read: Study the rhythm of the first section. Notice that the melody in the first two-measure phrase moves with one tone to the beat. In the remaining measures, the rhythm moves primarily with either one or two tones to the beat. Chant the words in rhythm while tapping the beat.

Study the rhythm of the second section. Observe that the rhythm in the upper part is the same as in the first section. **What happens to the rhythm in the low part?** Help the children realize that the rhythm of the melody is now "stretched out," sounding with one tone to *two* beats and that each note has become twice as long as in the original statement. **We call this rhythmic device** AUGMENTATION.

Divide the class into two groups and chant the first eight measures of the two parts simultaneously.

Play: Two children may play the rhythms on percussion instruments of contrasting tone quality, such as tone block and drum.

Create: Invite the children to take a familiar song, such as "Come, Follow Me," and augment the rhythm. Divide the class into two groups and chant or tap the original rhythm and the augmented rhythm together.

MELODY

Read: Scan the notation and discover that this song is in the key of E minor. **In which of the E-minor scales is this song written?** Help the children to realize that it is in the NATURAL MINOR because no accidentals occur on the sixth or seventh steps.

Sing: Sing the melody of the round in unison on a neutral syllable. Be sure that the children are singing D natural; they may have a tendency to sing D sharp, especially in the last measure.

HARMONY

Sing: When the children know the melody well, sing it as a four-part round.

Practice singing the second section. Discover that the melody of the upper part is the same as the melody in the first section for eight measures and that the melody of the lower part is the same, but in an augmented rhythm. Draw attention to the descending half steps in measures 9 and 10 in the lower part. Compare the two parts in measures 11 through 15 and discover that they move in contrary motion (opposite directions).

Try singing the two parts simultaneously. If problems arise, practice the parts separately, then sing in harmony immediately.

FORM

Play: Children will enjoy developing "spooky" introductions and codas for this song. Invite one child to improvise an appropriate melody on the bells or xylophone, using tones from the E-minor scale. Other children may improvise rhythm patterns on percussion instruments. For example:

SYMPHONY NO. 40 IN G MINOR (First Movement)

Many LP recordings available; consult record catalogues   Wolfgang Amadeus Mozart

FORM

Discuss: Review the things the class has learned about musical form. **What are some of the musical designs that you know?** (AB, ABA, ABACABA.) **What helps to create design in music?** (Repetition and contrast.) Remind the children that *variety* is also important because it provides interest and that *unity* is obtained through repetition. Help the children recall that each A, B, or C section has its own smaller design made up of single or groups of phrases.

Today we are going to hear one part of a very long composition called a SYMPHONY. **A symphony is an orchestral composition usually consisting of four contrasting parts or** MOVEMENTS. **Each movement has a complete design of its own. As you listen to one of these movements, you will notice that it is divided into smaller sections, each of which has a design of its own. The music we shall hear is the first movement of a symphony composed by Mozart; it has three large sections.**

Listen: **I am now going to play the opening section and as you listen, decide what is different about this and the first section of other forms that you are familiar with, such as the three-part form or the rondo.** Guide the children to conclude that this section is longer than usual and that it includes more than one musical idea.

Play Theme I, study its notation and determine its design: two eight-measure phrases (ab). Observe that this theme is in MINOR.

Symphony No. 40 *In G Minor*

Then play Theme II and note its contrasting nature, but similar design: two four-measure phrases (cd). Note that this theme is in MAJOR.

Listen again to this section and discuss details of its design:

1. Theme I is stated by the strings and repeated.
2. A linking section or bridge, made up of chordal figures and scale passages, occurs.
3. Theme II is introduced by the strings and woodwinds and is repeated.
4. The section is extended with additional figures, including some from Theme I, and ends with a vigorous passage.

Listen now while I play the middle section. What is different about this section from other middle sections you have heard? Help the children to realize that no new musical ideas have been introduced and that the composer has created this section out of ideas that were presented in the opening section. Play the middle section again and note that only materials from Theme I have been used.

Discuss the differences between the way this theme has been DEVELOPED and the way a theme may be VARIED in the "theme-and-variation" form they have studied previously. In this composition only small segments of the theme are used, whereas in a variation the complete theme is altered in some way.

As the children listen to this section once more, draw attention to the following:

1. In the first half of the section only the "a" part of Theme I is heard. Notice how this is passed from instrument to instrument and played in different keys.
2. When the theme passes to the low strings, a countermelody is played by the violins. Notice that a similar melody continues in the low strings as the theme shifts back to the high strings.
3. In the second half of the section only a three-note figure from the theme becomes the subject of a dialogue between violins and woodwinds. Listen for the occasional inversions of this figure.

Now listen for the final section of this movement. What do you expect to hear? New musical ideas? The same musical ideas treated in new ways? An exact repetition of the first section? As the children listen, agree that this section is almost identical to the opening section of the movement. The main differences are:

1. The bridge between the first and second themes has been extended.
2. Theme II is now in MINOR instead of major:

3. The closing section, which makes frequent references to the first theme, has been greatly extended and brings the movement to a vigorous close.

This complex design you have just studied is called a SONATA-ALLEGRO FORM. It is the form which composers usually use for the first movement of their symphonies. Help the children to summarize what they have learned about this form and give them the conventional names for the various sections.

The opening section contains statements of the two contrasting themes, the first in minor and the second in major. A bridge connects the two themes, and the section ends with a closing section. **This section is called the EXPOSITION.**

The middle section uses different segments from the first theme of the exposition in various ways. **This section is called the DEVELOPMENT.**

The final section is very similar to the exposition. The first theme reappears exactly as it was at the beginning, but the second theme is now in minor. The bridge and closing sections have been extended. **This section is called the RECAPITULATION.**

Discuss reasons why the names given to each section are good choices.

SWINGING ALONG

In marching tempo

Girl Scout Song

HARMONY

Read: This is a good example of how an arranger can create a DESCANT to a melody. The problem is to write an independent melody, interesting in itself, that will HARMONIZE with the original tune.

The first step is to find the chords that can be used to accompany the given melody. Number the measures for easy reference. Notice that the first eight measures of the melody are based on a two-measure motive:

What chord is outlined in the first motive? (The I chord.)

What chord is outlined in the second motive? (The V_7 chord.) **Yes, but the last tone of this motive (A) will not sound right with this chord. Which chord might we use on this note?** (The I chord, because A is a member of this chord.)

Which tones are used in the third motive? (D-G-B flat.) **None of our chords (I, IV, V_7) includes all these tones, so we must find a new chord for this motive. If we arrange these tones in thirds we shall have a new chord:**

What step of the scale is this chord built on? (The second.) **We call this a II chord. Is this chord major or minor in quality?** (Minor.) **So, on the autoharp, this would be called the Gm chord, since it is built on G.**

Use the same procedure to determine the chords for the fourth motive. (V_7, I.)

Measures 9 to 12 contain subtle modulations that may be beyond the children's comprehension. The teacher should explain, however, that each beat of these measures must be harmonized independently, and he should point out the modulating chords, A_7, D_7, G_7, C_7, F, in the last three measures.

Now, look at the DESCANT **melody.** Study the notation measure for measure and observe that the tones used for the descant belong to the same chords that were used for the corresponding measures of the original melody. Notice also the contrasting rhythmic patterns and the contrasting melodic direction of the two melodies. **A good descant must harmonize with the original chords, and it must have contrasting melodic and rhythmic patterns in order to be independent of the original tune.**

Create: Choose a song with a simple chord progression (I, V_7), such as "Sandy Land," and write a descant to it.

MELODY

Read: Draw attention to the chromatics in measures 10 and 11. Review the function of the "sharp" and the "natural" (cancel) signs in relation to the key signature.

Notice the sequential relationship of the two-measure motives in both voices, and also the contrary movement of the two melodies.

Sing: Use the chord sequence I-V_7-I-II-V_7-I as a "warm-up" to establish tonality and to develop sensitivity to the quality of secondary chords.

RHYTHM

Read: Draw the children's attention to the rhythmic notation in the ninth measure. **Do you see anything unusual about the notation in the descant in this measure?** (The notes with a "3" over them.)

These we call TRIPLETS. **Triplets are used whenever a composer wants to increase the number of notes he would use ordinarily on a certain beat.**

Notice the words "Swing along" in the melody. This can be written in the notation. But notice that in the descant we have "Swinging along," one more syllable than in the melody. The arranger has to get three syllables instead of two on one beat, so he has to use a triplet in order to notate this:

Whenever we have three notes of equal value within a beat unit that would ordinarily have two such notes, we call them TRIPLETS.

Move: To further the children's understanding and feeling for triplets, practice clapping the following rhythmic patterns while counting the beats:

Chant the words of the melody and the descant separately while clapping the beat. As soon as the children can do this accurately, divide them into two groups and chant both lines simultaneously, listening carefully to the rhythmic relationships of the two parts.

DONA NOBIS PACEM

Andante

Three-Part Round

1. Do - na no - bis pa - cem, pa - cem;

do - na no - bis pa - cem.

2. Do - na no - bis pa - cem;

do - na no - bis pa - cem.

3. Do - na no - bis pa - cem;

do - na no - bis pa - cem.

EXPRESSION

Sing: The words to this beautiful round mean "God, grant us peace." Discuss ways that tempo, dynamics, and tone quality can help convey the mood that these words suggest.

Read: Study the melodic line to decide where the CLIMAX should be in each of the four phrases. **Where is the climax of the whole song?** (In the second phrase.)

HARMONY

Sing: This ancient round is an excellent example of POLYPHONIC music. It should be learned thoroughly, and often enjoyed, as a unison song before children attempt to sing it as a round.

TUM BALALYKA

Jewish Folk Song
Words by Ruth Rubin

Animato

(*Boys*) 1. Maid - en, maid - en, tell___ me true,
(*Girls*) 2. Sil - ly lad, the an - swer true; A

What can grow with - out___ the dew?
stone can grow with - out___ the dew.

What___ can burn for years___ and years?
Love___ can burn for years___ and years; A

What___ can cry and shed___ no tears?
heart___ can cry and shed___ no tears.

MELODY

Read: Determine the D-minor tonality by studying the key signature and scanning the notation. Draw attention to the C # which occurs in the refrain. **What step of the scale is C? Why should this be altered?** To help the children determine their answer, play the D-minor scale, first with C natural and then with C sharp. Notice that the altered seventh step, C #, gives a stronger feeling of rest to the home tone, D. **When the seventh step in the minor scale is raised, we call it a HARMONIC MINOR SCALE.** The pattern of whole and half steps in the harmonic minor scale is:

1	2	3	4	5	6	7	8
whole step	half step	whole step	whole step	half step	whole-half steps	half step	

FORM

Read: Discuss the fact that knowing the form of a song will help one to learn it more efficiently and accurately. Study the score and describe the form. Discover that the song is in two sections, VERSE and REFRAIN, and that the verse is to be sung in UNISON, the refrain in HARMONY, also that the two first phrases of the refrain are HOMOPHONIC and the last two are POLYPHONIC.

Examine the notation for the verse and notice that phrases one and two form a sequence. Write the design of the verse with letters: AA₁BC.

As the children study the design of the refrain, help them realize that the melody of the first phrase is the same as the first phrase of the verse, only the rhythm has been changed. This is also true of the second phrase. The third and fourth phrases are identical to those of the verse.

Sing: Ask the children to sing the melody of the verse, reminding them to keep in mind the design as they practice each phrase.

HARMONY

Read: Study the notation of the first two phrases of the refrain. Discover that the two voices move primarily in THIRDS. Notice measures where the upper part remains on the same tone while the lower part moves stepwise.

Compare the two voices in the third and fourth phrases. In the third phrase the second voice imitates the first, either exactly or on a different pitch level.

Sing: Divide the class into two groups, establish the tonality, and encourage the children to sing as much as possible on a neutral syllable; practice both parts together.

STYLE

Discuss: This is a Jewish folk melody. Compare it with "Shalom Chaverim" studied in the fifth grade. Also review the Russian folk song "The Peddler" and discover that the two songs have common characteristics; this is not surprising as many Jews have come from Russia.

Jewish music is a blending of many styles, but there are some characteristics that can be classified:

1. Minor tonalities that are rooted in the ancient chants of the synagogue
2. Syncopation, resulting from the sounds of the Hebrew language
3. A "rhapsodic" nature, revealing intense feeling
4. Songs based on a "question-and-answer" form. This form goes back to the pattern of the ancient psalms in which two lines were used to complete one thought
5. Simple harmonic accompaniments, often using a simple OSTINATO figure to suggest the bare outline of a chord
6. Songs usually sung in unison
7. Much of the music influenced by the dance, which was very important in ancient religious rites
8. The use of instruments associated with ancient Jewish music: the *shofar* (a wind instrument made from a ram's horn), the *kinnor* (a lyre played with a plectrum), and the *tof* (an instrument similar to our tambourine used to accompany the dancing)

Discuss the list given above with the children and ask them to decide which of the characteristics can be heard in the three songs.

Play: Add an accompaniment on the tambourine. Use this rhythmic pattern or experiment with other patterns.

FUGUE IN G-MINOR ("Little")

Johann Sebastian Bach

Adventures in Music, Grade 6, Vol. 1

FORM

Listen: **This music is like a round. Listen carefully and see how many times you can hear the main theme, or SUBJECT as it is called in compositions of this form.**

Notice that, as one voice completes the subject, it goes on with another COUNTERSUBJECT, as a second voice begins the main subject.

After a voice has completed the subject and countersubject, it may rest or it may continue with a melody of its own that is not necessarily repeated by the other voices. These brief sections, containing new materials, are called EPISODES.

Usually one voice will complete the subject before another voice enters, but sometimes the composer will introduce the voices one after another very quickly. This "piling up" of the subject is called a STRETTO. Ask the children to listen for the stretto in the middle of this composition where the second voice enters right after the first voice has started on the subject.

Discuss: **A composition that is organized in this manner is called a FUGUE. A fugue is an example of POLYPHONIC music.**

A diagram of the opening section, or EXPOSITION, of a fugue might look something like this:

subject	countersubject				
	subject	countersubject		episode	*etc.*
		subject	countersubject		

Listen: **Listen to the composition again and see if you can identify the subject entrances, the countersubject, the episodes, and the strettos.** This is an interesting way to listen to a piece of music, but it does require concentration.

Can you identify the instruments that announce the subject the first three times? (The clarinet, the English horn, the viola and bassoon.)

STYLE

Discuss: This composition was written by Johann Sebastian Bach, who lived at the time when our country was first being settled. He is considered to be one of the greatest composers of all times, and his music is always interesting because every time you listen to it you find something new that you had not heard before.

Bach belongs to a group of composers referred to historically as BAROQUE musicians. The fugue form was perfected during the baroque period, and Bach's fugues are considered masterpieces of this form.

Listen: Much of Bach's music was written for organ or for small orchestra. This fugue was written originally for organ, which was his own favorite instrument. A modern composer, Lucian Caillet, made the orchestral arrangement that is heard in this recording. Even if Bach had written this work for orchestra, it would not have sounded like this version because his orchestra was smaller and "thinner" in sound. Have the children listen to one of Bach's original orchestral compositions, such as one of the Brandenburg Concertos, to compare the sonorities of the baroque and modern orchestras.

After listening to various examples of Bach's music, help the children to conclude that one can recognize baroque music by:

1. Melodies that are "ornamented"
2. Strict adherence to a set tempo; little use of ritardando or accelerando
3. Contrasting loud and soft phrases; little use of crescendo and diminuendo
4. Clear, balanced phrase structure
5. Use of a "running" bass below the melody line
6. Frequent use of contrapuntal writing—polyphony

PART III
PLANNING FOR MUSICAL LEARNING

Preparation of Daily Lesson Plans

The opening section of this book, devoted to the questions involved in planning for teaching, was designed to give the teacher some possible answers as to why, what, how, and when one teaches music. Part II further explored the answers to these questions by showing how musical growth might be furthered through the organization of musical activities in a sequential manner and by illustrating this sequence with specific musical materials. Nevertheless, some perplexing questions undoubtedly still remain unanswered as the teacher attempts to translate these principles of music teaching into day-to-day classroom experiences for his children. In this section teaching procedures for various activities are suggested in a manner consistent with the philosophy of this book.

Any teaching situation can be only as successful as its planning. The following pages are designed to help the teacher plan the kinds of learning experiences that will contribute to musical growth. There are some aspects of planning that are common to all learning situations. For each day's activities, the teacher should answer the following questions as he plans:

WHAT IS MY OBJECTIVE? Objectives such as "the enjoyment of music," "learning to read music," or "the appreciation of great composers," while certainly valid, are too general to be helpful in planning a specific day's activities. It will be helpful if the teacher states his objectives in two ways. He should first determine the concept to be stressed; he must then decide the behavior by which he expects the child to demonstrate understanding of the concept. Time spent on precise determination of the day's objectives will help ensure that the music class time is constantly focused on continuing musical growth. Although behavioral objectives may change, the same conceptual objectives will often be repeated because learning is dependent upon many experiences with the same concept.

WHAT ACTIVITIES SHALL I USE? The objective will determine the activities selected because certain learnings will be most easily grasped in a particular context. For example, rhythmic concepts might be more easily learned through moving or by playing percussion instruments. The present level of understanding of the class will also affect the choice of activity. The teacher will usually plan to include a variety of activities during each class period.

WHAT MATERIALS SHALL I NEED? The choice of musical materials should be based first on their musical value; from this body of worthy music, examples may be selected which are appropriate to the objective of the day. While any musical selection theoretically could lend itself to the teaching of a musical concept, teachers will need to keep in mind that conceptual learning is directly related to the complexity of the example.

Careful preplanning, including the collecting and checking of physical materials such as records, record player, autoharp, and so forth, will avoid needless delay and confusion during the music period.

WHAT WILL BE MY STEP-BY-STEP PROCEDURE? As the teacher plans the learning sequence, he will keep in mind his knowledge of how children learn, asking himself:

1. Have I taken into consideration my children's physical and emotional readiness?
2. Have I applied the principles of conceptual learning? (See page 15.)
3. Have I created an atmosphere in which the musical experiences of the day will be seen as meaningful and purposeful to the class?

As the teacher plans the day's activities, he may wish to organize the learning sequence into four stages:

1. *Review.* Provide time for the children to enjoy favorite songs and/or listening selections, recalling previous musical learnings.

2. *New Problem.* Move from review into exploration of new musical problems that grow logically out of the activities engaged in during stage one. Although emphasis will be on the conceptual objective of the day, all aspects of the music studied will be considered as the need arises. If the children have not easily accomplished the activities planned for review, they are not ready to proceed to the second stage, and additional review is needed. At this point the teacher must be flexible enough to reorient his lesson plan to fit the immediate needs of the children.

3. *Transfer.* During this stage, evaluative devices should be incorporated to provide the teacher with means of measuring children's achievement. Application of learnings begun in the second stage should be made in a new context. The accomplishments of the children during this stage will help provide direction for future planning.

4. *Summary.* Allow time at the end of the music period for the children to review the learnings of the day and to once again enjoy well-known songs and/or familiar listening selections.

A sample lesson plan based on the four questions a teacher should ask as he prepares daily classes follows. This lesson might be presented in the late spring to a first grade class.

OBJECTIVES

Conceptual: Melodies may move by steps, skips or repeated tones. Their movement may be represented on the staff with notes.

Behavioral: Children will correctly describe the melodic contour of a new song as they look at the notation.

ACTIVITIES

Singing, listening, playing bells.

MATERIALS

Musical: "My Pony" (page 74) and "Shoheen Sho" (page 76).

Supplies: Flannel board, felt stairsteps, disks, staff, notes, resonator bells.

PROCEDURE

Review: **I am going to show a picture of a favorite song. Who can tell me what it is?**

Place disks on stairsteps for first phrase of "My Pony."

Play first phrase of each song the children suggest.

Guide discussion toward relationship of picture to sound.

When the correct song is named, sing it together.

New Problem: Place notation of first phrase of "My Pony" on flannel board staff.

Here is a new way to show our melody. Can you see anything in this picture that would help you know how the melody moves?

Allow the children to make suggestions. Draw attention to note heads and their placement on the staff.

Introduce needed vocabulary: staff, lines, spaces, notes.

Put out bells E-F-G-A-B-C-D-E-F. Invite children to play short patterns of their own. As each is played, show it in notation; compare pictures with sound. Help the children to verbalize conclusions about the "pictures."

Transfer: Put notation of "Shoheen Sho" on the flannel board. **Here is a new song. Can you decide how it will sound?**

After the children have discussed the picture, sing the song for them. **Did it sound as you thought it would?** Sing the song again, pointing at the notation.

What kind of song is this? What is it about? Discuss meaning of "shoheen sho." Sing the song again and discuss the word sequence.

Can you sing the song for me? Point at notation as class sings. **Did the melody move the way the notes move?**

Discuss any problems encountered; resing the song for the class if needed. Repeat until the song is learned.

If there is time, place G-A-B bells on table; allow one child to find the melody on the bells.

Summary: Choose one child to select favorite song for class to sing. **How does it begin? Does it move up or down, by steps or skips?** As the children decide, place the notation for the first pattern on the flannel board.

Enjoy singing the familiar song together.

In addition to questions concerned with lesson planning, each activity—listening, singing, playing, moving, creating, and reading—has its own particular problems of presentation. Every teacher will, as he grows in teaching skill, develop techniques adapted to his own personality and his own teaching situation. The following discussion has been included to offer some procedures that might be used as points of departure by each teacher in developing his own teaching pattern.

PLANNING FOR LISTENING ACTIVITIES

While listening is a part of every activity in the music class, there will be some experiences devoted specifically to learning to listen with discrimination to the performances of others, either live or recorded. There are various procedures that may be followed in presenting listening situations. Any of them will be successful, however, only if the teacher knows the music well and has carefully determined the particular aspect of the recording toward which he wishes to guide the children's attention. There is much to hear in any composition. It will remain only a bewildering mass of sound, however, unless the teacher helps the children find the order that does exist. This can be done by directing their attention toward the individual parts that

make up the expressive whole: the melodic lines, the rhythmic patterns, the form, the instrumentation, and so on.

It is important to keep in mind that non-skilled listeners often find it difficult to simply sit and listen. The teacher should find ways of including other activities in the listening situation, such as playing the main theme on the bells or the piano, following the notation of the themes, responding with simple body movements, or accompanying a recording softly with appropriate percussion instruments.

In planning listening experiences it is well to remember that most music does not portray a specific mood or feeling that can be verbalized. By constantly drawing attention to "feeling" when there is no basis in the composer's known intent, one may create a false impression in the minds of children as to the purpose of musical expressiveness. When music is programmatic, the emphasis should primarily be on the manner in which the composer has combined the musical elements to create a particular mood or feeling. Emphasis should be not so much on *how* does this music make you feel, but *why?*

The same composition should be returned to frequently; a single hearing of most works is not enough. Competent skills and favorable attitudes cannot be acquired unless children discover the joy and satisfaction that can come from listening to a composition many times, each time discovering more and more until the music becomes as familiar and as dear as the proverbial "old shoe." As children develop a listening repertoire, they should be helped to determine standards of musical choice by discussing their reasons for preferring one composition to another. Familiarity does not necessarily mean memorization of specific compositions or themes. The purpose of the listening experience is to help children grow in listening skill, to develop an understanding of musical concepts, as well as to develop a repertoire of familiar musical works.

Children will grow in their ability to listen with discrimination in the same way that they improve in other skills, through constant guided practice. Although no one can provide a specific time schedule by which this ability develops, the teacher should constantly help the children become aware of the more subtle and more precise aspects of the musical totality. He may refer to the Charts of Musical Growth for suggestions of the concepts that may be emphasized as the child increases in listening skill. The sample listening lessons might also be consulted for examples of specifics emphasized in particular musical works.

A basic teaching procedure

An example of a basic teaching procedure follows.

1. Direct the children's listening. Before the recording is played, guide the children's attention to specific aspects of the music for which they are to listen.
2. Play the composition in its entirety. If the composition is unusually long, or if the children are unused to listening experiences, one section alone might be played.
3. Discuss the appearance of the specifics that have been brought to the children's attention, as well as any other aspects of the music they may have noticed.
4. Replay the composition. The decision to play the entire composition or a segment will be based on the same reasons as stated before.
5. Give the children a new listening problem. Repeat steps two, three, and four as often as necessary and desirable.

6. End the listening experiences with an uninterrupted performance. This may not occur on the same day as the listening experience was begun. Some listening activities will extend over a period of several days, before all aspects of the music that are pertinent to the present situation have been exhausted.

Selection of materials

Materials for listening experiences will consist primarily of recordings. In selecting recordings, the following questions should be considered.

Is the record of good fidelity and without blemishes? The finest of music is not appealing if it comes from a distorted recording.

Is the quality of the performance satisfactory? It should be technically accurate and expressively performed.

Is the composition of appropriate length and complexity? Music for early listening experiences should obviously portray the aspect of musical structure that is to be stressed. As children improve in listening skill, music of greater complexity, length, and subtlety of organization may be chosen.

Will this recording meet the interests and past experiences of the children? This question is primarily a problem of teaching technique rather than record selection. Many compositions will be suitable for various age levels if they are presented in a manner that meets the interests and experiences of that particular group.

Sources of recorded materials[1]

The sources of recorded materials are numerous. A listing of some of the sources that will be most useful in the elementary music classroom follows.

EDUCATIONAL RECORD SERIES. Certain of the major recording companies have compiled series of recordings especially designed for classroom use. These series have a definite advantage, particularly for the nonspecialist, because good teaching aids accompany each album. These series may well constitute the core

[1] See Appendix D for a list of recording companies and suppliers.

of the listening program for the classroom teacher.

1. Bowmar Orchestral Library. This series has been organized according to types of music. It is left to the teacher to determine the sequences by which he might present particular compositions. Volumes include such types as "Marches," "Dances," and "Pictures and Patterns." The teaching aids are printed directly on the album covers. Charts of the themes of most compositions are provided with each volume.

2. RCA Record Library for Elementary Schools. This series consists of three volumes for each grade: "Basic Listening Program," "Basic Rhythm Program," and "Basic Singing Program." There are also supplementary volumes such as "Indian Album," "Singing Games," and so forth. Many of the compositions included in this series are excerpts from lengthier works, introducing children to music they are not ready to hear in its entirety. Teaching suggestions are included in the front of each album.

3. RCA Adventures in Music. The volumes in this series are organized according to class levels. Extensive teaching suggestions accompany each volume. It is well to keep in mind that the suggested grading in this series is not meant to be absolute. Specific compositions may easily be used at grade levels other than that in which the composition is placed.

4. Musical Sound Books. The compositions in this series have been grouped primarily by type rather than by grade level. The teaching suggestions are published in a series of books by Lillian Baldwin: *Music for Young Listeners (The Green Book, The Crimson Book, The Blue Book)*. These compositions are also available on tape.

5. Recordings accompanying elementary music series. Many of the elementary music series are presently accompanied by record albums which include recordings of songs and instrumental selections. Both songs and instrumental compositions may be used as bases for listening lessons. Listening guides accompany some of the albums.

STANDARD RECORDINGS. The teacher will not wish to stop with the repertoire of compositions included in the educational series. There are many suites, overtures, operas, and so on, with which the children should become acquainted. The selection of these compositions requires some knowledge of music literature. The gaining of this knowledge can be an exciting and satisfying experience for the teacher, however, which will add to his own musical growth as he seeks ways of expanding the musical knowledge of his students.

RECORDINGS OF FOLK MUSIC. The teacher should know about the availability of many excellent collections of authentic ethnic recordings from all over the world as well as an abundance of fine folk music arranged and performed by professional musicians.

CHILDREN'S RECORDINGS. In recent years various recording companies have become aware of the huge youth audience and have produced numerous recordings especially designed for children. These recordings need to be screened carefully, but there are a number that are suitable for classroom use. The teacher must carefully evaluate them in terms of the contribution they may make to musical learning.

Selection of equipment

Equipment should be selected with the same care that was suggested in the selection of materials. Listening situations will require the following equipment.

PHONOGRAPH. It was suggested that fine music is unappealing when played on a distorted recording. This is equally true of the machine upon which the recording is played. It should be a three-speed machine of the finest possible fidelity.

TAPE RECORDER. More and more standard recordings are becoming available on tape. The teacher may wish to investigate the possibility of using tapes, because there are some advantages in operation and storage.

PICTURES OF INSTRUMENTS, THEME CHARTS. These materials can be purchased from various educational music suppliers. Theme charts can also be made by teachers and/or children to become part of a permanent collection.

PLANNING FOR SINGING ACTIVITIES

Singing is second in importance only to listening as a basic classroom activity. Most music experiences will be based on, or grow out of, the learning of songs. Helping the child gain skill in singing is, therefore, an important aspect of the music class, and his development of this skill can be guided in a number of ways. The first problem facing the teacher of the primary grades is that of helping children gain pitch control, which may be a major problem for some children and may never be surmounted if not solved during the early grades.

There may be several causes for the appearance of problem singers in the early grades. One may well be simply a lack of experience. Some children come to kindergarten without ever having had a song sung *to* them, and with no realization of the possibilities of singing. Other children have never realized that they were not singing. They may be perfectly happy "droning" away, because it has never come to their attention that they are not singing correctly. Another reason for problem singers may be lack of interest. Unless the child sees singing as a skill that is satisfying and enjoyable, he will have no motivation to attain this skill. There may be other reasons for children's being unable to sing accurately, including both physical and emotional disturbances. These problems, however, are generally beyond the power of the teacher to solve within the singing situation.

How to help these children develop pitch control is a constant problem, since no one approach will work with every child. Here are some suggestions that may prove valuable in working not only with children who have special pitch problems, but with all young singers.

Provide a wide variety of singing experiences. Sing to, and with, the child often, until singing becomes as much a part of his aural world as is the spoken word.

Draw the child's attention to pitched sound and to melodic movement through playing the song bells, moving to melodic direction, or exploring the differences in pitches of various instruments.

Emphasize the melodic movement of new songs through discussion and by picturing the movement on the chalkboard or by hand levels.

Provide a music time involving a variety of activities that are appealing and challenging, in which singing may be seen as a desirable skill.

Help the child to face his own problems objectively. A problem cannot be solved until one realizes that there *is* a problem.

Associate the spacial concepts of high-low, up-down that the children already possess with these concepts as they relate to pitched sound. Stretch "way up" for high tones, climb "up and down the stairs" vocally as well as physically.

Make use of tone games and action songs where the melodic direction and the actions match to help the children gain concepts of melodic movement.

Use dialogue songs requiring individual participation where the child may find singing both important and satisfying.

As the teacher strives to help each child find his singing voice, it is imperative to keep the emphasis on accurate singing in perspective. This skill is a very important one, but musical understanding and enjoyment may be attained without it. Undue stress may result in the exact opposite of the desired goal. The child may not only not learn to sing, but may well develop unfavorable attitudes toward the whole world of music. Help him to learn to sing, of course, but it is more important to help each child find *some* facet of musical expression in which he can find satisfaction.

As the child gains control over a limited range, the teacher will wish to work for the expansion of range. Children's voices seem to follow a natural range expansion, but we cannot take this for granted and must consciously work for an ever-widening range. Along with expanding range should go increasing independence, which is attained only as the child learns to listen to himself and to evaluate his own performance in terms of both accuracy and quality.

Learning to sing is developed as the child expands his repertoire of songs. Many of the songs children sing, particularly during the primary grades, will be learned by listening to the teacher sing or by listening to a recording. This learning period is most important, for it is *as* the child learns a new song, as well as later, that the singing activity becomes a time of musical learning for the child.

A suggested teaching procedure

1. The teacher sings the entire song (first establishing tonality and tempo) or plays a recording of it. Give the children some specific aspect for which they are to listen during this initial hearing. These should usually relate to the text or over-all mood of the song.
2. Discuss the text. Resing the song whenever the children are not sure of the content or the word sequence.
3. Discuss the musical content. It is at this point that the musical objective of the day may be stressed. The objectives may be to expand children's awareness of phrase pattern, melodic direction, rhythmic repetition, and so forth. As in step two, resing whenever the children cannot correctly identify the patterns. You may also wish to use additional aids at this point in the lesson, such as playing the patterns on the bells, drawing contour lines of the melody on the chalkboard, and so on.
4. Invite the children to sing the entire song, or a single phrase if the song is long and complex. This performance should be an independent rendition without the teacher's help. Musical independence comes only if there is a need for independence. Sing *for* the children, but not *with* them during the learning period.
5. Ask the children to identify problems that they may have experienced.
6. Help the children correct their errors, returning to steps two to four as often as necessary.
7. The children may sing the entire song, followed by an evaluation of their performance for its expressive character as well as its accuracy.
8. Use the song as a vehicle for further learnings, experimenting with instrumental accompaniments, physical movement, different expressive interpretations, and so on.

When the children have gained independence and accuracy in singing, they are ready to expand their singing skill to include the ability to harmonize. No single outline can be given for the introduction of part-singing experiences, because development of this ability is a long process that should include a variety of types of part-singing activities. It is dependent on a sequence of activities, which includes listening to multiple sounds and playing harmonic accompaniments for class songs as well as singing. The following is a description of some ways in which children can participate in progressively more demanding part-singing experiences.

CHANTS. A chant is a repetitious pattern of few tones, usually lower than the melody, which can be continued throughout the song with a minimum of alteration necessary to fit the harmonic demands. In early experiences it is generally wise to select a chant pattern that uses only one or two tones. Later, use more complex chants with older children, or help them plan their own chants to use with favorite songs. ("Get on Board," "Buffalo Gals.")

ROUNDS. Rounds are very simple examples of polyphonic music; they are the combination of two or more independent melodic lines. The number of sections of a round is usually determined by the number of phrases in the round. Many rounds may be combined with chants. ("Are You Sleeping," "Canoe Song.")

DIALOGUE SONGS. There are many songs that are designed to be sung as question and answer. These songs may sometimes be turned into harmonic experiences by having one group hold the last tone of its phrase while the other group answers. ("Old Texas," "Vreneli.")

ADDED CHORD TONES. In place of a repetitious chant, one group may add a simple harmonizing part by singing the root of the harmonizing chord. They may sing this on a neutral syllable or they may sing the words of the melody. Adding the autoharp will help reinforce correct tones and will indicate needed changes. Other chordal tones may be used in the same manner. ("Down in the Valley.")

DESCANTS. Descants are examples of polyphonic music. The descant is an independent melodic line, usually higher than the main melody, which is based on the same harmonic progressions. As with chants, in early experiences the descant may be taught independently before combining it with the main melody. ("Lullaby," "This Land Is Your Land.")

IMPROVISED HARMONIZATIONS. Listening to the multiple sounds will be stressed in all part-singing experiences. One of the aims of such emphasis should be to develop the capacity to add a second part spontaneously, by ear.

One of the simplest ways to do this is to sing the same melody a third higher or lower. Many songs lend themselves to this treatment. Any song that can be sung in thirds can also be sung in sixths; experiment with both intervals. Gradually, songs that require additional intervals may be introduced. Help the children to decide through experimentation where other intervals are needed. ("Au clair de la lune," "French Cathedrals.")

READING PART-SONGS. Every new notational problem must first have been experienced aurally before children can solve it successfully. Reading part-songs should therefore probably be delayed until the fourth grade, after the children have enjoyed many of the experiences described above. In learning part-songs from notation, the teacher should recognize the importance of learning all parts simultaneously, particularly those songs harmonized in homophonic style. Problems should always be considered in relation to the harmonic totality, seeing and hearing individual lines in relation to the whole. Separate rehearsal of parts should be resorted to only after the class has studied the song as a unit. Then the problem sections may be practiced separately and immediately replaced in context.

Selection of song materials

In selecting songs to be used as a basis for the singing experience, the teacher should refer to the suggestions for selection of repertoire discussed in the section, "What Shall We Teach?" In addition, the teacher will need to consider such factors as range, complexity, length, and appropriateness of the subject matter. The possibility of correlation should also be considered when selecting songs. *Meaningful* correlation may result in added interest and increased learning for both the music and the correlated subject, but correlation that is artificial and unnatural has no place in the curriculum.

Sources of song materials

The major source of song materials for the elementary grades will be the music series published by various book companies. (See Appendix D for a complete listing of the more recent series.) The teacher should keep in mind that no one book will supply all the material needed for his class, so that he will wish to refer to other grade levels within the basic series used in his school, as well as to other music series. In addition, there are countless song collections that the teacher will wish to investigate.

Selection of equipment

The only equipment needed for singing activities is some pitched instrument by which to establish tonality—a chromatic pitch-instrument, bells, a piano, or an autoharp.

PLANNING FOR PLAYING ACTIVITIES

An important part of music time through the elementary grades will be spent in learning to use instruments in a variety of ways. Many concepts of musical organization may be more easily acquired through the kind of concrete experiences that can be provided with musical instruments. Intervallic relationships and concepts of duration and of multiple sound may be much more clearly grasped when heard and played on an instrument than when experienced only through singing.

Good quality instruments have a place in every music class; they provide one more way of exploring the world of musical expressiveness or of developing performing skills, as well as helping the children to become aware of musical concepts.

Experiences in the elementary classroom should include the exploration of pitched and nonpitched instruments. The instrumental collection should be selected with care, avoiding homemade instruments unless the end product is *musical* in sound. Children learn to appreciate musical quality when surrounded by music of quality. Instruments that are little more than noisemakers or toys have no place in the music classroom. Fewer instruments of better quality are of far more value than many instruments of poor quality. Older children should be encouraged to share their ability to play standard orchestral instruments with members of the general music class.

Playing percussion instruments

Once we believed that percussion instruments, the "rhythm band," belonged to the primary grades. When the child left the third grade, the instruments were put away, never to be used again. Today we know that good quality percussion instruments have a place at every grade level.

It is important that, as new instruments are introduced to the children, time be taken to discover the proper way to produce a musical sound on each instrument. Teachers who are unskilled in this area may find that the instrumental teacher in the local school can be helpful in this field. The children should also be encouraged to experiment with various ways of playing the instruments and be helped to decide which ways seem to produce the most musical sound.

The teacher must keep constantly in mind that the purpose of playing experiences is to further musical understanding and to participate in a *musical* performance. One way to help ensure this is to use only a few instruments at a time. One pair of sticks or a single tambourine may be very effective—multiplying by ten or twenty does not necessarily increase the effectiveness.

Because there is such a variety of percussion instruments, it is difficult to suggest a specific procedure for their introduction. The following are some suggested ways in which they may be used; as the teacher and the children explore together, they will find many other possibilities.

Using nonpitched percussion instruments

Use drums, sticks, and so forth, to establish tempos for songs or to underline the beat in recordings.

Select different instruments to play repetitious patterns as song accompaniments. Patterns may be created by:

(1) Using word patterns from the song. ("Who's That Tapping at the Window?")
(2) Making up word patterns that are related to the song text as a basis for the rhythmic pattern. ("Lone Star Trail.")
(3) Finding patterns from the melodic notation. ("Angel Band.")
(4) Using a different instrument for each note in the pattern. ("Fengyang Drum.")

Add instrumental introductions, interludes, and codas based on repetitious patterns similar to those under (2). ("Little Black Train.")

Select instruments to add special sound effects at appropriate places in the song. ("Hickory, Dickory, Dock.")

Use instruments to add expressiveness to the choral reading of favorite poems.

Use instruments to help tell a familiar story, using a different instrument to describe each character. ("Compose a Musical Story," page 98.)

Create a "sound drama," using instruments to describe in rhythmic patterns the sounds associated with a fire, a storm, a walk in the woods, and so on.

Select percussion instruments and plan rhythmic accompaniments that will be characteristic of the song's style. ("Mary Ann.")

Nonpitched percussion instruments:

Rhythm sticks
Drums
Wood block
Triangles
Sand blocks
Cymbals
Finger cymbals
Jingle bells
Tambourines
Claves
Maracas
Castanets
Gongs
Guiro
Bongo drums
Temple blocks
Conga drums

Using pitched percussion instruments

Associate the aural concepts of high-low, up-down, and step-skip with visual concepts through the use of step bells.

Help the children to develop the scale concept by having them place "scrambled" resonator bells in order.

Improvise bell descants for pentatonic songs. ("The Rain Sings a Song.")

Use bells to add appropriate introductions and codas to familiar songs. ("Sleep, Baby, Sleep.")

Encourage the children to play familiar melodies on the bells by ear. Begin by placing before them only those resonator bells that are needed. Later, help them locate the melody, using the entire scale.

Use the bells, the xylophone, or the meloharp for simple one-, two-, or three-tone ostinato accompaniments. At first, give each child a single bell. ("Turn the Glasses Over.")

Write familiar tunes in number notation for the children to play on the bells. ("Dance in the Circle.")

Add harmonic accompaniments, giving each child a single resonator bell. Try a variety of accompaniment patterns. ("Down in the Valley.")

Make use of pitched instruments to help the children develop an understanding of tonality by "figuring out" scales on the bells, thus discovering the placement of whole and half steps. (Make use of the step bells in this activity also.)

Help the children learn chord construction by grouping the resonator bells in the correct order.

Pitched percussion instruments:

Song bells
Step bells
Resonator bells
Xylophone

Playing the autoharp

Children should be familiar with the autoharp and its sound long before they begin to use it themselves. In the early primary grades the teacher will want to accompany the children as they sing. Later, children may begin to develop skill in stroking the autoharp strings while the teacher changes the chords. When the children are ready to begin to accompany the class, the following procedure might be used:

Select a familiar song that can be accompanied with only one or two chords.

Place on the chalkboard the names and numbers of the chords that are to be used:
F C$_7$
I V$_7$

Choose a child who has a good sense of rhythm to be the first accompanist. Give him an opportunity to practice moving from one chord to another. The class may practice on autoharp charts if they are available.

The accompanist should establish tempo and tonality by strumming the I chord.

The members of the class listen as they sing softly, raising their hands when they wish the chord to be changed.

Sing through the first phrase; discuss suggested chord changes. In case of a disagreement, try both ways and ask the children to decide which seems the most appropriate.

As the class decides the accompaniment, write the chord names on the blackboard in the order in which they are to be used; refer to the chart for future performances if needed.

The autoharp can be a valuable means of developing sensitivity to multiple sounds. For this reason the development of accompaniments should always be through the *ear* rather than the eye. Determine the accompaniments first by sound; later the chord markings can be used as reference. As the children improve in skill and discrimination, songs requiring more than three chords may be used. Encourage them to experiment with various chordal progressions for the same song. They may also experiment with different ways of playing the autoharp to represent the stringed instruments of various countries. Try different kinds of "picks" and various rhythmic patterns to add an authentic stylistic flavor.

The diffculty of tuning an autoharp cannot be minimized. If the teacher is not sure of his own ability to discriminate, he should call on the assistance of a trained musician to tune the instrument regularly.

Playing the piano

The piano will be an integral part of all classroom music activities throughout the elementary school. The teacher who has had some piano training will often accompany the children in their singing and moving, but the use of the piano should not be limited to the teacher only. Although the teacher is not expected to instruct the children to play the piano as part of the general music curriculum, he will want to introduce them to the keyboard, using it in a variety of ways to further their musical learning. Even though the teacher may not be a skilled performer, he and the children may explore together. Older children often have developed considerable facility at the keyboard as a result of class or private piano instruction; these children should be encouraged to share their abilities with the class through solo performance and accompaniment of class songs.

The purchase of a piano may represent a major part of any elementary music budget; it should be selected with care. Again, expert help is needed. Many major piano companies have developed special schoolroom models.

Using the piano

Help the children associate up–down and high–low with right–left at the keyboard.

Use the piano freely to create special "sound effects" in dramatic play situations.

Add repetitious one- or two-tone ostinato accompaniments, or use such patterns as introductions and codas. ("Vesper Hymn.")

Improvise piano descants for pentatonic songs by encouraging the children to create a pattern on the black keys as other children sing.

Use the keyboard to help the children discover scale organization. One child may select the tone on which he wishes to start his scale. With the help of the class, he may experiment to determine which black and white keys are needed to make the scale "sound right." This new skill may be used to establish the tonality of songs.

Introduce the children to simple chording, helping them to apply the knowledge gained from their use of the autoharp to the piano.

1. Find the roots of the I and V chords on the piano; use them as accompaniments for songs.
2. Add the full chord to songs, using the I and V chords.
3. Experiment with different rhythmic patterns for accompaniments.
4. Later, introduce the IV chord.

Playing recorder-type instruments

Easy-to-play instruments such as the flutophone, the song flute, the tonette, and the traditional recorder can provide children with many opportunities for exploring music. These instruments are usually introduced in the third or fourth grade. They can only be used for playing music that can be notated within a range of nine tones:

(This is the playing range of all the above-mentioned instruments except the recorder.) It is possible, however, to play all the chromatic tones between these two tones. A suggested procedure for introducing a recorder-type instrument is:

Hold the instrument at the far end with the *right* hand, leaving all holes open.

Place the thumb of the *left* hand over the hole at the back of the instrument and the index finger of the same hand on the hole closest to the mouthpiece.

Next, place the mouthpiece between the front teeth, cushioned by the lips, and blow softly into it, releasing the breath as if trying to say the word, "too."

Proceed by placing the middle and ring fingers on the second and third holes in succession, blowing "too" for each note in turn.

After a little practice on these separate tones, play the following tune by ear, using the numbers 1-2-3 for the index, middle, and ring fingers of the left hand.

1 2 | 3 – | 1 2 | 3 – | 3 3 3 3 | 2 2 2 2 | 1 2 | 3 –|

While keeping the holes for the left hand covered, place the thumb of the *right* hand under the "thumb-rest" at the back of the instrument and the index (4), middle (5), and little (6) fingers on the remaining holes in succession, again blowing "too" for each new tone. It may take a little practice to produce a good tone on the lowest (last) note. *Be sure to cover all the holes firmly with the cushion part of the finger tips.*

"Hot Cross Buns" can now be played on the lower part of the instrument in this manner:

4 5 | 6 – | 4 5 | 6 – | 6 6 6 6 | 5 5 5 5 | 4 5 | 6 –|

(Be sure that the children understand that these numbers refer to the number of the fingers, and not to the steps in the scale.)

After practicing this tune on each part of the instrument, the children will be ready to play other songs, referring to the fingering chart which comes with the instrument for new notes.

Using recorder-type instruments

Play one part of a round on the instrument while the class sings the other parts.

Play descants or harmony parts to class songs.
Play short themes from compositions listened to in class.
Some children may wish to form a small ensemble to rehearse compositions especially written for these instruments.

There are many recorder-type instruments on the market, the most common of which are:

Song flute
Tonette
Flutophone
Recorder (soprano, alto, tenor, bass)

One drawback of many of these instruments is the difficulty of tuning them. The recorder, while the most expensive, may also be the most rewarding musically.

PLANNING FOR MOVING ACTIVITIES

Young children need active participation; they learn best when they are completely involved in the learning situation. Physical response to music provides this involvement; for many children it will be the most effective way to attain the basic concepts of musical organization. For some, this mode of expression may prove to be the most satisfying.

Observing children as they respond physically to music offers the teacher an opportunity to evaluate their musical growth. For these reasons, bodily response to music will form an integral part of many classroom activities. Sometimes physical movement will be the focus of the daily music class; on other occasions it will serve a supplementary role, as when children indicate physically their recognition of the elements of music to which they are listening. In whatever way it is used, the teacher will keep the role of physical movement in its proper perspective, remembering that it is the musical response with which we are concerned and not merely the development of good physical coordination. The teacher will also recognize that the terms "physical movement" and "rhythmic response" are not necessarily synonymous and will use movement to help the children grow in their understanding of all aspects of musical organization.

As in playing, there are many aspects of moving; no one approach is suitable to all types of physical activities. In all, however, the focus will remain on the music and on physical movement as a means of reflecting *musical* movement. The following teaching procedure is suggested primarily for free interpretive dance, but could be easily adapted for other kinds of musical movement.

The children listen quietly to the music. Do not expect the children to move expressively to music they have not previously heard. (See suggestions under "Planning for Listening Activities.")

The children move freely and spontaneously to the music, respond with an appropriate fundamental movement, or respond with an appropriate patterned dance step.

Discuss the various responses, encouraging the children to tell why they feel their movement is appropriate and to make suggestions for other movements that would be even more exact. The degree of exactness will depend upon the age and the previous musical experiences of the class.

The children again move to the music, this time attempting new movements or improving on previous ones.

Steps three and four may be repeated as often as time permits and interest dictates.

Guide the children to concentrate in their responses on reflecting a specific aspect of the music such as the meter, rhythmic pattern, the melodic direction, phrase, repetition and contrast, or harmonic changes.

Using physical movements

Use physical movement to accompany songs (finger play, action songs, and dramatic characterization). Following similar procedures as outlined above, remembering that the primary goal is the faithful representation of the music rather than the learning of a specific set of movements.

Encourage the children to use their entire bodies in a variety of free interpretive responses. Help them to move constantly toward more and more exact reflection of the musical line.

Respond to music with appropriate fundamental movements: walk, run, sway, skip, gallop, hop, jump, stamp, and so forth.

Explore all the possibilities of a particular movement. For example, different ways of walking are forward, backward, sideways; big steps, little steps, on tiptoe, on heels, prancing, shuffling, hopping, and so on.

Explore the possibilities of combining the above variations into patterned steps to reflect a particular meter or rhythmic pattern to fit a particular mood or style. For example, combine one big step and two little steps into a pattern to match a waltz meter, or combine toe and heel steps into an Indian dance.

Learn traditional folk dances, emphasizing in the learning process the manner in which the steps suit the musical organization.

Help the children develop their own folk dances. Discuss the kinds of formations possible: single or double circle, line, square. Make decisions as to appropriateness based on knowledge of music and on the children's research into types of dances typical of specific cultures or periods.

Develop group interpretations, with a different group assigned to each new phrase or to each new musical idea. Older children may group themselves according to melodic lines: group one representing the main melody, group two reflecting the countermelody, and other groups responding to the bass line or to the harmonic accompaniment.

PLANNING FOR CREATIVE ACTIVITIES

Creative experiences grow out of the activities previously described. One can be creative as he sings, plays or moves; however, because there are some problems peculiar to the planning of creative activities we shall consider this facet of the music program separately.

The term "creative" implies the organization of materials into a product that is original and unique; it is in this sense that we shall consider activities in the music curriculum as creative. The children's efforts will be primitive and simple, but to the degree that they represent the children's own choices of the organization of musical materials into new wholes, these efforts can be considered creative.

It is wise to remember that creativity does not follow a time table. The teacher cannot plan to "create a song on February 18th." He *can* be prepared to take advantage of situations where the creative act is a natural sequence. It is also important to recognize that true creativity is an individual effort. The teacher should provide opportunities for children to work on creative projects by themselves, or in small groups.

Young children often create "songs" spontaneously as they play. Encourage this spontaneous creation, even though the beginning efforts will be primitive and seldom repeated. Gradually, as children grow in their musical knowledge and skills these expressions can be guided into more formal creative efforts. The creating of a song as a class project might follow the sequence described below:

Select a text. It may be a familiar poem, or the class may choose to create new words.

Read the poem together; discuss its expressive purpose.

Discuss the ways in which music might support this expressiveness. The degree of specificity of this discussion will depend on the musical maturity of the class. Some questions that might be considered are:

1. Should the melody move smoothly or jerkily; by steps or by skips?
2. Are there any words that suggest a particular melodic contour, such as "high in the sky" or "hopping along the path?"
3. Where is the most important part (the climax), of the poem?
4. Is the general mood happy, sad, frightening, or funny?
5. What type of rhythmic pattern might help to reflect the mood of this song?

Read the poem together several times to establish the rhythmic movement and the accent grouping.

Determine the tonality and the starting pitch.

1. For early experiences, the teacher may simply establish a tonality and a starting pitch.
2. For later experience, the children may discuss and select an appropriate tonality and agree on a starting pitch.

With the tempo, the rhythmic pattern of the words, and the tonality well in mind, individual children sing the first phrase.

Discuss the results and make suggestions for improvement.

1. The teacher may sing the pattern he has heard.
2. Individuals may sing alternative melodic patterns.
3. The class may discuss various alternatives and decide which is most appropriate.

The entire class resings the first phrase and proceeds directly to the second phrase, which should grow out of the first.

Proceed similarly for each phrase of the song.

Sing the entire song; discuss suggestions for improvement.

Notate the song for future reference.

1. First and early second grade—the teacher notates.
2. Second and early third grades—the children notate the melody with numbers (syllables) and rhythm in line notation.
3. Fourth, fifth, and sixth grades—children notate, with the teacher assisting only as needed.

Using creative activities

Create songs, encouraging the children to combine words and melodic patterns both individually and as a group. ("Clouds.")

Develop percussive and melodic accompaniments for familiar songs. ("Get on Board," "Ghost of Tom.")

Create interpretive dances to reflect the musical organization of composed music. As the children grow in understanding and skill, this creative effort should become more exact. ("Parade," "March of the Siamese Children.")

Create instrumental compositions to be played by class members who are studying orchestral and band instruments (fifth and sixth grades).

Take advantage of various experiences as an incentive for creative activities, such as unusual classroom occurrences (the arrival of a pet turtle, or the construction of a new building across the street), or the anticipation or remembrance of a special occasion (holidays, field trips, unusual weather, and so forth).

Correlate creative activities with other classroom experiences:

1. Compose in the style of a country being studied in social studies.
2. Set to music poems created in language arts.
3. Create ballads or operettas based on stories learned in reading class.

Use creative activities as a means of expanding musical learning:

1. Compose in a particular form—a three-part song form, theme and variations, or rondo.

2. Make a setting of a familiar folk tale, creating a melodic or percussive pattern for each character in the tale (as in "Peter and the Wolf").
3. Combine a variety of creative efforts—songs, instrumental compositions, dances, and so forth, into large-scale projects such as an operetta or a cantata.

PLANNING FOR READING ACTIVITIES

Before the child is ready to begin to use standard musical notation to help him expand his musical understanding, he must have had an opportunity to explore music in many ways. His understanding of the basic musical concepts should be demonstrated in various ways before he is introduced to musical notation. Such symbolism will be meaningless if the child has not first grasped the basic concepts of musical organization through listening, singing, moving, and playing. Before he is presented with the problems of standard musical notation he should be able to:

Sing what he hears.

Respond physically to what he hears.

1. Picture up-down melodic movement with hand levels as he listens to songs or instrumental selections.
2. Step and clap the beat and rhythmic pattern of familiar songs.
3. Show through dance his recognition of repetition and contrast of melodic movement, rhythmic pattern, phrase structure.

Diagram what he hears.

1. Picture melodic direction with line notation.
2. Picture rhythmic pattern with long and short lines.
3. Picture phrase sequence with contour lines.

Verbalize what he hears.

1. Describe music as moving up or down, by step or by skip.
2. Discuss rhythmic movement, using terms such as long-short, even-uneven.

"Transcribe" what he hears.

1. Write numbers (syllables) for simple melodic patterns that he hears, such as 1–2–3 (*do-re-mi*) and 1–3–5 (*do-mi-so*).

Convert diagrams and numbers (syllables) into sound.

1. Play or chant simple rhythmic patterns from line notation.

2. Play simple melodies on bells from number (syllable) notation.
3. Sing simple melodic patterns from number (syllable) notation.

The day the music books are first used should be a SPECIAL day. On this day the purpose of song books is established—to read music. From then on, the books should never be in the children's hands unless they are to be *purposefully* used. This does not mean that second graders will be expected to try to read all of every new song learned. It does mean, however, that they should read those sections (melodic and/or rhythmic) that are within their grasp, so that they can feel that they have contributed to the learning of each new song. Only if music reading is presented in such a manner—as a meaningful and desirable skill—will it become a satisfying experience rather than a frustrating drill.

Children will realize the need for this skill only if they are expected to make use of it by solving musical problems independently. In other words, *do not* sing with them when learning a new song, but *do* be ready to suggest ways by which they, themselves, can solve each new problem. Essential to this ability to solve notational problems independently is an understanding of the musical concept for which the symbol stands. An aural awareness is necessary before reproduction of any notational pattern can be accomplished. We do not expect children to read before they understand the spoken word; neither can we expect them to read music before they have an aural comprehension of musical organization.

Comprehension of the function of musical notation will be expanded if experiences with such include other activities in addition to studying the notation of new songs. One of the best ways for children to realize the importance of notation is to allow them to notate their own compositions. Ask other children to play the new music. "Does it sound as you intended it to?" "Did you communicate your intentions clearly?" Early experiences may be accomplished by using number and line notation. This simple notation may then be transferred to the staff. Later, help the children to notate their own compositions directly on the staff.

Provide ear-training experiences regularly for the class. At first give the children just one notational problem: "Can you notate the rhythm of this pattern?" "Can you show the direction of this melody, using whole notes on the staff?" First attempts at notating rhythmic and melodic patterns should be class projects. Later invite each child to write what he hears; play what the children have written, compare the results, discuss errors made.

Music reading involves the dual process of interpreting both rhythmic and melodic notation. Each category of symbols has problems peculiar to itself, but there are some principles of learning that should be kept in mind in all music reading experiences.

Move from whole to part. Early experiences should be concerned with the over-all unevenness or evenness of rhythmic pattern or with melodic movement as an entity. Later experiences will explore more specific relationships of duration and interval.

Move from the known to the unknown. Relate to previous experiences. No rhythmic or melodic problem is entirely new.

Move from the concrete to the abstract, associating musical symbols with physical movement and spacial concepts when meaningful: walking-running, long–short, up–down, and so on.

Help the children to see the value of recognizing repetition, sequence, and variation as an aid in learning new melodic or rhythmic patterns.

Make sure a strong sense of tonality and of accent grouping has been established before starting to read a new song.

Some problems of reading rhythmic notation may be avoided by heeding the following suggestions:

Always teach rhythmic relationship rather than absolutes: Tones move in 2–1 or 3–1 relationships (twice as long as, or three times as long as). Never teach something you will have to *unteach* later. For example, *do not* teach that a quarter note gets one beat. *Do* teach that a quarter note is half as long as a half note.

Emphasize the flow of the melodic line by avoiding the mechanical droning of note names or words. Chanting and clapping should always reflect the continuity of the rhythmic movement.

In teaching melodic notation, the following suggestions might be taken into consideration:

Introduce the children to some means of naming tonal relationships: numbers, syllables, letters, and so forth. Each device has its particular advantages and disadvantages. Because they are most commonly used, numbers and syllables have been referred to throughout this book.

Be sure the children realize the existence and importance of the spaces as well as the lines in the musical staff.

Focus the children's attention on scale-line and chord-line melodic patterns, beginning with the 1-3-5 (*do-mi-so*) pattern. Constant reference should be made to this central tonal pattern in all elementary reading experiences.

As the children increase in music reading skill, use numbers or syllables only when necessary. *Do not* waste time with them when the children do not need them; *do* return to them to solve new problems.

Introduce key signatures only after they have grasped the concept of scale organization and can see the purpose of keys. In the meantime, the teacher may simply tell them where the home tone is located.

Help the children to develop techniques for solving new intervallic problems by referring to the familiar 1-3-5 tonal pattern as a starting point. For example, if the new interval is 1-6, the children may sing 1-3-5-6, listening carefully. Then they may sing 1—think 3-5—sing 6. Finally, sing 1-6.

Make use of melodic instruments to help the children grasp intervallic relationships.

Introduce letter names in association with the staff as a convenient means of communication.

A suggested teaching procedure

Survey the song; discuss the words, the expressive intent of the song, its origin, and so on.

Examine the form of the song.
1. Discover the number of phrases.
2. Determine those phrases which are the same, similar, or different.

Study the rhythm.
1. Determine how the song will move.
2. Discover which note will sound with the beat.
3. Scan the notation:
   Look for notes that sound with the beat, that sound two to the beat, that last for two beats.
   Look for repetition of rhythmic patterns and for distinctive patterns that include dotted notes, syncopation, or other rhythmic variations.
4. Establish the meter by clapping lightly.
5. Practice tapping difficult rhythm patterns.
6. Tap or chant the rhythm of the entire song.

Study the melody.
1. Determine the home tone by examining the key signature.
2. Scan the notation:
   Look for melody patterns that move by scale steps.
   Look for patterns that include skips using tones from the I chord.
   Look for patterns that use tones from other common chords, V_7 or IV.
   Look for wide skips and unusual intervals.
3. Establish key feeling by playing 1-3-5-8 on the bells or piano, or by playing I-V_7-I on the autoharp.
4. Sing 1-3-5-8-5-3-1 (*do-mi-so-do-so-mi-do*).
5. Practice singing any unusual intervals.
6. Sing the melody with number (syllables) or with words.

Classroom
Instruments

NONPITCHED PERCUSSION INSTRUMENTS

1. Rhythm Sticks

2. Jingle Bells

3. Tambourine

4. Tone Block

5. Triangle

6. Sand Blocks

7. Drum

8. Finger Cymbals

9. Cymbals

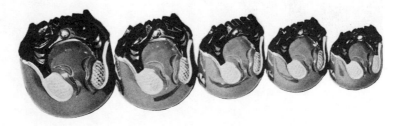

10. Temple Blocks

11. Castanets

12. Claves

13. Maracas

14. Guiro

15. Gong

17. Conga Drum

16. Bongo Drums

**PITCHED
PERCUSSION
INSTRUMENTS**

Resonator Bells

Courtesy Peripole, Inc., Far Rockaway, N. Y.

Xylophone

Courtesy Peripole, Inc., Far Rockaway, N. Y.

Step Bells

Courtesy Peripole, Inc., Far Rockaway, N. Y.

RECORDER-TYPE INSTRUMENTS

1. Song Flute   *2. Tonette*   *3. Flutophone*   *4. Soprano Recorder*

1–4 Courtesy Peripole, Inc., 51–17 Rockaway Beach Boulevard, Far Rockaway, N. Y.

AUTOHARP

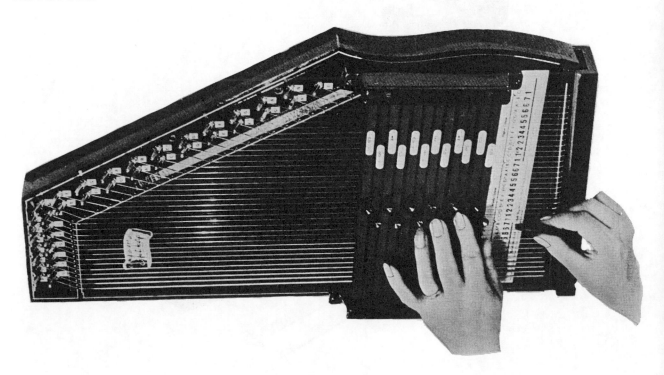

Autoharp

Courtesy Oscar Schmidt International, Inc., Union, N. J.

APPENDIXES

Appendix A
Elements
of Music Theory

I. PITCH NOTATION

Staff Five lines and four spaces, numbered from bottom and upward, used to notate pitches:

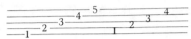

Staff degree A line or space on the staff identified by one of the letters A, B, C, D, E, F, G.

Grand staff The combination of two staves, *treble* and *bass,* used to indicate a wide range of pitches.

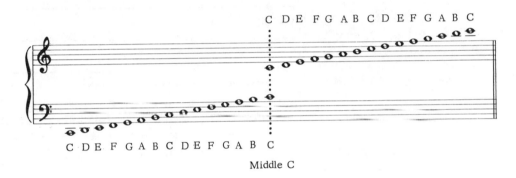

Middle C

Treble clef or G-clef A symbol establishing G above middle C on the second line of the staff.

Bass clef or F-clef A symbol establishing F below middle C on the fourth line of the staff.

Ledger Line A short line above or below the staff used to extend the range of pitches.

Accidental A sign used to alter the pitch of a given staff degree.

Sharp (♯) Raises the pitch by a half step.

Flat (♭) Lowers the pitch by a half step.

Natural (♮) Cancels the influence of a sharp or flat.

II. NOTE AND REST VALUES

Duration   The length of time assigned to a note or a rest.

	NOTES		RESTS
𝅝	whole note	▬	whole rest
𝅗𝅥	half note	▬	half rest
𝅘𝅥	quarter note	𝄽	quarter rest
𝅘𝅥𝅮	eighth note	𝄾	eighth rest
𝅘𝅥𝅯	sixteenth note	𝄿	sixteenth rest
𝅘𝅥𝅰	thirty-second note	𝅀	thirty-second rest

Relative duration   The following are examples of the relative duration of note values (rest values are comparable):

Triplet   A 3 to 1 instead of a 2 to 1 relationship of note values:

$$
\text{♩} = \text{♫} = \text{♫♪}_3
$$

$$
\text{𝅗𝅥} = \text{♩ ♩} = \overline{\text{♩ ♩ ♩}}^{\,3}
$$

$$
\text{𝅝} = \text{𝅗𝅥 𝅗𝅥} = \overline{\text{𝅗𝅥 𝅗𝅥 𝅗𝅥}}^{\,3}
$$

Dotted notes and rests   A dot adds half the value to whatever note or rest that it follows:

DOTTED NOTES			DOTTED RESTS		
𝅗𝅥· =	𝅗𝅥 +	𝅘𝅥	▬· =	▬ +	𝄽
𝅘𝅥· =	𝅘𝅥 +	𝅘𝅥𝅮	𝄽· =	𝄽 +	𝄾
𝅘𝅥𝅮· =	𝅘𝅥𝅮 +	𝅘𝅥𝅯	𝄾· =	𝄾 +	𝄿
𝅘𝅥𝅯· =	𝅘𝅥𝅯 +	𝅘𝅥𝅰	𝄿 =	𝄿 +	𝅀

Tie   A slur used to connect two tones of the same pitch, which prolongs the time value of the first note by the amount indicated by the second note:

III. METER AND RHYTHM

Beat   The underlying pulse of the music upon which the rhythm is organized.

Meter   The systematic grouping of beats resulting from *accenting* certain beats.

Bar lines   Vertical lines across the staff to indicate metric groupings.

Measure   One unit of a metric grouping between two bar lines.

Meter signature   Indicates the kind of accent grouping and the duration of beat units. The upper number signifies how many beats there are in each measure and the lower number indicates what kind of note value (𝅗𝅥 , ♩ , ♪) should receive one beat.

Simple meters   DUPLE METER.   Two beats to each measure.

2/4 indicates that there are two beats to the measure and that a quarter note gets one beat ($\frac{2}{♩}$):

$$\frac{2}{4} \ \ \overset{>}{♩} \ ♩ \ | \ \overset{>}{♩} \ ♩$$

1   2   1   2

2/2 or C (*alla breve*) indicates two beats to the measure and that a half note gets one beat ($\frac{2}{𝅗𝅥}$):

$$\frac{2}{2} \ \text{or} \ ¢ \ \overset{>}{𝅗𝅥} \ 𝅗𝅥 \ | \ \overset{>}{𝅗𝅥} \ 𝅗𝅥$$

1   2   1   2

TRIPLE METER. Three beats to each measure.

3/8 indicates three beats to the measure and that an eighth note gets one beat ($\frac{3}{𝅘𝅥𝅮}$):

$$\frac{3}{8} \ \overset{>}{♪} \ ♪ \ ♪ \ | \ \overset{>}{♪♪♪}$$

1   2   3   1   2   3

3/4 indicates three beats to the measure and that a quarter note gets one beat ($\frac{3}{♩}$):

$$\frac{3}{4} \ \overset{>}{♩} \ ♩ \ ♩ \ | \ \overset{>}{♩} \ ♩ \ ♩$$

1   2   3   1   2   3

QUADRUPLE METER.   Four beats to each measure.

4/4 or C indicates four beats to the measure and that a quarter note gets one beat ($\frac{4}{♩}$):

$$\frac{4}{4} \ \text{or} \ C \ \overset{>}{♩} \ ♩ \ \overset{>}{♩} \ ♩ \ | \ \overset{>}{♩} \ ♩ \ \overset{>}{♩} \ ♩$$

1   2   3   4   1   2   3   4

4/16 indicates four beats to a measure and that a sixteenth note gets one beat ($\frac{4}{𝅘𝅥𝅯}$):

$$\frac{4}{16} \ \overset{>}{♬} \ ♬ \ \overset{>}{♬} \ ♬ \ | \ \overset{>}{♬♬} \ \overset{>}{♬♬}$$

1 2 3 4   1 2 3 4

Compound meters   DUPLE METER.   Two accent groupings to each measure.

6/8 indicates that there are six beats to the measure with an accent on 1 and 4 and that an eighth note gets one beat ($\frac{6}{𝅘𝅥𝅮}$):

1 2 3 4 5 6   1 2 3 4 5 6

May also indicate two beats to the measure and that a dotted quarter note gets one beat (♩.):

TRIPLE METER.   Three accent groupings to each measure.

9/8 usually indicates three beats to the measure and that a dotted quarter note gets one beat (♩.):

QUADRUPLE METER.   Four accent groupings to each measure.

12/8 usually indicates four beats to the measure and that a dotted quarter note gets one beat (♩):

Combination meters
Meters made up of mixed simple meters.

5/4 indicates five beats to the measure and that a quarter note gets one beat (♩):

7/4 indicates seven beats to the measure and that a quarter note gets one beat (♩):

Rhythm
The patterned movement of tones related to, but independent of, the metric structure. Rhythmic patterns may be short or lengthy.

RHYTHM OF THE BEAT. The accented grouping of beats.

RHYTHM OF THE MELODY.   The rhythmic pattern of melody.

Syncopation
The shifting of the accent from its normal position within the measure:

IV. INTERVALS, SCALES, AND CHORDS

Interval:
The distance between two pitches, described in terms of the number of staff degrees included:

| prime (unison) | second | third | fourth | fifth | sixth | seventh | octave |

HALF STEP.   The smallest interval in a scale, as represented by the distance between two consecutive keys, whether white or black, on the piano keyboard.

WHOLE STEP.   An interval including two half steps.

PERFECT INTERVALS.   Prime (unison), fourth, fifth, and octave.

MAJOR INTERVALS.   Second, third, sixth, and seventh.

MINOR INTERVAL.   One half step smaller than a major interval.

DIMINISHED INTERVAL.   One half step smaller than a minor interval.

AUGMENTED INTERVAL.   One half step larger than a major interval.

INVERTED INTERVALS.   Primes become octaves, fourths become fifths, octaves become primes, seconds become sevenths, thirds become sixths, sixths become thirds, and sevenths become seconds. Major intervals become minor, minor become major, perfect intervals remain perfect.

Scale   A group of tones arranged in a particular pattern of whole and half steps.

DIATONIC SCALE.   A group of eight tones arranged consecutively on different staff degrees, from low to high.

MAJOR SCALE.   A diatonic scale arranged in the following pattern:

NATURAL MINOR SCALE.   A diatonic scale arranged in the following pattern:

HARMONIC MINOR SCALE.   The natural minor scale with the seventh step raised:

MELODIC MINOR SCALE.   The natural minor scale with the sixth and seventh steps raised a half step ascending and unaltered descending:

RELATIVE MINOR SCALE.   A minor scale with the same key signature as a major scale, like:

F major   D minor

PENTATONIC SCALE. A five-tone scale; some common patterns are:

WHOLE-TONE SCALE.   A scale of six tones, all one whole step apart:

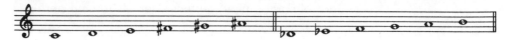

CHROMATIC SCALE.   A scale of twelve tones all one half step apart:

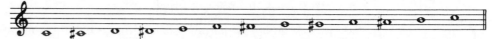

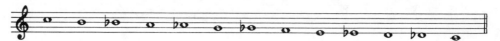

(Sharps are used in the ascending scale and flats in the descending scale.)

KEY CENTER.   The tone on which a scale is built.

KEY SIGNATURE.   The sharps or flats placed on the staff following the clef to designate the key center (*tonic*) and to alter the pitches on the staff degrees to provide the correct arrangement of whole and half steps:

D major   D minor

SCALE SYLLABLES.   Italian names for the tones in a major scale:

1	2	3	4	5	6	7	8
do	*re*	*mi*	*fa*	*so*	*la*	*ti*	*do*

Syllables for the chromatic scale are as follows.

Ascending:

do   di   re   ri   mi   fa   fi   so   si   la   li   ti   do

Descending:

do   ti   te   la   le   so   se   fa   mi   me   re   rah   do

TWELVE-TONE ROW.   Not a scale, but a distinctive pattern of the twelve tones of the chromatic scale created by a composer as the basis of a specific composition. Example:

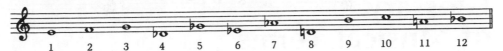

Triad   A chord of three tones built in thirds.

MAJOR TRIAD.   A triad in which the lower third is a major third and the upper third is a minor third.

MINOR TRIAD.   A triad in which the lower third is a minor third and the upper third is a major third.

DIMINISHED TRIAD.   A triad containing two minor thirds.

AUGMENTED TRIAD.   A triad containing two major thirds.

TRIADS OF C MAJOR SCALE.   Classified as to quality, number, and chord name:

Chord root   The tone upon which a chord is built.

Seventh chord   A four-tone chord built in thirds. The most commonly used seventh chord is the one built on the fifth step of the scale, the *dominant seventh:*

Chord inversion   Arranging a chord so that a tone other than the root becomes the lowest tone:

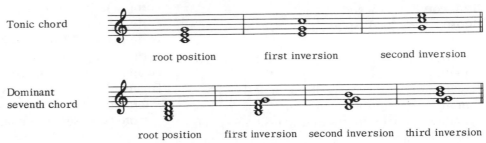

Chord progression   The movement from one chord to another. Common chord progressions, utilizing inverted chords, in the key of C are:

Appendix B
Glossary
of Musical Terms

Absolute music Music that is dissociated from extramusical implications.

A cappella Choral music without accompaniment.

Accelerando, accel. Becoming gradually faster.

Accent The stress of one tone over others.

Accidental Chromatic alteration of single notes within a measure.

Adagio Slowly; leisurely.

Agitato Agitated; excited.

Al fine To the end.

Allegretto Moderately fast; slower than allegro.

Allegro Lively; brisk; quick.

Anacrusis Up-beat (see *up-beat*).

Andante Moderately slow.

Animato Animated.

Arpeggio Executing a chord by playing one tone after another, from the bottom up, instead of playing all tones simultaneously.

Assai Very.

A tempo Return to the original tempo.

Augmentation Doubling of note values in a section.

Atonal Music without a fixed key center.

Binary form An AB form; a two-part song form.

Bridge passage Section of a musical composition serving to connect two themes.

Brio, con With vigor or spirit.

Brioso Fiery; with spirit.

Cadence The ending of a musical phrase, period, or section.

Cadenza A solo passage for technical display.

Canon A composition in which one part is imitated strictly in another part at any pitch or time interval.

Cantabile In singing style.

Cantata A composite vocal form consisting of arias, recitatives, duets, and choruses, based on a narrative text.

Capriccio Humorous; capricious.

Coda A supplement to the ending of a composition.

Concerto A composition for a solo player and an orchestra.

Contrapuntal In the style of counterpoint.

Counterpoint A weaving together of melodies horizontally to form a musical texture.

Crescendo, cresc. < Increasing in loudness.

Da capo, D.C. From the beginning.

Dal segno, D.S. From the sign.

Decrescendo, decresc. > Decreasing in loudness.

Diminuendo, dim. > Gradually softer.

Diminution Contraction of note values (opposite of augmentation).

Dolce Sweet and soft.

Doloroso Sadly; dolefully.

Embellishment Ornamentation.

Espressivo, espress. With expression.

Exposition Initial section of a sonata or fugue, which contains the statement of the main subject or themes.

Fermata ⌒ Hold; pause.

Figure A melodic or rhythmic fragment consisting of two or more tones.

Fine End; close.

Form Design in music.

Forte, *f* Loud.

Forte-piano, *fp* Accent strongly, diminishing.

Fortissimo, *ff* Very loud.

Fugato A short passage in fugal style.

Fugue A composition based on imitative counterpoint. "Fugue" means "flight": the two or more parts seem to chase each other.

Giocoso Playful.

Glissando Execution of consecutive notes rapidly and smoothly by a sliding movement of the hand.

Grandioso In a grand manner; pompous; majestic.

Grave Slow; solemn.

298

Grazioso   Gracefully.
Ground bass   A repeated bass-line melody over which new melodies or harmonies are created.

Homophonic   Music in which one leading melody is supported by a chordal accompaniment.

Imitation   The restatement in close succession of a motive or theme in different voices of a contrapuntal composition.
Interval   Difference in pitch between two tones.
Introduction   An opening section to a composition.

Largo   Very slowly.
Legato   Smoothly connected.
Leggiero   Light and graceful.
Lento   Slowly; between andante and largo.
L'istesso tempo   In the same tempo.

Maestoso   Majestic; dignified.
Marcato   Marked; emphasized.
Meno   Less.
Mezzo   Halfway; medium.
Mezzo forte, *mf* Moderately loud.
Mezzo piano, *mp* Moderately soft.
Moderato   Moderate speed; between allegro and andante.
Modulation   Change of key within a composition.
Motive, motif   A short melodic, rhythmic, or harmonic pattern.

Neighboring tone   A tone one staff degree above or below a chord tone from which the melody departs and returns.
Non troppo   Not too much.

Opera   A drama sung throughout with an orchestral accompaniment and staged with scenery, costumes, and action.
Opus, op.   Used in conjunction with numbers (op. 1, op. 2) to indicate the chronological position of a composition within the entire output of a composer.
Oratorio   A drama of a religious character performed by solo voices, chorus, and orchestra without staging.

Ostinato   A continuously repeated melodic figure or motive.
Overture   An instrumental introduction to an opera or oratorio; or a one-movement composition for orchestra or band.

Passing tone   A nonharmonic tone that is touched in passing from one chord to another.
Period   A unit of music consisting of two contrasting phrases, called *antecedent* and *consequent* phrases.
Phrase   A natural division of the melodic line, comparable to a sentence in speech. "The distance between two cadences."
Phrase group   Usually three phrases of parallel or contrasting construction.
Pianissimo, *pp* Very soft.
Piano, *p* Soft.
Più   More.
Poco   Little.
Polyphonic   Music written for two or more simultaneous parts of pronounced individuality.
Polyphony   Polyphonic texture.
Polyrhythm   Simultaneous use of contrasting rhythms in different parts.
Polytonality   Simultaneous use of two or more tonalities in different parts.
Prelude   A piece of music serving as an introduction to a larger composition.
Presto   Very quick.
Program music   Music inspired by, or suggestive of, story, event, situation, and so forth; opposite of *absolute music.*

Rallentando, rall.   Gradually slower.
Repeat   The signs ‖:   :‖, at the beginning and at the end of a section that is to be repeated.
Ritardando, rit.   Gradually slower.
Ritenuto   Same as *ritardando.*
Rondo   A musical form resulting from the alternation of a main theme with contrasting themes: A   B   A   C   A, and so forth.
Round   A "circle canon," that is, a canon in which the melody is repeated on the same pitch level.

Scherzando   Playfully; sportively.
Sequence   Immediate repetition of a tonal pattern at a higher or lower pitch level.

Sforzando, *sfz* Forcibly; with sudden emphasis.

Slancio, con With impetuosity.

Sonata An extended composition for one, two, or three instruments in one or more movements.

Sonata-allegro form A three-sectional instrumental form consisting of *exposition, development,* and *recapitulation.*

Sostenuto Sustained; prolonged.

Staccato Detached; separate.

Stretto The overlapping of the subject in a fugue due to the entrance of a new voice before the first voice has completed its statement.

Style "Characteristic language" with reference to melody, rhythm, harmony, form, and so on.

Subito Suddenly.

Suite A group of related compositions.

Symphonic poem An orchestral composition based upon extramusical ideas, poetic or descriptive.

Symphony A sonata for orchestra.

Tempo Rate of speed.

Ternary form An ABA form or three-part song form.

Tessitura The general "lie" of a vocal part, whether high or low in average pitch.

Theme A definite, complete musical subject.

Timbre Tone color; the difference between tones of the same pitch produced by different instruments or voices.

Toccata A keyboard composition in free style.

Tonality Feeling for a key center; "loyalty to a tonic."

Tone poem Same as *symphonic poem.*

Tranquillo Quietly.

Troppo Much.

Un poco A little.

Up-beat One or several initial notes of a melody occurring before the first bar line.

Variation Modification of a theme.

Vivace Quick.

Vivo Lively; spirited.

Appendix C
Bibliography

I. BOOKS FOR THE TEACHER

Alvin, Juliette, *Music for the Handicapped Child.* London: Oxford University Press, 1965.

Andrews, Gladys, *Creative Rhythmic Movement for Children.* Englewood Cliffs, N.J.: Prentice-Hall, Inc., 1954.

Baldwin, Lillian, *Music for Young Listeners: The Blue Book, The Crimson Book, The Green Book.* Morristown, N.J.: Silver Burdett Company, 1951.

Bernstein, Leonard, *The Joy of Music.* New York: Simon and Schuster, Inc., 1959.

Coleman, Jack L., *et al., Music for Exceptional Children.* Evanston, Ill.: Summy-Birchard Company, 1964.

Copland, Aaron, *What to Listen for in Music.* New York: McGraw-Hill Book Company, Inc., 1957.

Daraz, Arpad, and Stephen Jay, *Sight and Sound.* Oceanside, N.Y.: Boosey and Hawkes, Inc., 1965.

Doll, Edna, and Mary Jarman Nelson, *Rhythms Today.* Morristown, N.J.: Silver Burdett Company, 1964.

Elliott, Raymond, *Learning and Teaching Music.* Columbus, Ohio: Charles E. Merrill Books, Inc., 1966.

Ellison, Alfred, *Music with Children.* New York: McGraw-Hill Book Company, Inc., 1959.

Garretson, Robert L., *Music in Childhood Education.* New York: Appleton-Century-Crofts, 1966.

Gary, Charles L. (ed.), *The Study of Music in the Elementary School.* Washington, D.C.: Music Educators National Conference, 1967.

Ginglend, David R., and Winifred E. Stiles, *Music Activities for Retarded Children.* Nashville, Tenn.: Abingdon Press, 1965.

Heffernan, Charles W., *Teaching Children to Read Music.* New York: Appleton-Century-Crofts, 1968.

Lloyd, Norman, *The Golden Encyclopedia of Music.* New York: Golden Press, a Division of Western Publishing Company Inc., 1968.

Lomax, Alan (ed.), *Folk Song Style and Culture.* Washington, D.C.: American Association for Advancement of Science Publications, 1968.

McMillan, Eileen, *Guiding Children's Growth through Music.* Boston: Ginn and Company, 1959.

Monsour, Sally, *et al., Rhythm in Music and Dance for Children.* Belmont, Calif.: Wadsworth Publishing Company Inc., 1966.

Murray, Ruth L., *Dance in Elementary Education,* 2nd edition. New York: Harper & Row, Publishers, 1963.

Myers, Louise K., *Teaching Children Music in the Elementary School,* 3rd edition. Englewood Cliffs, N.J.: Prentice-Hall, Inc., 1961.

Nordoff, Paul, and Clive Robbins, *Music Therapy for Handicapped Children.* New York: Rudolf Steiner Publications, 1965.

Nye, Robert E., and Bjornar Bergethon, *Basic Music,* 3rd edition. Englewood Cliffs, N.J.: Prentice-Hall, Inc., 1968.

Nye, Robert E., and Vernice T. Nye, *Music in the Elementary School,* 2nd edition. Englewood Cliffs, N.J.: Prentice-Hall, Inc., 1964.

Orff, Carl, and Gunhild Keetman, *Orff "Schulwerk/Music for Children,"* Vol. I–V (German). (American Edition by Doreen Hall and Arnold Walter, Vol. I–V; English Edition by Margaret Murray, Vol. I–IV.) New York: Associated Music Publishers, 1956.

Raebeck, Aleta, and Lawrence Wheeler, *New Approaches to Music in the Elementary School.* Dubuque, Iowa: Wm. C. Brown Company, Publishers, 1967.

Richards, Mary Helen, *Threshold to Music* (The First Three Years). Palo Alto, Calif.: Fearon Publishers, Inc., 1964.

Richards, Mary Helen, *Threshold to Music* (Fourth Year). Palo Alto, Calif.: Fearon Publishers, Inc., 1967.

Runkle, Aleta, and Mary Lebow Erikson, *Music for Today's Boys and Girls.* Boston: Allyn and Bacon, Inc., 1966.

Saffran, Rosanna, *First Book of Creative Rhythms.* New York: Holt, Rinehart and Winston, Inc., 1963.

Schubert, Inez, and Lucille Wood, *The Craft of Music Teaching.* Morristown, N.J.: Silver Burdett Company, 1964.

Shetler, Donald J., *Film Guide for Music Educators.* Washington, D.C.: Music Educators National Conference, 1968.

Sheehy, Emma Dickson, *Children Discover Music and Dance.* New York: Holt, Rinehart and Winston, Inc., 1959.

Slind, Lloyd H., and Evan D. Davis, *Bringing Music to Children.* New York: Harper & Row, Publishers, 1964.

Stringham, Edwin J., *Listening to Music Creatively,* 2nd edition. Englewood Cliffs, N.J.: Prentice-Hall, Inc., 1959.

Swanson, Bessie, *Music in the Education of Children,* 3rd edition. Belmont, Calif.: Wadsworth Publishing Company, Inc., 1969.

Timmerman, Maurine, *Let's Teach Music.* Evanston, Ill.: Summy-Birchard Company, 1958.

II. BOOKS FOR CHILDREN

Arnold, Elliot, *Finlandia: The Story of Sibelius.* New York: Holt, Rinehart and Winston, Inc., 1941.

Bakeless, Katherine, *Story-Lives of Great Composers.* Philadelphia: J. B. Lippincott Company, 1953.

_____, *Story-Lives of American Composers.* Philadelphia: J. B. Lippincott Company, 1962.

Britten, Benjamin, and Imogen Holst, *Wonderful World of Music.* Garden City, N.Y.: Doubleday & Company, Inc., 1968.

Bulla, Clyde R., *Stories of Favorite Operas.* New York: Thomas Y. Crowell Company, 1959.

_____, *Ring and the Fire: Stories from Wagner's Nibelung Operas.* New York: Thomas Y. Crowell Company, 1962.

_____, *More Stories of Favorite Operas.* New York: Thomas Y. Crowell Company, 1965.

Burch, Gladys, *Famous Composers for Boys and Girls.* New York: A. S. Barnes & Company, Inc., 1942.

_____, *Modern Composers for Boys and Girls.* New York: A. S. Barnes & Company, Inc., 1941.

_____, *Richard Wagner Who Followed a Star.* New York: Holt, Rinehart and Winston, Inc., 1941.

Craig, Jean, *The Heart of the Orchestra.* Minneapolis: Lerner Publications Company, 1963.

_____, *The Story of Musical Notes.* Minneapolis: Lerner Publications Company, 1963.

_____, *The Woodwinds.* Minneapolis: Lerner Publications Company, 1963.

Davis, Lionel, and Edith Davis, *Keyboard Instruments.* Minneapolis: Lerner Publications Company, 1963.

Davis, Marilyn, *Music Dictionary.* Garden City, N.Y.: Doubleday & Company, Inc., 1956.

Deucher, Sybil, *Edvard Grieg, Boy of the Northland.* New York: E. P. Dutton & Co., Inc., 1946.

_____, *The Young Brahms.* New York: E. P. Dutton & Co., Inc., 1949.

Fletcher, Helen, *The First Book of Bells.* New York: Franklin Watts, Inc., 1959.

Gilmore, Leo, *Folk Instruments.* Minneapolis: Lerner Publications Company, 1962.

Higgins, Helen Boyd, *Stephen Foster, Boy Minstrel.* Indianapolis, Ind.: The Bobbs-Merrill Company, 1947.

Hughes, Langston, *First Book of Jazz.* New York: Franklin Watts, Inc., 1955.

_____, *First Book of Rhythm.* New York: Franklin Watts, Inc., 1954.

Kaufman, Helen L., *History's 100 Great Composers.* New York: Grosset & Dunlap, Inc., 1957.

Kettlekamp, Larry, *Drums, Rattles and Bells.* New York: Thomas Y. Crowell Company, 1960.

_____, *Horns.* New York: Thomas Y. Crowell Company, 1960.

Krishef, Robert K., *Playback: The Story of Recording Devices.* Minneapolis: Lerner Publications Company, 1962.

Lyons, John H., *Stories of Our American Patriotic Songs.* New York: Vanguard Press, 1942.

Mirsky, Reba P., *Beethoven.* Chicago: Follett Publishing Company, 1963.

_____, *Bach.* Chicago: Follett Publishing Company, 1965.

_____, *Haydn.* Chicago: Follett Publishing Company, 1963.

_____, *Mozart.* Chicago: Follett Publishing Company, 1960.

Posell, Elsa, *American Composers*. Boston: Houghton Mifflin Company, 1967.

——, *Russian Composers*. Boston: Houghton Mifflin Company, 1967.

——, *This Is an Orchestra*. Boston: Houghton Mifflin Company, 1950.

Scotin, L., *Let's Go to a Concert*. New York: G. P. Putnam's Sons, 1960.

Surplus, Robert, *The Beat of the Drum*. Minneapolis: Lerner Publications Company, 1963.

Tetzlaff, Daniel B., *Shining Brass*. Minneapolis: Lerner Publications Company, 1963.

Wheeler, Opal, and Sybil Deucher, *Curtain Calls for Joseph Haydn and Sebastian Bach*. New York: E. P. Dutton & Co., Inc., 1935.

——, *Franz Schubert and His Merry Friends*. New York: E. P. Dutton & Co., Inc., 1939.

——, *Handel at the Court of Kings*. New York: E. P. Dutton & Co., Inc., 1943.

——, *Joseph Haydn, the Merry Little Peasant*. New York: E. P. Dutton & Co., Inc., 1936.

——, *MacDowell and His Cabin in the Pines*. New York: E. P. Dutton & Co., Inc., 1940.

——, *Mozart, the Wonder Boy*. New York: E. P. Dutton & Co., Inc., 1934.

——, *Paganini, Master of Strings*. New York: E. P. Dutton & Co., Inc., 1950.

——, *Robert Schumann and Mascot Ziff*. New York: E. P. Dutton & Co., Inc., 1947.

——, *Stephen Foster and His Little Dog Tray*. New York: E. P. Dutton & Co., Inc., 1941.

——, *The Story of Peter Tschaikowski*. New York: E. P. Dutton & Co., Inc., 1953.

Young Keyboard Jr. (Monthly magazine), New Haven, Conn.

Appendix D
Sources for School
Music Materials

I. BASIC MUSIC SERIES

Birchard Music Series. Evanston, Ill.: Summy-Birchard Company, 1962.

Discovering Music Together. Chicago, Ill.: Follett Publishing Company, 1970.

Exploring Music. New York: Holt, Rinehart and Winston, Inc., 1966.

Growing with Music. Englewood Cliffs, N.J.: Prentice-Hall, Inc., 1963.

Making Music Your Own. Morristown, N.J.: Silver Burdett Company, 1965.

Music for Young Americans. New York: American Book Company, 1966.

The Magic of Music. Boston, Mass.: Ginn and Company, 1965.

This Is Music. Boston, Mass.: Allyn and Bacon, Inc., 1962.

II. BASIC RECORD SERIES

Adventures in Music, RCA Victor Record Division, New York, N.Y.

Bowmar Orchestral Library, Bowmar Records, Inc., Glendale, Calif.

Musical Sound Books, Sound Book Press Society, Inc., Scarsdale, N.Y.

Victor Record Library for Elementary Schools, RCA Victor Record Division, New York, N.Y.

III. FILMS AND FILM STRIPS

Films

Beethoven and His Music, Coronet Instructional Films, Chicago, Ill., 1954. Color or b/w—14 minutes. Shows relation of Beethoven's environment to his work as a composer.

Brahms and His Music, Coronet Instructional Films, Chicago, Ill., 1957. Color or b/w—14 minutes. Story of Brahms' life with explanation of his music.

Design to Music, International Film Bureau, Chicago, Ill., 1949. Color—6 minutes. Children drawing and painting to music.

Development of a Musical Instrument, NET Film Service, Indiana University, Bloomington, Ind., 1956. B/w—30 minutes. Historical development of harpsichord and piano with musical examples.

Discovering Form in Music, Film Associates of California, Los Angeles, Calif., 1967. Color—19 minutes. Introduction of musical forms through listening and utilization of common classroom visual aids.

Discovering Melody and Harmony, Film Associates of California, Los Angeles, Calif., 1967. Color—16 minutes. Illustrates the use of instruments in introducing melodic and harmonic concepts to elementary school children.

Discovering Rhythm, United World Films, Inc., New York, 1967. Color—11 minutes. Depicts rhythm as an outgrowth of physical movements: walking, running, skipping and marching.

Discovering Sound and Movement, Film Associates of California, Los Angeles, Calif., 1967. Color—16 minutes. Demonstration lesson with second graders focusing on high-low concepts with corresponding movement.

Elements of Composition, NET Film Service, Indiana University, Bloomington, Ind., 1956. B/w—27 minutes. The New York Woodwind Quintet explains and demonstrates the elements of composition.

Flute and Harp, NET Film Service, Indiana University, Bloomington, Ind., 1956. B/w—23 minutes. History of the harp and explanation of tuning, pedal technique, and special effects.

Handel and His Music, Coronet Instructional Films, Chicago, Ill., 1957. Color or b/w—14 minutes. Traces Handel's musical life and discusses his operas, oratorios, and orchestral music.

Instruments of the Orchestra, Contemporary Films Inc., New York, 1947. B/w—20 minutes. Introduction of orchestral instruments through performance of Britten's *Young Person's Guide to the Orchestra.*

Mozart and His Music, Coronet Instructional Films, Chicago, Ill., 1954. Color or b/w—10 minutes. Life of Mozart with excerpts from his music.

Peter and the Wolf, Walt Disney Productions, Burbank, Calif., 1964. Color—14 minutes. Animated cartoon with narration of the story.

Reading Music Series (three films), Coronet Instructional Films, Chicago, Ill., 1960. B/w— 11 minutes each. Children and a teacher demonstrating music reading procedures. Includes: *Learning About Notes, Finding the Rhythm,* and *Finding the Melody.*

Science of Musical Sounds, The, Academy Films, Los Angeles, Calif., 1964. B/w—11 minutes. An introduction to basic elements of musical tones.

What Is Rhythm? Film Associates of California, Los Angeles, Calif., 1966. Color—11 minutes. Illustrates concepts of beat, tempo, rhythm pattern, and meter.

Film Strips

Biographies of Great Composers Series, Bowmar Records, Inc., Glendale, Calif., 1967. Six sets of two colored film strips and one LP recording for the following composers; *Mozart, Verdi, Schubert, Puccini, Haydn,* and *Beethoven.*

Great Composers and Their Music, Jam Handy Organization, Detroit, Mich., 1966. Six color film strips and accompanying LP recording for the following composers: *J. S. Bach, Handel, Mozart, Beethoven,* and *Schubert.*

Meet the Instruments of the Symphony Orchestra, Bowmar Records, Inc., Glendale, Calif., 1960. Two color film strips, with accompanying LP recording, showing children performing on orchestral instruments.

Musical Books for Young People, Society for Visual Education, Inc., Chicago, Ill., 1965. Set of six film strips and three LP recordings based on books of the same title published by Lerner Publishing Co.: *The Heart of the Orchestra, Shining Brass, The Woodwinds, The Beat of the Drum, Keyboard Instruments,* and *Folk Instruments.*

Music Stories, Jam Handy Organization, Detroit, Mich., 1953. Six color film strips and correlated LP recordings telling the stories of: *Peter and the Wolf, Hansel and Gretel, Peer Gynt, The Nutcracker, The Firebird,* and *The Sorcerer's Apprentice.*

Stories of Music Classics, Jam Handy Organization, Detroit, Mich., 1956. Six color film strips with correlated LP recordings presenting stories of *The Sleeping Beauty, William Tell, Midsummer Night's Dream, The Bartered Bride,* and *Scheherazade.*

IV. CLASSROOM INSTRUMENTS

Chicago Musical Instrument Company, Chicago, Ill. (Tonette.)

Conn Corporation, Elkhart, Ind. (Song flute.)

David Wexler and Co., Chicago, Ill. (Rhythm, melody, and harmony instruments.)

Educational Music Bureau, Inc., Chicago, Ill. (Rhythm, melody, and harmony instruments.)

Hargail Music Press, New York, N.Y. (Recorders.)

B. F. Kitching and Company, Inc., Brookfield, Ill. (Resonator bells and other mallet-type instruments.)

William Kratt Company, Union City, N.J. (Chromatic pitch instruments.)

Peripole, Inc., Far Rockaway, Long Island, N.Y. (Rhythm, melody, and harmony instruments.)

Oscar Schmidt-International, Inc., Jersey City, N.J. (Autoharp and meloharp.)

Rhythm Band, Inc., Fort Worth, Texas (Rhythm, melody, and harmony instruments.)

Trophy Products Company, Cleveland, Ohio. (Flutophone.)

Walberg and Auge, Worcester, Mass. (Song bells, resonator bells, and other percussion instruments.)

Appendix E
Autoharp Keyboard

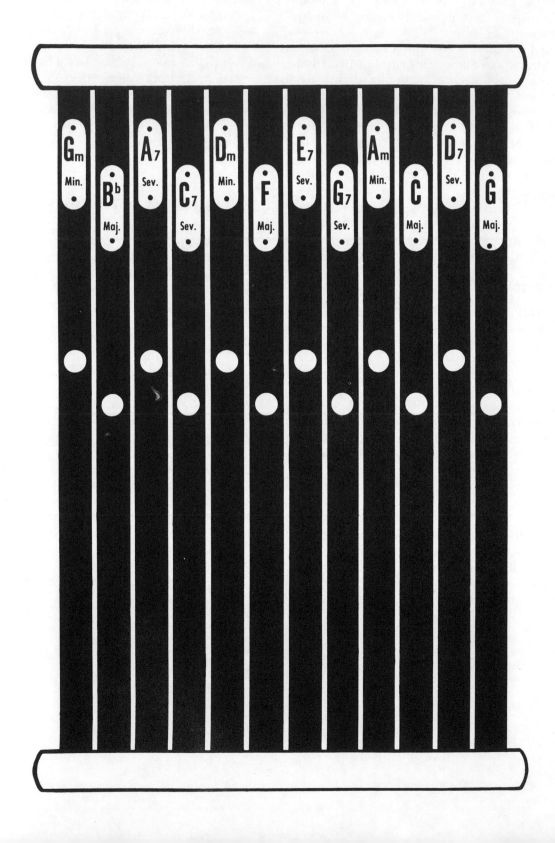

Index A

Index B

INSTRUMENTAL COMPOSITIONS

Selections marked with an (*) are available on the supplementary recording issued with this book.

Index C

CREATIVE ACTIVITIES